W9-BVH-036

CALVIN AND THE REFORMATION

CALVIN AND THE REFORMATION

BY

JAMES MACKINNON
Ph.D., D.D., D.Th., LL.D.

Regius Professor-Emeritus of Ecclesiastical
History, University of Edinburgh

NEW YORK
RUSSELL & RUSSELL · INC
1962

FIRST PUBLISHED IN 1936
PUBLISHED, 1962, BY RUSSELL & RUSSELL, INC.
L. C. CATALOG CARD NO: 62—10690

PRINTED IN THE UNITED STATES OF AMERICA

TO

My Colleagues, Past and Present,
and Valued Friends of the United
Divinity Faculty of Edinburgh
University and New College.

PREFACE

THERE has been a revival of interest in Calvin in recent years. This revival has found resounding expression in the neo-Calvinism of the Swiss theologian Karl Barth and his associates and disciples in Germany and Switzerland, though the quickened interest in him is not confined to this movement. It has led me to work over afresh the material for my lectures on Calvin and supplement it by further study. Hence this volume on " Calvin and the Reformation "—a pendant, on a smaller scale, to my " Luther and the Reformation "—in commemoration of the four hundredth anniversary of the beginning, in 1536, of his career as a Reformer, which was lately celebrated at Geneva. In the spring of that year he published at Basle his " Institutes of the Christian Religion " (*Institutio Christianæ Religionis*)—the theological *Magnum Opus* of the Reformation period. In the summer he began his reforming activity, in association with Farel, at Geneva.

The book is an attempt to portray his work as a leader of the Reformation at Geneva and far beyond it. He is an international, not merely a local or national figure, who had his finger on the pulse of the Reformation in many lands outside the little Republic on the shore of Lake Leman. Though not so original a religious thinker as Luther, he was more systematic in the expression of his thought, and he greatly surpassed him as an organiser and an ecclesiastical statesman. Moreover, he developed the movement in essential respects, particularly in his system of ecclesiastical discipline and polity. He thereby imparted to it a driving force which made itself

vii

felt in the social and political as well as the religious history of the Western lands, particularly France, Holland, England, and Scotland, from which it ultimately expanded into the New World beyond the Atlantic. Calvinism, in its developed form, became, in fact, " a live wire " in modern political as well as religious history. " Calvin and the Reformation " thus means far more, in ultimate result, than the local religious history of Geneva. It is the history of a widespread movement, of which, by his powerful intellect, his force of conviction and character, his organising genius, he made Geneva the headquarters.

The monumental work of Émile Doumergue, " Jean Calvin, L'Homme et les Choses de son Temps," the seven folios of which have appeared at intervals from 1899 to 1927, has also contributed to the current interest in Calvin and his work as a Reformer. It is the most exhaustive of the Lives of Calvin. It contains a wealth of archæological and historical as well as biographical material, and, while erudite in content and inconveniently ponderous in format, is written with characteristic French lucidity and vivacity. The venerable biographer is a whole-hearted admirer and protagonist of Calvin alike against his contemporary antagonists and his later critics. His great contribution has one defect. It is too partisan at times for the critical historian, who finds occasion enough in the career of Calvin for legitimate dissent and even animadversion. In some respects I prefer the solid and more critical, if less brilliant, work of Kampschulte, the former old Catholic professor of History at Bonn, " Johann Calvin, Seine Kirche und Sein Staat " [1] (1869-99), with whom M. Doumergue is often at feud,

---

[1] Vol. ii., covering the period 1546-59, was edited after his death in 1872 by W. Goetz, who also edited the valuable " Historische Arbeiten " of Cornelius, the old Catholic professor at Munich, on Calvin's career to 1549 (1899).

and who was, indeed, to some extent influenced by the anti-Calvinist works of J. B. G. Galiffe (1862-63). Other veterans in the field of Calvin research, to whom every student of the subject is indebted, are August Lang of Halle, Eugène Choisy of Geneva, Paul Wernle of Basle, and Jacques Pannier in France.

For the extensive modern literature on Calvin, as far as I have made use of it (a portion of it is antiquated), I must refer the reader to the notes. Of biographies in the stricter sense there is a large number in English and other modern languages. Among those in English two are fairly recent— those of Williston Walker (1906) and Reyburn (1914)—and that of Hunt is as recent as 1933. " Calvin and the Reformation " is not a biography, but primarily a critical survey of the Reformer's work and influence, into which the biographical element only enters as far as it is relevant to this survey. Its basis is mainly the standard edition of his " Opera " in the " Corpus Reformatorum," edited by Baum, Cunitz, and Reuss (1863-1900), and the " Correspondance des Réformateurs " (to 1544), edited by Herminjard (1866-97).

In the Introduction I have given a necessarily rapid sketch of the Reformation at Zürich under the leadership of Zwingli —*Nomen clarum et venerabile*, worthy to stand with Luther and Calvin in the front rank of the Reformers, though rather over-shadowed by them. In its general features Zwingli provided the model for the Reformation in the rest of Switzerland, though Calvin, in adopting, sought to modify it in certain respects, more particularly in the direction of striving to maintain the inherent autonomy of the Church in purely spiritual things. The method of its establishment at Geneva by public discussion and vote under the auspices of the civil power was identical with that previously applied at Zürich and in other Swiss Protestant cantons.

The Reformed Churches are under no small obligation to John Calvin. If Luther was the creator of the Reformation, Calvin was its great organiser, developer, and propagandist. The Reformed Church of Scotland, in particular, whilst honouring Luther as the religious genius of the movement, venerates Calvin as the moulder, through Knox and others, of its Confession and Polity, albeit no longer subscribing unreservedly to his theology, and totally at variance with his intolerant spirit and practice.

TABLE OF CONTENTS

xi

Calvin and the Reformation

CHAPTER I

INTRODUCTION

THE REFORMATION IN WESTERN EUROPE

THE Reformation in Western Europe is, in many essential features, the reflex of the movement originated and directed by Luther in Germany. It is part of the revulsion from the mediæval Church and religious life, though this revulsion had to a certain extent an independent origin in Switzerland, France, and England. Luther's doctrine of justification by faith, his denial of the papal supremacy as anti-Christian, his antagonism to the current ecclesiastical, and particularly the monastic conception of the Christian life, for instance, are characteristic of the developing movement in the Western lands as influenced by Calvin and his disciples. This movement had, however, marked individual features which distinguish it, more or less, from the Lutheran Reformation. Along with the doctrine of justification by faith characteristic emphasis is laid on the sovereignty of God and the operation of the Divine will in the work of salvation. Luther, indeed, in his conflict with Erasmus had stressed the doctrine of predestination and election. But this doctrine ultimately recedes into the background of the Lutheran theology as influenced by Melanchthon. In that of Calvin it is and remains a fundamental of the first importance, and though it is less prominent in the early French and Scottish Confessions of Faith, the Divine sovereignty is nevertheless a basic belief of Western Protestantism. Moreover, it exercises a far-reaching influence on character and is a potent force in the sphere of practical life. It lends to the movement a staying power, an aggressiveness which make themselves felt in the political as well as the religious sphere. In virtue of this doctrine alone, Calvinism, in its more developed form, is more forceful, more militant, than Lutheranism, and its effects are correspondingly far-reaching.[1]

In the sphere of the religious and ethical life it shows an equally marked individuality. It allows less individual liberty in the matter of religious usages, and exacts a more thorough surrender of self to its narrower and more intense moral ideal. In respect of religious usages Luther was more accommodating, more latitudinarian. Zwingli, Calvin, Knox on the other hand, not only " sned the branches of the papistry," but " struck at the root to destroy the whole " as Knox's listeners said of his first public sermon at St Andrews. In matters of conduct it applies a more systematic and vigorous " discipline " which, by minute external regulation and excommunication, strives to renovate, not always successfully, the lax moral conditions bequeathed by the old Church to the new. In contrast to Lutheranism, Zwinglianism and Calvinism are thus more distinctively " Puritan " in regard both to ecclesiastical usage and the practical life. They inaugurate and direct an extension of the Reformation programme, in this respect, of far-reaching effect.

In the sphere of Church government the contrast is equally striking. Zwingli and Calvin worked in a more democratic atmosphere than Luther, who ultimately turned fiercely on the democratic elements that were attracted to the religious movement, and sought to turn this movement to account in the

[1] Max Weber, whilst noting that Protestantism in general, as against Catholicism, gave an impulse to the practical life, seeks to show that this feature is especially characteristic of Calvinism and the Puritan sects. He remarks on the curious fact that the industrial development and capital of Germany were largely in Protestant hands, and explains it by saying that the majority of the wealthy German cities went over to the Reformation. He ascribes it to the conception of the Christian life as " a calling " to be realised in all the relations of life, in the secular as well as the religious sphere, whereas the Catholic conception found its distinctive expression in monasticism. He emphasises, however, that this feature is particularly characteristic of Calvinism. " Die Protestantische Ethik und der Geist des Kapitalismus," Archiv für Social Gesetzgebung und Statistik, Neue Folge, xx. and xxi. Included in "Gesammelte Aufsätze," i., 2nd ed., 1922, Eng. trans. by Parsons. See also Troeltsch, " Social Teaching of the Christian Churches," Eng. trans., ii. 641 f. (1931). Weber's theory has been adversely criticised by Rachfahl, " Internat. Wochenschrift," 1909-10; Seeberg, " Dogmengeschichte," iv. 625 (1917); Robertson, " Aspects of the Rise of Economic Individualism " (1933).

redress of social as well as religious grievances. Zwingli was less antagonistic to the aspirations of the people. Though Calvin's predilections were aristocratic, his disciple Knox, to his infinite credit, displayed a warm interest in the grievances of the tillers of the soil and pleaded for justice for the common man at the hands of his oppressive superiors. Moreover, all three lived in an environment more favourable to the development of a democratic Church polity than obtained in the Lutheran principalities, though even in Germany this more democratic influence found a certain scope in the German cities and states of the south and west, where the Zwinglian or Calvinist influence erelong made itself felt. Zwingli and Calvin were citizens of a republic, whilst Knox belonged to a nation in which the monarchic government was weak and was ever in jeopardy from a factious and turbulent nobility. All three were, too, imbued with a profound sympathy with the early system of Church government, which they rediscovered in the New Testament and on which they sought to model the organisation of the Church. Hence the development of a representative system of ecclesiastical government which recognised the rights and more or less gave scope to the activity of the laity in ecclesiastical administration and legislation, in contrast to the ecclesiastical bureaucracy of the Lutheran principalities.

Very marked, too, is the influence of the movement in the political sphere which made Calvinism, in its later development, so powerful an adjunct of political liberty in the Western lands. Calvin himself takes up pretty much the standpoint of Luther in the sphere of political thought. He is by no means a political or social revolutionist and is, generally speaking, a legitimist in politics. While preferring an aristocracy, he recognises the rights of established authority, whatever its constitutional form. His followers, under the influence of persecution and in defence of the Reformed Church, were by no means so accommodating. In France, the Netherlands, England, and Scotland their leaders became the protagonists of political liberty. Hence the rise of a series of publicists such as Ponet and Goodman in England, Knox and Buchanan in Scotland, Hotman and Duplessis-Mornay in France, and the apologists of the Revolution in the Netherlands, who champion the political rights of the subject, based on the Bible, history, the doctrine of the sovereignty of the people. They thus evolve the theory of the right of resistance to oppressive government, which found its application in these Western lands in a series of revolutions in the sixteenth and seventeenth centuries. In this respect, too, the Calvinist Reformation took a wider sweep than that directed by Luther and exercised a far-reaching influence, the effects of which are still felt in the opposing forces, of political absolutism and political freedom, which the Great War has bequeathed to Europe.

Whilst Calvinism thus rendered inestimable service to political liberty, it did not, unfortunately, materially improve upon the Lutheran Reformation in the sphere of liberty of thought and conscience. It was too dogmatic to anticipate or to contribute to a real emancipation of mind and conscience from their mediæval trammels. It produced indeed a Castellion and it gave rise to the sects, especially in the English-speaking nations, which became the champions of toleration in Britain, Holland, and North America. But Calvinism pure and undefiled was, in its narrowing development, alien to this great cause, and, like Lutheranism in this respect, it was untrue to its root principle in substituting rigid theological formulas for the religion of the New Testament and the emancipated reason and conscience.

THE SWISS CONFEDERATION ON THE EVE OF THE REFORMATION

The Swiss Confederation began in the union at the end of the thirteenth century of the three Forest Cantons—Uri, Schwyz, and Unterwalden—around the Lake of Lucerne. It grew until, at the beginning of the sixteenth, when it had practically, if not formally secured from the Emperor Maximilian the recognition of its independence of the Empire,[2] it numbered thirteen, with certain allied or subject territories.[3] Some of these Cantons were city states, such as Bern and Lucerne, in which the Government was aristocratic, or Zürich and Basle

---

[2] Oechsli, " Hist. of Switzerland," 13 f. (Eng. trans., 1922). Martin, " Cambridge Med. Hist.," vii. 212 (1932).
[3] Zugewandte and Unterthan Länder.

in which it was more democratic. The others were rural democracies. The bond of union between them was the Federal Diet, which deliberated on matters of general concern, but whose resolutions could not become law without the assent of each Canton. There was no central government to enforce the laws so made, and each Canton could practically ignore them if it so pleased. It was only in the direction of external relations that the Diet, to which the making of treaties was entrusted, had any real power. The Confederation was thus a very loose one, each Canton having the fullest right of self-government, and this practical autonomy is represented in the Swiss Reformation. Each state exercised the right to accept or reject the religious revolution.

From the day on which the battle of Morgarten was fought (15th November 1315) the Swiss Confederation had given proof on many a hard-fought field of their invincible valour and independent spirit, notably in their victories over Charles the Bold of Burgundy in the second half of the fifteenth century. Their prestige and their warlike reputation were very high, and towards the end of the century their active alliance was eagerly sought by the contending powers. But the honour of the Confederation was tarnished by the practice of mercenary service, and the morality of the people undermined by the corrupting influence of foreign gold. The hiring of soldiers to fight in the wars of foreign states, the bribes, in the form of bounties to the Cantonal Governments and pensions to individuals, offered by the various powers that sought their support, resulted in widespread demoralisation. Protests and attempts at reform by the Federal Diet were unavailing to counteract the evil. It was against this evil that Zwingli began his career as a reforming preacher, though his efforts were actuated by patriotism rather than evangelical zeal. Sumptuary and other laws were equally ineffective to check the luxury and other vices to which the influence of foreign gold gave rise, and it is instructive to remember that before the days of Calvin the Swiss had grown accustomed to this kind of tutorial legislation without profiting by it.

Against the growing demoralisation the Church was helpless to effect any amendment. Not only did the papal legates vie, in bribery, with the agents of secular princes in their efforts to raise mercenary contingents for the papal service. They were only too ready to sell dispensations of various kinds in order to fill the papal treasury. The scandalous traffic in benefices for the same purpose inevitably tended to secularise the clergy both higher and lower. Priests and monks were to a large extent ignorant and immoral, and too many of their superiors, who were themselves by no means paragons of morality, did not shrink from deriving a considerable revenue from the fines levied for breaches of the law of celibacy, for which there seems to have been a regular tariff. From this source the Bishop of Constance, for instance, though he is found in a pastoral of 1513 bewailing the rampant clerical immorality, derived, according to Zwingli, a yearly revenue of 4000 gulden.[4]

The power of the clergy does not, in fact, seem to have been very extensive, though there was much zeal among the people in the matter of pilgrimages, image worship, and other external observances. They were amenable to the civil tribunals, and the Cantonal Governments were not slow to assert their jurisdiction in ecclesiastical affairs, in opposition to the bishops and abbots, with whom they were often at variance. The republican spirit was incompatible with clerical privilege and domination, and was more restive than in other lands under the oppressive régime of feudal ecclesiastical superiors like the powerful abbot of St Gall. " The democratic form of Government," says Staehelin, " to which the people was accustomed, as well as the Allemanic spirit of freedom, engendered also in the relation to the ecclesiastical authority a larger measure of independence which, just at the end of the fifteenth and the beginning of the sixteenth centuries, showed itself in constant quarrels over their respective jurisdiction between the civil and the episcopal authorities. In the dispatches of Aleander from Worms to the Pope, for instance, we find the complaint that the authority of the bishops in Switzerland is but weak, and Zwingli himself did not shrink from reminding a bishop, who threatened him with excommunication, that the Swiss, in the consciousness of their native freedom, were not wont to fear everyone that might accost

[4] Staehelin, " Huldreich Zwingli, Sein Leben und Wirken," i. 10 (1895).

them." [5] Even the papal authority had come to be treated with scant respect, for the closer acquaintance which the Swiss mercenaries had made with the corruption rampant at Rome, and the worldliness of the papal legates did not tend to raise the papal prestige.

ULRICH ZWINGLI

Unlike that of Luther, Zwingli's early youth was not clouded by poverty and hardship. His father was the " Amman " or bailiff of Wildhaus, the village and district of the Toggenburg valley where he was born on 1st January 1484, and where his uncle was priest. Unlike that of Luther, too, his boyhood was that of a sturdy and buoyant mountaineer, whose school-days at Wesen, of which his uncle had become dean, and at Basle and Bern, seem to have been carefree and happy. At Bern, under the instruction of the humanist Wölflein (Lupulus) he came in contact with the new culture, of which he was subsequently to become the ardent adherent. The Dominicans of Bern, impressed by his musical talent, would fain have attracted him into their order. But his father and his uncle intervened in time and in 1500 [6] sent him to continue his education at the university of Vienna, which, under the patronage of the Emperor Maximilian, had become a centre of humanist culture and counted Conrad Celtes among its teachers. During the two years that he remained at Vienna he appears to have notably amplified his knowledge of Latin literature. At Basle, where he spent the next four years [7] and took his Master's degree in 1506, and where he had as fellow-student his future reforming colleague Leo Juda, he ploughed through the usual courses in the scholastic philosophy and theology, which had regained their predominance in the university after the departure of Reuchlin and Sebastian Brant shortly before

[5] Staehelin, i. 13-14.
[6] His name appears in the matriculation list of the university for the winter session 1498-99. But for some reason it was scored out, and it was only at the beginning of the summer session 1500 that he was actually admitted. Where he was in the interval (Paris, Tübingen ?) is unknown. W. Köhler, " Das Buch der Reformation U. Zwingli's," 14 (1926). Valuable collection of extracts from contemporary documents and sources, including the " Vita Zwinglii," by Myconius, and Bullinger's " Reformationgeschichte."
[7] Whilst a student at Basle he taught the Latin classes in a school attached to St Martin's Church.

his arrival. The effect was only to confirm him in his preference for the new culture. He found more satisfaction in
the writings of Pico della Mirandola, an edition of which
appeared at Strassburg in 1504, and in the lectures of Thomas
Wyttenbach, who became professor of theology at Basle in
1505 and expounded the Epistle to the Romans as well as the
Sentences of Peter Lombard. From Wyttenbach he learned
to seek the truth in the Scriptures and the Fathers rather than
in the schoolmen, and in the combination of humanist and
Biblical studies, which he owed to him, he had already, when
he left Basle, towards the end of 1506, to become parish priest
of Glarus, made a start towards his future vocation as a
reformer.

At Glarus he continued during the next ten years his
humanist studies and carried on a literary correspondence
with Glareanus, Vadianus, and other humanist friends.[8] The
broadening effect of these studies appears in the large-minded
outlook which could comprise Socrates, Plato, Aristotle,
Seneca among the Apostles and the Fathers as exponents of
truth. " All truth," he subsequently declared, " is from God,
through whomsoever it has been revealed. Plato and Seneca
were taught by the Holy Spirit." [9] He was even prepared,
with Lambertus de Monte,[10] to find a place for Aristotle among
the saints. He was by this time an enthusiastic Erasmian,
and under this influence began the study of Greek,[11] " in order,"
as he said later, " that he might learn the teaching of Christ
from the original sources." [12] Erasmus, to whom he paid a
visit at Basle in the spring of 1516, intensified the tendency
to independent Biblical studies, which he had derived from
Wyttenbach, and in the enthusiastic letter which he wrote to
him shortly after this visit he tells him that he never went
to bed without reading some portion of his works.[13] Like
Melanchthon and other young humanists, it was by the

---

[8] See the letters to and from these friends in vol. vii. 1 f. (1911) of
" Sämmtliche Werke," ed. by Egli, Finsler, W. Köhler, and Farner from
1905 onwards. This has superseded the older edition by Schuler and
Schulthess (1828 f.). For his humanist studies during this period at Glarus
see Usteri, " Initia Zwinglii," " Theol. Studien und Kritiken," 1885, 614 f.
[9] Staehelin, i. 50.
[10] " Werke," vii. 14, and see Usteri, " Initia," 628 f. ; Staehelin, i. 50.
[11] " Werke," vii. 21 f.
[12] *Ibid.*, ii. 147.   [13] *Ibid.*, vii. 36.

humanist approach that he reached his mission as a militant reformer. He underwent no convulsive spiritual experience like Luther, and in this process of gradual enlightenment, which ultimately led him to break away from the Church as well as the scholastic theology, he owed much, on his own confession, to Erasmus.[14]

With his humanist studies he combined, as beseemed the citizen of a free state, a keen interest in the political affairs of his people. On political and ethical grounds he denounced by pen and voice the evil of mercenary service and the corruption which was its fruit. His earliest writings were, in fact, two poems, " The Ox and Other Beasts " and " The Labyrinth,"[15] which though very poor as poetry, gave vent to his indignation at this demoralising system. The personal acquaintance which he made with it as chaplain of the mercenary contingent of Glarus in the Italian campaigns of 1513 and 1515 only increased his zeal against it. He was present at the battle of Novara, in the former year, which ended in the crushing defeat of the French, and at that of Marignano in the latter, which reversed this defeat and put an end to the long period of Swiss invincibility. He was, however, the protagonist of the papal cause against the French[16] and proud of the exploits of his countrymen as the defenders of the Church, though the closer knowledge of the worldly spirit and methods of the Roman Curia seems to have somewhat shaken his confidence in its head. He himself was the recipient of a pension from the Pope, which he used for the purpose of collecting a considerable library, and the fact is not creditable to the moralist who espoused so warmly the political cause of his patron, whilst denouncing so boldly the practice of others of taking pensions for the support of the interests of foreign potentates.

On the other hand, his uncompromising attitude towards political pension-holders roused against him the hostility of the more influential section of his congregation. Their intrigues led him in 1516 to accept the post of preacher in the Abbey Church of Einsiedeln,[17] whilst retaining his official status as parish priest of Glarus and employing a vicar to

---

[14] In his " Exposition of the Conclusions," " Werke," ii.
[15] See " Werke," i. 10 f., 53 f.
[16] See Staehelin, i. 66 f.   [17] " Werke," vii. 54.

perform the duties of the charge. The abbey possessed a black image of the Virgin supposed to be endowed with the power to work miracles, and its fame drew yearly a large concourse of pilgrims from Switzerland and Southern Germany. Whilst their presence contributed to spread his reputation as a preacher, this reputation did not rest on any pandering to the popular superstition, on which the cult of the wonder-working image was based. Though not as yet directly attacking ecclesiastical institutions, his sermons became more evangelical in tone in the emphasis laid on the necessity of seeking in the work of Christ the forgiveness of sins and in His teaching the norm of a good life. These sermons have not been preserved, but Zwingli himself afterwards claimed that during the two years of his sojourn at Einsiedeln from 1516 to 1518 he had already anticipated Luther as an evangelical teacher. " I began," wrote he in 1523, " to preach the Gospel of Christ before I ever heard the name of Luther mentioned." [18] Though " the Gospel of Christ " at this early period was by no means the Gospel in the more developed sense of his later preaching as an evangelical reformer, these two years mark a distinct progress in the process of self-illumination by the continued study of the Scriptures, and in the growth of his conviction of the need of a practical reformation of the Church. He read the Greek Testament of Erasmus and copied the Epistles of Paul in the original. He even made an attempt to learn Hebrew,[19] which he afterwards pursued with more success at Zürich. He amplified his knowedge of Greek under the instruction of Bombasius,[20] the distinguished Italian scholar and secretary of Cardinal Schinner, who accompanied the cardinal on a visit to Einsiedeln. Whilst studying, in addition, the works of Origen, Jerome, Augustine and other Fathers, he came more and more to regard the Bible as the ultimate authority in matters of faith as against the Fathers as well as the School-men.[21] At the same time, he was still a loyal churchman and was on intimate terms with Cardinal Schinner, the highest

[18] " Werke," ii. 147.
[19] " Zwingliana," i. 153 (ed. by Egli, 1904).
[20] There is a letter of Bombasius to Zwingli, March 1518, in " Werke," vii. 75.
[21] For his Biblical and patristic studies during this Einsiedeln period, see Usteri, " Initia," 655 f. See also Staehelin, i. 95 f.

dignitary of the Swiss Church. He was promoted by the Pope to the rank of acolyte chaplain,[22] and though he attacked the abuse of Indulgences as practised in the Swiss Cantons by the Franciscan monk Samson,[23] a worthy counterpart of Tetzel, he did so, not on his own responsibility, but at the instigation of his superior, the Bishop of Constance.

Unfortunately, his private life was not at this period free from the taint of immorality which dishonoured that of so many of his fellow-priests, and which does not seem to have lain very heavily on his conscience.[24] Despite this ugly fact, he was called from Einsiedeln to assume the post of people's priest (*Leutpriester*) in the Great Minster at Zürich in December 1518, after he had convinced the majority of the chapter of the falsity of the version of his offence circulated by his enemies. He amply justified their choice by his power as a preacher. He discarded the method of preaching on the passages prescribed by ecclesiastical regulation (the Pericopes), and beginning with the Gospel of Matthew, expounded systematically during the next seven years [25] the writings of the New Testament. His theme was the Gospel as he found it in these writings, and from the outset he laid stress on the practical application of this Gospel in the individual, social, and national life. He was the social reformer and the moralist as well as the theologian in the pulpit, and his earnestness and forcible eloquence drew crowds to hear him. During the first three years his attitude was still that of a reformer within the Church. It was again with the sanction of the Bishop of Constance that he renewed the attack on the Indulgence traffic carried on by Samson,[26] this time with such effect that the papal emissary was forbidden to exercise his mercenary calling not only in Zürich but throughout the Confederation. Even this onslaught on an abuse which had the papal sanction did not bring him into collision with the Pope, as in the case of Luther, for

---

[22] " Werke," vii. 95 f., 1st September 1518.
[23] On Samson's Indulgence mission, see " Das Buch der Reformation U. Zwingli's," 36 f. (Bullinger's account).
[24] See his letter to Utinger, canon of the Great Minster of Zürich, in explanation of the reports against him, " Werke," vii. 110 f.
[25] Staehelin, i. 135. Owing to the fact that he preached without notes, few of his earlier sermons have been preserved.
[26] See Bullinger's account in " Das Buch der Reformation U. Zwingli's," 50 f.

Leo X. was anxious to cultivate the goodwill of the Swiss for political purposes. He was besides not minded to conjure a new Indulgence Controversy, and was fain to add his approval.

Various influences were, however, tending to bring him into conflict with the traditional Church. An attack of the plague, which broke out in Zürich in the summer of 1519, brought him face to face with Death. In the verses in which he gave vent to the emotions of this critical experience, it is to Christ alone, not to the Church or the saints, that his thoughts turn, though these verses do not justify D'Aubigné's inference of a spiritual crisis such as that which resulted in the conversion of Luther. They only reflect a deepening of existing religious convictions to which he now gave more emphatic expression in his preaching. His personal religious experience and his study of the New Testament combined to accentuate the sense of antagonism to the traditional religion. He was no longer content to expound the teaching of Christ as contained in the New Testament. He attacked the intercession of the saints, the doctrine of purgatory, monasticism, and even the authority of the Pope, and denied the divine obligation of tithes.[27]

He renounced his papal pension in 1520,[28] for the loss of which he was compensated by his election as canon of the Great Minster in the following year. His antagonism to the papacy was, however, at this stage, actuated by political rather than ecclesiastical motives. In the inevitable conflict between the Emperor Charles V. and Francis I., as the result of the imperial election in Germany, Leo X. was fain to side with the young Emperor against his disappointed rival. Both the French King and the Pope strove to gain the support of the Swiss Confederation in the forthcoming struggle, and Zwingli once more raised his voice in the pulpit against the evil of mercenary service in the interest of foreign powers, and on behalf of Christian pacifism. It was, in part at least, due to his sermons against it that Zürich refused to join the other Cantons on the side of Francis. Though he was unable to prevent Cardinal Schinner obtaining the sanction of the Zürich Government for the raising of a mercenary contingent for the papal

---

[27] Staehelin, i. 181.   [28] " Buch der Reformation," 77 f.

service, he did not hesitate to denounce a policy which would array the Confederates in a fratricidal strife on foreign battle-fields, and the corrupting influence of the papal agents in support of it. " We cry aloud against the savage wolf which devours the sheep, but no one lifts a hand against the wolves which destroy human beings." [29] The subsequent experience of papal tergiversation and perfidy erelong roused against the Pope and his agents a storm of indignation at Zürich, which made it easier for him to transfer his antagonism to the papacy from the political to the ecclesiastical sphere. On the 11th January 1522 the Zürich Council forbade all mercenary service, whether on behalf of the Pope, the Emperor, or the French King.[30] Two months later, Zwingli preached a sermon on the question of fasting in Lent (29th March). The sermon was the prelude to the evangelical reformation for which his three years' ministry at Zürich had been the gradual preparation.

During these three years he had taken a keen interest in the resounding conflict which Luther, on religious grounds, was waging with the papacy and the mediæval Church. Early in 1519 he eagerly read and helped to circulate a collection of Luther's early writings, which Froben had published at Basle.[31] He continued throughout the next two years to follow with unabated interest the course of his heroic struggle in the main-tenance and defence of his evangelical teaching. In his corre-spondence he expressed his general approval of his developing views in the course of his expanding controversy with Eck and other opponents.[32] He welcomed in him a fellow-reformer on a larger scale, though he refrained from publicly espousing his cause in order, apparently, not to give a handle to his own ecclesiastical opponents at Zürich and elsewhere, who were already aspersing his heterodoxy. At the same time, he resented the assumption of these opponents that he was but an echo of Luther, and emphatically declined to own him as his leader. His master in theology, he maintained, was not Luther, but Erasmus, and along with him, Wyttenbach, who, unlike Erasmus, ultimately became an evangelical reformer. Its

[29] " Werke," i. 73.
[30] " Buch der Reformation," 77.
[31] " Werke," vii. 175 f.
[32] See, for instance, his letter of 31st December 1519 to Myconius, " Werke," vii. 245.

source was the teaching or Word of Christ in the oirginal Greek, not that of any man. Whilst ready to learn from others, he claimed the right to use his own judgment in considering their views, and refused to set up any theologian, ancient or modern, even an Erasmus, as an infallible authority. There can be no doubt about his sturdy individuality, and in view of this independent spirit, it is unwarrantable to see in his emphatic disclaimer of Luther's leadership mere jealousy of a rival.[33] Moreover, with Luther himself, he objected to the tendency to label the new evangelical teaching as " Lutheran," and rightly claimed that in maintaining and vindicating this teaching, as reflected in the New Testament, he was a disciple of Christ, not of any party leader. " I object," he subsequently protested in his " Exposition of the Articles or Conclusions " of 1523, " to be called a Lutheran by the papists, for I have learned the teaching of Christ, not from Luther, but from the Word of God itself (dem selbstwort Gottes). In preaching Christ, Luther only does what I myself have done, though, God be praised, he has brought to Him a far greater multitude than I or others have done. But I will be known by no other name than that of my captain, Christ, whose soldier I am and in whose service I stand." [34]

In some respects, in fact, he was, in his early Zürich period, in advance of Luther in his polemic against current ecclesiastical practice. He dissented from his more conservative attitude in his early writings on such questions as the intercession of the saints, priestly absolution, purgatory.[35] He was and remained more rational than Luther in some of his views—witness his doctrine of the Lord's Supper—and allowed more scope to the humanist influence, which Luther was only too disposed unduly to limit, if not altogether to reject. On the other hand, it is probable that in his progress beyond the Erasmian standpoint to a deeper insight into the Pauline teaching on sin and grace, faith and works, and on the impotence of the will in the religious sense, he owed to Luther's writings more than he realised or was willing to admit. Equally probable that Luther's attack on the papal authority and even on

---

[33] Jackson, " Ulrich Zwingli," 130 (1901), for instance.
[34] " Werke," ii. 146 f.
[35] Staehelin, i. 176.

that of a General Council contributed to his emancipation from the mediæval conception of both the papacy and the Church. Equally so that the condemnation of Luther opened his eyes to the futility of the idea of a reformation within the Church even on Erasmian lines.

THE ZÜRICH REFORMATION

In the establishment of the Reformation at Zürich, the chief part, next to that of Zwingli himself, was played by the Cantonal Government, which, as elsewhere in the Confederation, had been exercising, in an increasing degree, its authority in ecclesiastical affairs at the expense of that of the hierarchy. At Zürich the government was vested in two Councils—the Great Council and the Small. The Small Council was the administrative body and consisted of fifty members, representing the various guilds, half of whom carried on the administration for six months, when the other half took their place, each half being presided over by a burgomaster. The Great Council, which was the supreme legislative body, was composed of the members of the Small Council, plus additional delegates from the guilds, to the number of 200 in all.[36] It was this Council which—practically, if not directly, representing the citizen—carried out the Reformation at Zürich. Legislatively, it was the work of the civil authority, as instructed and counselled by Zwingli, on the assumption that, so instructed and counselled, to it belonged the right to reform the Church. Whilst it might seem an audacious claim on the part of the Government of a single Canton, it was in line with the tendency throughout the Swiss Confederation to encroach on the ecclesiastical jurisdiction.

Characteristically the Swiss Reformation began in an appeal on behalf of individual liberty in the matter of fasting. As the result of Zwingli's teaching, some members of his congregation, including the distinguished printer, Christopher Froschauer, ventured to eat meat during the Lent of 1522 in order to vindicate their Christian freedom. In defence of their action Zwingli preached a sermon on the " Liberty of Foods," and

[36] See Vincent, " Switzerland at the Beginning of the Sixteenth Century." Introduction to Jackson's " Zwingli," 42 f.

Froschauer adduced his teaching and that of the New Testament on the subject in his own vindication and that of his fellow-delinquents.[37]

The Bishop of Constance promptly sent a deputation to complain of the violation of ecclesiastical usage. The Small Council referred the question to the Great Council, which accorded a hearing to Zwingli as well as the bishop's representatives, who had striven unsuccessfully to exclude him, against whom the complaint was in reality, if not nominally, directed, from the sitting. After hearing the arguments on both sides, it decided that abstinence from meat in Lent should continue to be observed, whilst urging the Bishop of Constance to settle the question in dispute in accordance with the teaching of Christ and convene a provincial synod to this end (9th April 1522).[38]

A week later Zwingli sent forth from the press his first Reform manifesto in the form of an amplified version of his sermon.[39] It is not only a plea for Christian liberty on the ground of the teaching of Christ and the apostles on the subject, which he examines in detail, but an exposition of the Gospel, as reflected in this teaching. Abstinence from meats is, in itself, of no real religious value. Nor is it a Christian obligation, though it may be expedient in the exercise of self-discipline or for the sake of others till they learn to be free. Nor has the Church the right to fetter the Christian with men-made regulations. Did not Christ denounce the legalism of the Pharisees and Paul that of the Judaisers ? Such legalism is a perversion of the Gospel, " which is nothing but the Good News of the Grace of God." [40] Salvation does not depend on the attempt, in this legalist spirit, to fulfil the law, which no one can keep by his own powers. It is due not to our works, but solely to the mercy of God through Christ, in distrust of works and in the spirit of the publican, " God be merciful to me a sinner." To seek salvation by way of the law is to return to " the

---

[37] " Buch der Reformation," 88.

[38] Egli, " Actensammlung zur geschichte der Zürcher Reformation in den Jahren 1519-33," No. 236. Zwingli's account of the debate over the question in a long letter to Fabricius, " Werke," i. 142 f. Eng. trans. in Jackson's " Selected Works of Zwingli," 9 f. (1901).

[39] " Von Erkiesen und Fryheit der Spysen," " Werke," i. 88 f. Eng. trans. in Jackson's " Zwingli," App., 404 f.

[40] " Werke," i. 97.

weak and beggarly elements," against which Paul warned the Galatians.[41] The evangelical note has thus become as distinctive of the preaching of Zwingli as of that of Luther. The manifesto seems, in fact, to reflect the influence of Luther's " Liberty of a Christian Man."

Instead of complying with the request of the Council for the reform of abuses in accordance with Christ's teaching, the Bishop of Constance, at the instigation of his vicar-general Faber, who, though a friend of the new learning, had become an opponent of Luther, retorted by admonishing the Council and the chapter of the Minster to maintain established usages and repress heresy (May 1522). Some weeks later he appealed to the Federal Diet, which convened at Baden in July, and the Diet responded by issuing a warning to the Cantons to suppress the preaching of the new doctrines.[42] On his side, Zwingli and ten other reforming priests sent a petition to the bishop and the Diet respectively in favour of the free preaching of the Gospel and the sanction of clerical marriage.[43] It is a very human, and, it must be added, humiliating document. It exposed the prevalent breach of the law of celibacy by the clergy, and the petitioners frankly confess that they form no exception to the rule. They simply cannot observe chastity, and on the ground of human weakness, the scandal of free concubinage, and the scriptural sanction of marriage, they beg the bishop to permit lawful wedlock to the clergy or at least wink at their marriage. The document reflects the low view of marriage as a gratification of the flesh, all too current in this gross age. It is not pleasant reading as coming from priests who are professedly zealous for the Gospel and might be expected to expend a portion of their zeal in the exercise of self-control befitting their profession. It laid them open to the sharp criticism of the opponents of an evangelical reformation, though they were themselves by no means immaculate. At the same time, the case for the abolition of celibacy, apart from personal grounds, was a very strong one. It was certainly not a scriptural institution and was responsible for the general

---

[41] " Werke," i. 101 f.   [42] Staehelin, i. 216 f.
[43] " Werke," i. 197 f. The petition to the bishop is in Latin and is signed by Zwingli and his fellow-priests (dated 2nd July). That to the Diet is in German and is unsigned (13th July). Eng. trans. of the Latin in Jackson's " Selected Works," 25 f.

clerical immorality which was working great harm to religion. In the diocese of Constance as many as 1500 children of clerics were born by their concubines in one year.[44] The testimony of Erasmus in a letter to the Bishop of Basle, advocating the concession of this reform, is equally conclusive. To wink at this abuse, and even make a revenue out of it in the shape of fines, was only to aggravate the evil, and the proposal of the petitioners, in the face of the actual state of things, might well seem to be the only effective remedy. It was, however, impossible for the bishop, on his own responsibility, to defy canon law by granting it,[45] and thus the breach was widened, on this additional ground, between the opponents and the votaries of the old usages. Zwingli was, in fact, already secretly married to Anna Reinhard, and others of his coadjutors were in the same case.[46]

He aggravated the attack on established usages by refuting the intercession of the saints in a debate with the French Franciscan, Lambert,[47] the future Reformer of Hesse. His growing temerity arrayed against him the monks, who inveighed against his teaching in their sermons, and the controversy became so bitter that the Small Council intervened. To the proposal to refer the quarrel to the chapter of the Minster, Zwingli would on no account consent. In deference to his arguments the Council ultimately ordained that henceforth all preaching should be based on the Scriptures and nothing maintained that was not in accord with them. Appeals to Aquinas, Scotus, or other schoolmen were expressly forbidden.[48]

On the 23rd August appeared his answer to the "Admonition" against the new preaching, which the bishop had directed in May to the chapter and the Great Council. In this apology, which he entitled "Archeteles,"[49] he elaborated his principle of the supreme authority of Scripture

---

[44] "Werke," i. 225.

[45] The petitioners are quite conscious of this, and in that to the Diet ask protection from the civil power from punishment on the part of the Pope and the hierarchy.

[46] Staehelin, i. 224 f.

[47] "Werke," vii. 548.   Lambert went over to the Reformation after a visit to Wittenberg and became the Reformer of Hesse and Professor of Theology at Marburg.

[48] See Zwingli's letter to Beatus Rhenanus, 30th July 1522. "Werke," vii. 548 f., and his "Archeteles," i. 257.

[49] Its full title was "Apologeticus Archeteles Appellatus."

as the arbiter of both doctrine and usage, and refused absolutely
to accept any belief or institution that could not stand this
test. " We prove everything by the touchstone of the Gospel,[50]
the fire of Paul. Whatever we shall find to agree with the
Gospel, we shall hold to it ; whatever does not so agree we
shall reject . . . we must obey God rather than men." " The
Gospel stands in need of no Pope, no Council, no ecclesiastical
unity to assert its claim as divine truth on the heart." [51] In
order to strengthen his appeal to Scripture as the supreme
standard of belief, he had resumed his study of Hebrew. " I
have begun the study of Hebrew," he wrote to Beatus Rhenanus
on the 25th March 1522. " Ye gods ! what a dry and dreary
business. Nevertheless, I shall not desist till I have brought it
to an effective result." [52] In his appeal to the original sources,
in the Erasmian spirit, as the arbiter of faith and practice,
he had by this time overpassed the theological standpoint of
the great humanist. A fortnight after the publication of
" Archeteles " Erasmus, in a letter to him on the 8th September,
remonstrated against what he conceived to be his reckless
zeal, and advised him to consult his learned friends before
rushing such questionable effusions through the press.[53]

The " Archeteles " (the beginning and end), as its title
indicates, was meant to be the last word on the subject. It
was anything but this. The effort of Pope Hadrian VI., who
wrote him a kindly letter [54] in January 1523, to win him over
by the prospect of high promotion, he treated with contempt.
According to Myconius, he might have had a cardinal's hat,
everything in fact short of the papal chair itself, if only he
could have suited his convictions to his worldly interests.[55]
That he was prepared, on the other hand, to sacrifice even the
office he held for what he deemed the truth appears from his
resignation of his charge as people's priest rather than perform

[50] Explorabimus omnia ad lapidem evangelicum et ad ignem Pauli,
ch. lx., " Werke," i. 319.
[51] It is the same principle that he expounded in his sermon on the
" Clearness of the Word of God," published in September 1522.
[52] " Werke," vii. 497. On his ultimate proficiency in Hebrew see
" Zwingliana," i. 153 f. In this study he was greatly helped by Boschenstein,
formerly professor at Wittenberg and teacher of Melanchthon in this
subject, and by Ceporin, teacher of Greek and Hebrew at Zürich.
[53] " Werke," vii. 582.
[54] " Buch der Reformation," 80.
[55] *Ibid.*, 81.

functions to which he was conscientiously opposed, the Council nevertheless continuing to him the right to preach in the Minster pulpit. He had already entered the lists against the Pope himself with a pamphlet [56] in defence of the German Reformation.

At his instigation the Small and Great Councils at length resolved to hold a public disputation between the champions and the opponents of the Reformation before the united Council as the arbiters of the controversy, on the assumption that the supreme test of truth is the Word of God. To this disputation, to be held on the 29th January 1523, it summoned all the clergy of the city and Canton and invited the bishop to be present personally or by deputy. It extended the invitation to the other Cantons, to which only Bern and Schaffhausen unofficially responded. Whilst in the controversy over fasting it had referred the decision to the bishop and a clerical assembly, it now, under Zwingli's prompting, ignored the traditional right of bishop or hierarchy to decide in matters ecclesiastical, and arrogated this function to itself. This extraordinary development appears in the authoritative tone of the summons to the clergy. For the settlement of the prevailing religious dissension the clergy are not only required to attend the disputation, but to argue only from the divine Scripture and in the German tongue. To this discussion the Council will, with the aid of certain learned men, if it deems fit, give close attention, will decide in accordance with what it shall find to agree with Scripture, and will direct the clergy henceforth to preach accordingly, with threat of punishment for contravention of this decision.[57]

To prepare the way for it Zwingli set forth in a series of sixty-seven Articles (*Schlussreden*) the truths which he was prepared to defend and which involved nothing less than an ecclesiastical revolution. The Gospel, he insists, does not depend for its confirmation on the Church, and the substance of the Gospel is the revelation of the Father by Christ, His atonement for sin, and the reconciliation of the sinner to God by His death. The drift of the following Articles is to put Christ in

---

[56] " Suggestio Deliberandi super Propositione Hadriani Nerobergæ facta." " Werke," i. 434 f., November 1522. .
[57] " Werke," i. 466 f.

the place of the traditional Church, and to emphasise the importance of the relation of the Christian to Him. Christ being the eternal High Priest, the claim of the Pope to be the chief priest of Christendom is, therefore, untenable. Nor is the Mass a sacrifice, but only the memorial of one. The whole sacerdotal system of the Church, in fact, is unwarrantable, Christ being the only mediator between God and man. Equally so the multifarious usages based upon it. There is nothing in the New Testament to warrant the priestly order as it has developed in the Church, which consists of the body of its members, of whom Christ is the head. The civil authority has its sanction in the teaching of Christ, and if it is Christian, it possesses all the rights that the so-called spiritual power claims as belonging to it. To it all Christians are bound to render obedience as long as it enjoins nothing that is contrary to God. A reformation of the abuses rampant in the Church is essential and inevitable. " The axe," he concludes, " is already laid at the tree." [58]

In his opening address to the conference, which assembled in the hall of the Great Council on the 29th January, the burgomaster dwelt on the prolonged contention and disorder which the teaching of Zwingli had aroused among both clergy and laity, and the necessity of putting an end to it in the interest of truth and public order. The question to be decided was whether the charge of heresy which had been so often levelled against him, and which he was prepared to refute, could be proved or not from the Word of God.[59] After the bishop's major-domo (Hofmeister) had expressed the willingness of himself and his fellow-deputies to restore harmony, Zwingli rose and declared his readiness to defend his teaching as contained in the sixty-seven Conclusions, " Let us proceed in God's name. Here I stand." [60] Whereupon the Vicar-General Faber, the chief representative of the Bishop of Constance, retorted that he and his colleagues were there to hear complaints, not to discuss the doctrines and usages of the Church, and were ready to judge these complaints and thereby bring about peace. Only a General Council could authoritatively deal with matters of doctrine or usage, and this Council the Imperial Diet had resolved to hold in Germany within a year.

[58] " Werke," i. 458 f.   [59] Ibid., i. 483 f.   [60] Ibid., i. 486 f.

How could such as assembly presume to decide what was to be believed without the co-operation and consent of the Christians of other nations ? In any case, they ought to refer such questions to the universities—say, Paris, Cologne, Louvain. " Why not Erfurt or Wittenberg ? " interrupted Zwingli, amid the laughter of the audience. " No," retorted the vicar-general, " these are too near Luther. All bad things spread from the north." [61] Zwingli claimed that the present assembly, containing a majority of men of goodwill and anxious to find the truth, was a true Christian Council. Had not Christ said, he forcibly asked, " Where two or three are gathered together in my name, there am I in the midst of them." The primitive assemblies were not comprised of powerful, worldly prelates, but of simple pastors, bishops and pastors in primitive times being interchangeable terms. Knowledge of the truth as contained in God's Word, the enlightenment of the Spirit of God is no prerogative of pope, bishop, or imperial magnate. This belongs to every pious Christian. He was sceptical as to the meeting of the projected General Council, and even if it met, its ability to achieve any effective reformation. Catch the Pope and the hierarchy allowing the Scriptures alone to witness to the truth. Moreover, in reply to the vicar-general's proposal to refer the dispute to the universities for judgment, the Scriptures in the original languages were on the table, and the present assembly, in view of the scholarship of many of its members, was as capable, under the guidance of the Spirit, of understanding and expounding them as any Council or university.[62]

There ensued a prolonged silence, which was at length broken by Zwingli, who demanded that those who had attacked his teaching should prove him a heretic from Scripture. Still no response. " Step up now, you braggards, who swagger so loudly in the streets," at length called out the town fool from the door of the hall. " Here's your man. You can be loquacious enough over wine-cups. But not one of you will say cheep here." [63] At this there was more laughter, and then, in response to another appeal from Zwingli, a priest rose and reminded the assembly that the parson of Fislisbach had been arrested

[61] " Werke," i. 489 f.
[62] Ibid., i. 494 f.   [63] Ibid., i. 500.

and imprisoned at Constance for his evangelical views.[64] This brought Faber once more to his feet to announce that the priest in question had recanted his heresy on the intercession of the saints, and would presently be released.[65] Zwingli at once seized the opportunity to draw the vicar-general, in spite of himself, into a discussion on this and other questions in dispute, which filled out the remainder of the forenoon sitting. He made some strong points in support of his contention that Councils had erred and that both they and the Fathers had contradicted one another. His extensive knowledge of early Church history and patristic literature enabled him to show, for instance, that ecclesiastical practices, for which there was no warrant in Scripture, had grown up gradually and that they had no other sanction than that of canon law. Were there, then, no true Christians before these things existed? Had there not been, was there not at present, constant friction on the part of the nations with papal decrees—about ecclesiastical property, for instance? His opponent strove to invalidate his argument by distinguishing between general and particular Councils, the decisions of the former being universally binding. This Zwingli refused to admit in regard to many matters such as the marriage of the clergy. For him the decisions of Councils were simply a matter of historical development, and human reason had a large share in moulding them. "What do you mean by the term Church?" demanded he of Dr Martin Blansch, of Tübingen, who expatiated on the dictum that the Church cannot err. "If you mean the Pope and the hierarchy, then I say that this Church has often erred, because it has often acted solely in the interest of its worldly power, and has made use of force and barbarous methods to maintain its tyranny, not the will of Christ. But there is another Church, the Church invisible and spiritual, which the Pope does not recognise, but which eschews such an arbitrary worldly dominion, and this Church, relying upon the Word and Will of God, does not err." [66]

Both had so far conducted the dispute with ability and dignity — Faber from the ecclesiastical, Zwingli from the historical and Biblical point of view. The one strove to vindicate existing ecclesiastical institutions, the other to show that

[64] " Werke," i. 501 f. [65] *Ibid.*, i. 502 f. [66] *Ibid.*, i. 536 f.

they were incompatible with original Christianity. Zwingli
had certainly succeeded in showing the glaring contrast between
the Church of the present and the Church of the New Testament, and his arguments led the Council, which, from the
outset, was predisposed in his favour, to the conclusion that
the charge of heresy had not been made good. His opponents
having failed to refute his " Conclusions " or disprove them
from Scripture, it accordingly decided, on reassembling in the
afternoon, that he should continue to preach the Gospel and
that all other preachers should set forth nothing that could not
be substantially proved from the Scriptures. None should
henceforth accuse or revile another as a heretic, under penalty
of punishment for disobedience.[67] The deliverance revealed
a strong sympathy with Zwingli and his teaching. He rightly
regarded it as a virtual recognition of the truth of his " Conclusions." " God be praised and thanked," he exclaimed,
" who will have His Word prevail in heaven and on earth." [68]

Faber was not disposed to bow to this decision and resumed
the debate, notwithstanding, with special reference to the
" Conclusions," of which he had received a copy in the interval.[69]
On the fundamental point, which Zwingli stressed throughout
the whole disputation, he could not accept his contention that
Scripture is the only test of Christian truth and practice. The
Scripture had by no means prescribed everything bearing
on the Christian life and had left scope for the usages which
the Fathers, enlightened by the Spirit, had ordained and the
Church rightly observed. Moreover, in such a contention
there must somewhere be an authority to judge between the
disputants. What, he asked ironically, would you say if I
suggested that the Great Council should decide on the points
in dispute between us ? It was an embarrassing question in
view of the deliverance of the Council, which had claimed the
right to decide and had already given judgment. " I readily
accept the Council," retorted Zwingli, " as judge in temporal
matters. But in regard to religious truth I accept no judge
but the Scriptures and the Spirit of God speaking from the
Scriptures." [70] " Did not Christ say, ' Search the Scriptures,'

[67] "Werke," i. 546 f.   [68] Ibid., i. 547.
[69] According to Zwingli, a copy had been sent him, but he had not
received it before his arrival at Zürich. " Werke," i. 548-549.
[70] " Werke," i. 557 f.

and thus preclude any human judge in such matters ? " [71] His disclaimer was rather ingenuous. In reality the disputation was initiated by him and arranged by the Council on the assumption that, the truth having been ascertained by the theologians, the civil power was to give judgment accordingly.[72] To this extent he did perforce ascribe to the Council a certain judicial function in matters spiritual, whilst assuming that it only endorsed what had been proved from Scripture—the supreme authority—to be the truth.

The disputation was the prelude to the actual Reformation. Zwingli could not indefinitely go on demonstrating from the Word of God that the traditional Church was unscriptural in it beliefs and practices, as he proceeded to do more at length in his " Exposition of the Sixty-seven Articles," [73] and yet leave things as they were. He himself was prepared to move slowly in the actual work of reformation. But some of his hearers were less restrained and demanded the abolition of objectionable ecclesiastical usages, especially images and the Mass. His colleague Leo Juda, who became people's priest at St Peter's, Zürich, assumed a more aggressive attitude and openly advocated in the pulpit the removal of the images (September 1523). The exhortation led to spasmodic and furtive attempts to carry it into effect in some of the churches, and the Council, whilst imprisoning the authors of these outrages, was fain to institute a second disputation on the 26th October 1523 to discuss the question of images and the Mass. To this disputation it sent invitations to the Diet and the bishops of the Confederation as well as to the clergy of the city and Canton. The bishops declined to have anything to do with such a presumptuous enterprise, and of the Cantons only St Gall and Schaffhausen sent deputies.

In the discussion, which lasted three days, Zwingli joined Leo Juda in maintaining the thesis that, as the worship of

[71] " Werke," i. 561.

[72] An account of the disputation was written by Hegenwald, who was present and wrote it immediately after its conclusion. It was probably edited by Zwingli, and was contradicted in many points by Faber, who published his own account. This divergent version is given in the notes along with that of Hegenwald in " Werke," i. A reply to Faber appeared in the *Geyerrupfen* by seven Zürichers, in which he is charged with making false statements.

[73] " Auslegung und Begrundung der Schlussreden," " Werke," ii. 14 f. (1908).

images was forbidden in the Scriptures, it was inadmissible in the Christian Church.[74] Konrad Schmidt, who championed the more moderate view, urged the expediency of reckoning with the scruples of weaker brethren until they should be able to rely on Christ alone. Let them first destroy idolatry in the heart and the need of images would disappear of itself.[75] Against this halting attitude Zwingli insisted on the imperative necessity of obeying the Word of God, whose testimony, he held, was explicit and left no other alternative. In this matter the Gospel had not done away with the law.[76] On the question of the Mass, the discussion of which occupied the following ten days, he contended that the primitive Mass was no sacrifice, but merely the memorial of the death of Christ.[77] Whilst the Council did not venture to give a definite decision, the discussion revealed the fact that a large proportion of the assembly was in favour of Zwingli's views on both questions, though leaving to the civil power the means of putting them in operation as it should see fit. Only a few, following the lead of Grebel, advocated an immediate and radical reformation, even if the civil power should refuse its sanction.

Meanwhile the Council appointed a commission, of which Zwingli, Schmidt, and Juda were members, to continue the work of enlightening the people of the city and Canton on the points discussed. In addition to preaching, Zwingli, with the official sanction of the Council, published a short treatise on the subject, " A Short Christian Introduction," [78] which was sent to the bishops and the other Cantons. The process of further educating public opinion was a speedy one, and in three months, after two further discussions on a smaller scale by the champions and the opponents of the proposed changes (28th December 1523 and 19th and 20th January 1524), the Council definitely lent its authority to the gradual abolition throughout the years 1524 and 1525 of these and other practices of the Roman Church. One after another relics, images, processions, festivals, pilgrimages, Masses for the dead, monasteries and convents, even organs and choirs, and finally, in April 1525, the Mass itself [79] were swept away, and this in spite of the remonstrances

[74] " Werke," ii. 690 f.   [76] *Ibid.*, ii. 707 f.
[75] *Ibid.*, ii. 699 f.   [77] *Ibid.*, ii. 732 f.   [78] *Ibid.*, ii. 628 f.
[79] Zwingli retained, however, a portion of the old liturgy in the Communion Service, modified and translated into Swiss German.

of the Federal Diet and the bishops. Among the innovations we may include Zwingli's public marriage (April 1524) to Anna Reinhard, to whom he had secretly been married two years before. Whilst scandalising his enemies, the event gave great satisfaction to his friends, who had been rather perturbed by the secrecy which he had hitherto deemed incumbent to observe.[80] Many of his fellow-reformers followed his example, and the frequency of the marriage of ex-priests gave rise to the witticism of Erasmus that the Reformation was a comedy rather than a tragedy, since it always ended in a marriage.

Characteristic of the Zürich Reformation was the free discussion in the presence of the sovereign authority as representing the people, which preceded and led up to it. The movement was initiated within the Church by Zwingli and his fellow-reformers, who came to their reforming standpoint by the humanist approach. At the outset they were the champions of a reformation in the Erasmian sense, though they erelong went beyond Erasmus, who ultimately renounced his friendship with Zwingli as well as Luther. They appealed to the civil authority in support of their contentions. Hence the two public disputations, at which laymen as well as clerics were present, and which were intended to enlighten the civil authority on the questions at issue in order that it might prescribe accordingly. The civil authority did not claim the right to formulate the truth. It only claimed the right to decide on which side, as the result of the discussion, the truth lay. Neither side, in fact, attributed to it the function of propounding theological or ecclesiastical dogmas. The opponents of the Reformation explicitly reserved this power to the Church and referred the dispute to a General Council. Zwingli and his associates, on the other hand, set up the Scriptures as the supreme and sole authority and ascribed to the civil power only the right of deciding in accordance with scriptural testimony, as established in the course of the discussion.

The appeal to the civil authority in such a contingency was, for them, a practical necessity. Since the Pope and the hierarchy refused to reform the Church on evangelical lines, there was

[80] See, for instance, the letter of Melchior Dürr to Myconius, Mörikofer, " U. Zwingli," i. 211 (1867).

no other alternative open to them, if they were to carry the movement to a practical issue. To attempt to reform the Church independently of the civil authority might well seem, in the circumstances, impracticable. Moreover, it was natural that they should resort to the civil authority in a community in which the Government had asserted its right to a voice in ecclesiastical affairs, and was assumed to represent the people. At the same time, the ultimate authority in religion is for Zwingli and his fellow-theologians not the civil power, but the Word of God, of which the Government is only the executive. Only those who are sufficiently versed in the original languages can adequately (with the additional aid of the Holy Spirit) interpret the Scriptures. Given this indispensable condition, which reveals the humanist influence, it is assumed that the Scriptures are the real arbiter of both doctrine and practice. It was open to the objector to urge that the interpreters might err, and that from the point of view of religious liberty it was risky to invest the Government with the function of sanctioning and executing theological judgments, even assuming that the Scriptures, competently interpreted, are the real arbiter of Christian truth. But Zwingli and his fellow-theologians did not appreciate this danger to liberty of opinion which they only imperfectly understood. He held, moreover, that the Word of God was, in itself, clear and consistent, and that its testimony is surely ascertainable by those who adequately strive to discover it.[81] In so doing, he applied to a certain extent the critical method. He distinguished between the letter and the spirit of the Scriptures—the external Word and the revelation contained in it—and emphasised the necessity of " penetrating from the husk to the kernel." He had no taste for the Apocalypse, for instance.[82] As little as Luther did he share the later theory of the verbal inspiration of the whole Bible. To this extent he was no fundamentalist. His critical method does not, however, go very deep, and he insists on the general principle of its infallibility as an offset to the infallible authority of the Church. On this ground he will " restore the true lordship of God on earth in place of the lordship which the

---

[81] He set forth this principle in popular fashion in his sermon, for instance, " Von Klarheit und Gevissheit des Wortes Gottes," September 1522. " Werke," i. 358 f.

[82] See Usteri, " Initia Zwinglii," 660.

Pope arrogates to himself." In so far at least as he strove to test existing ecclesiastical doctrines and institutions by the touchstone of the New Testament, he was, from the historic point of view, on the right track, even if his principle of an infallible Book and his exegesis of both the Old Testament and the New are by no means always convincing.

In virtue of this principle, the Bible in the original languages is laid on the table and appealed to in the course of the disputations as the infallible and decisive arbiter of Christian truth. In virtue of this principle, the civil power is further requested to establish the truth. The result was the abolition of the Roman worship and the mediæval theology and the substitution of a scriptural worship and creed. Accordingly, the Zürich Reformation represents a wider breach with the traditional Church than in the case of that directed by Luther, who did not carry the principle of scriptural authority in regard to usages so far. It was Puritan in this respect, and its puritanism went to the extreme of banishing music and choir singing from the Church services. The fact is all the more singular inasmuch as Zwingli, like Luther, was a lover of music and himself no mean musician.

As the result of this ecclesiastical revolution, the Church was transformed into a State Church, independent of pope and hierarchy, and the State became a virtual theocracy. Church and State are closely interwoven, and civic and religious life are strictly regulated. Zwingli was fain to recognise this development on the ground that the civil authority was the representative of the Christian community as well as the State, though he had in an earlier tract differentiated the two spheres.[83] The State not only authorises the demands of the reformers and by a series of legislative acts separates the Church from Rome. It takes over the education, appointment, and maintenance of the clergy, the ecclesiastical organisation and discipline, the care of the poor, the consistorial jurisdiction of the bishop in matrimonial causes, and the supervision of morals. It entrusted the ecclesiastical administration, including the supervision and discipline of the clergy, to a synod, which met twice a year and consisted of all the ministers of

[83] "Von Göttlicher und Menschlicher Gerechtigkeit," "Werke," ii. 471 f., see especially 524.

the city and Canton,[84] two lay representatives from each parish, and eight members from both Councils. It thus recognised the co-operation of clergy and laity in the government of the Church, which Occam had advocated in the fourteenth century. But it reserved the legislative function to itself.[85] It reserved, too, the filling of vacant parishes, which Zwingli had at first proposed to entrust to the congregation.[86] It required the ministers on oath to preach in accordance with the Word of God, and made church attendance obligatory under legal penalty.[87] Under Zwingli's influence, the Synod even went the length of attributing to the State the right of excommunication in the exercise of its ethical function.[88] In place of the episcopal consistory, it instituted a court, consisting of two ministers and two members from each of the Councils, to deal with matrimonial suits and offences,[89] and erelong empowered it to take cognisance of all moral delinquencies. The court thus became the guardian and upholder of both public and private morality. Its institution in this enlarged form was a necessary and, in the circumstances, a salutary expedient for coping with the rampant demoralisation of the community. It was, too, in keeping with the tutorial régime of the mediæval municipality. At the same time, its procedure, as its records show,[90] was apt to be inquisitorial and legalist, and its puritan spirit led it to infringe unduly on personal liberty in purely social life. In this respect the Zürich consistory was the forerunner and the prototype of that of Geneva, and, as Walther Köhler has shown, its régime under Zwingli's auspices, which was based on the theocratic principle, was as comprehensive and inquisitorial as that of Geneva under the auspices of Calvin.[91]

[84] There was parity among the clergy. But Zwingli, and after him Bullinger, his successor, occupied a position of eminence, equivalent to an informal episcopacy. A similar position was held by the Antistes at Basle and Schaffhausen. See Schaff, " History of the Christian Church: the Swiss Reformation," i. 68.

[85] Staehelin, ii. 92.   [87] Ibid., ii. 84.
[86] Ibid., ii. 96.   [88] Ibid,, ii. 144.
[89] Ehegericht, 1525.

[90] See W. Köhler, " Das Zürcher Ehegericht und seine Auswirkung in der Deutschen Schweiz zur zeit Zwingli's " (1932).

[91] Ibid., 154 f. Köhler forcibly maintains that there is no ground for the assumption of Farner (" Die Lehre von Kirche und Staat bei Zwingli," 17, 1930) and Staehelin (ii. 144), for instance, that Zwingli was less exacting than Calvin in the maintenance of public and private morality by legal means.

THE ZÜRICH ANABAPTISTS

Radical though the Zürich Reformation was, it was not radical enough for the more extreme party, which under Grebel, Haetzer, Manz, Blaurock, and Hubmaier, and influenced apparently by the German radicals Carlstadt and Münzer, demanded a more thoroughly religious transformation, in accordance with what they deemed the teaching of the New Testament. Grebel, Haetzer, Manz, and Hubmaier had received a university education, and Haitzer and Manz were distinguished Hebrew and classical scholars. They became known as Anabaptists (Rebaptizers) on account of their rejection of infant in favour of adult baptism. This designation, which implies the rebaptism of those baptized in infancy, they disowned on the ground that infant baptism, not being a scriptural practice and therefore invalid, baptized infants had never really been rightly baptized. Baptism in the primitive Church was, they held, performed only after personal confession of faith, and such confession infants could not make. It was the sign and symbol of the regeneration of the adult believer by the Spirit of God, of which personal faith was the indispensable condition. Hence the imperative necessity of discarding the traditional practice and substituting for it the primitive practice of adult baptism. The question at issue with those early Baptists was thus not whether immersion or sprinkling was the right method, but whether adult baptism was the only permissible practice.

The antagonism between them and the Reformers was not confined to the question of adult as against infant baptism. It included a radically different conception of the Church and the State, the rejection of the idea of a State Church as established at Zürich, the recognition of the autonomy of the Church as a spiritual, self-governing community and its radical separation from the world, the literal application of the teaching of the New Testament in its life, organisation, and discipline. The Church is exclusively the community of regenerate, baptized believers—" the true, holy Christian Church "—and this Church the Anabaptists claimed to be.[92]

[92] Kessler, " Sabbata," 142, edited by Egli and Schock (1902) ; Johann Stumpf, " Chronica von Leben und Wirken des U. Zwingli," 64 f. (edited by Weiss, 1932).

For them the Church could not contain the tares and the wheat—the regenerate and the unregenerate—as in the parable of Jesus. It could only consist of baptized believers, regenerated by the Holy Spirit. All outside this narrow sect, even if professedly Christian, were outside the Church.[93] This association of regenerate baptized believers, living in strict obedience to the Gospel or Law of Christ, as reflected in the Sermon on the Mount, is a self-governing community, which exercises an inherent jurisdiction (the power of excommunication and self-regulation), apart from State control or even co-operation. They refused point blank to allow even a limited jurisdiction to the State in relation to the Church, though the more moderate of them recognised its lawfulness in its own sphere as a divinely ordained institution, and repudiated the revolutionary violence of a Münzer in Germany.[94] As a secular institution, the State can possess no right to legislate or judge in the spiritual sphere. Nor is it permissible to the members of the regenerate community to exercise office in the secular administration,[95] to take oaths, bear arms, or inflict civil penalties. The supreme obligation of the regenerate believer is to suffer wrong, to renounce the world and all its ways, to bear the cross. Hence, too, the self-denying philanthropy in obedience to the Gospel ideal, which led them to share their goods with one another in the Communist spirit of early Christianity. Hence also their thoroughgoing biblicism, in which they carried Zwingli's principle of the sole authority of the Scriptures to its logical extreme in the practice of a minute literalism. They could have no compromise with traditional institutions and usages which had not the express sanction of the Word of God. For the individual and the community the Law of Christ, as they interpreted it, is the only norm, and any later deviation from or development of it

[93] " Sabbata," 141 f.

[94] See the letter of the early Zürich Anabaptists to Münzer, Tumbült, " Die Wiedertäufer," 14 f (1899), and Hubmaier's " Tract on the Sword," Vedder, " Balt. Hubmaier," 279 f. (1905).

[95] Kessler, " Sabbata," 143, and see also Zwingli's philippic in 1527, " In Catabaptistarum Strophas Elenchus," " Werke," vi. (1936), edited by W. Köhler. Eng. trans. in Jackson under the title " Refutation of Anabaptists' Tricks," 200 f. Hubmaier, however, did not debar the Christian from holding office in the State. Denck, on the other hand, disallowed it. Coutts, " Hans Denck," 182 f. (1927).

is invalid, even if it is not expressly opposed to Scripture and might, therefore, be assumed to be in accord with it.

Zwingli was at first inclined to admit that, normally, baptism in the early Church was preceded by instruction and confession of faith. The radical party claimed, in fact, that, in his earliest preaching and in the private discussions of his sermons with them he was in favour of adult baptism. But in view of the strong attachment of the more conservative party in the Council and in his congregation, he was not prepared to abolish infant baptism and substitute adult baptism. Accordingly he ultimately joined issue with their leaders and, at the instigation of the Council, he strove in a series of private conferences, and later in a number of controversial works [96] on the subject, to convince them of the validity of the traditional practice. Christian baptism, he maintained, on the ground of Col. ii. 10-12, is the equivalent of circumcision among the Jews. As Hebrew children were circumcised under the Old Covenant, the children of Christian parents are baptized under the New.[97] Moreover, among those baptized in the primitive Church children were undoubtedly included—Cornelius and his whole household, for instance. He was no believer in baptismal regeneration. Baptism does not wash away sin. Salvation does not depend on any external rite of this kind. It is symbolic of the consecration of Christian children to God. Nor is the Church exclusively the community of baptized and regenerate believers. The visible Church consists of all professing Christians. It contains the tares as well as the wheat. Only the Church invisible consists of the regenerate of all the ages. It is no narrow sect, but is coextensive with the whole Christian community embraced within the Christian state. In this Christian state it is the function of the Government to further the interest of morality and religion, and the duty of its Christian members to take part in the administration.[98] The emphasis on such external rites is merely the revival of the old monkish righteousness in a new guise, and is an unwarrantable legalist shackling of the freedom of the Gospel. His reasoning is, on

[96] In addition to his " Refutation " he wrote in 1525 his tract, " Von der Taufe, von der Wiedertaufe, und von der Kindertaufe," " Werke," iv. 206 f.

[97] " Selected Works," 236

[98] *Ibid.*, 206.

the whole, forcible, though his aspersion of the moral character and seditious tendency of the sectaries in general is unwarranted.

To put an end to the contention, which was seriously jeopardising the Reformation, the Council was fain to institute a disputation in January 1525, in which Zwingli and Leo Juda maintained, and Grebel and Manz controverted, the validity of infant baptism. It decided in favour of Zwingli and his colleague, and accordingly directed all Anabaptists to have their children baptized within a week under penalty of banishment for non-compliance. Protesting that they must obey God rather than man, they withdrew to the village of Zollikon and organised themselves into a brotherhood on the basis of adult baptism, to which they now definitely submitted themselves, Grebel first baptizing Blaurock, by pouring water on his head, and Blaurock in turn baptizing fifteen others.[99] A second disputation in March and a third in November were equally fruitless, and ultimately the Council, in March 1526, decreed the penalty of death by drowning against these stubborn sectaries on the ground that their tenets were subversive of civil order as well as religion.[100] In the following January Manz, the first victim of this brutal policy, was drowned in the lake of Zürich, protesting to the last his fidelity to his convictions in obedience to Christ. On the same day Blaurock, as an outsider, was publicly scourged out of the city. Several others were also drowned and several more died from the effects of their maltreatment in prison.

Zwingli's approval of this barbarous method of dealing with dissenters from his teaching is a sad blot on his memory, even if he only reluctantly abetted the use of force in the service of religion, which he had rebutted so strongly in the case of the Romanists. His personal animosity against those opinionated but conscientious sectaries, who denounced him as " the Antichrist of the Great Minster," may explain and palliate to some extent his inconsistency. It was none the less a gross violation of the teaching of the New Testament, on which he professed to base the Reformation, and to which he had taught these sectaries to appeal as the norm of both faith and practice.

[99] Kessler, 142.
[100] Mandate in " Buch der Reformation," 187, which gives also Bullinger's account of the controversy.

In his controversial works against them he allowed his personal resentment to overcloud his judgment, and indiscriminately and, for the most part, unwarrantably, charged them with immorality and hypocrisy, as well as heresy.

His attitude towards the demands of the peasants who, as in Germany, took advantage of the religious movement to press for the redress of grievances, does him more credit. Whilst maintaining the duty of the peasants to obey the powers that be and submit their case to their discretion, he urged the Council to abolish serfdom and at least the small tithes, and energetically condemned the fierce outburst of Luther against the revolted German peasants.[1] It was due to his energetic advocacy as well as the threatening attitude of the peasants that the Council, whilst refusing to sacrifice the tithes, conceded the demand for the abolition of serfdom.[2]

THE SEQUEL OF THE ZÜRICH REFORMATION

Whilst the Diet of the Confederation had declined to take part in the Zürich disputations, it ultimately accepted the proposal of Eck, Luther's redoubtable antagonist, to debate with Zwingli and others at Baden in Aargau in May 1526. Zwingli declined the invitation on the ground that he could not with safety take part in it, and the task of defending the Reformation before the deputies of the Cantons and the bishops devolved on Oecolampadius of Basle and Haller of Bern. The disputation lasted several weeks and ended in the triumph of Eck, who received a large majority of votes in support of the real presence, the invocation of the saints, purgatory, and images.[3] But the time had gone past for such dialectic triumphs either to regain the allegiance of Zürich or to prevent the spread of the movement to the other Cantons. In 1528 the Great Council of Bern, where Haller had prepared the way by his preaching, decided, after the usual disputation (6th to 26th January), to adopt the ten evangelical Conclusions which had formed the subject of discussion, abolish the episcopal juris-diction, and introduce the Reformed worship. At Basle the

[1] Staehelin, i. 508.
[2] " Das Buch der Reformation," 177 f. ; Staehelin, i. 497 f.
[3] Staehelin, ii. 30.

transformation was still more expeditious. Basle, which Erasmus, in the later period of his career, chose as his residence, was the great humanist centre of the Confederation, and was fortunate in possessing in Oecolampadius, preacher and professor in the University, a scholar who combined the love of humanist studies with zeal for the Gospel. He became the staunch associate of Zwingli in the propagation and defence of the Reformed doctrines as well as the associate of Erasmus in his critical labours. Under the stimulus of his preaching his adherents in February 1529 destroyed the images in the churches and compelled the Council to introduce the Reformed worship,[4] to the disgust of Erasmus, Glareanus, and Beatus Rhenanus, who withdrew to Freiburg. St Gall under the leadership of Vadianus (Joachim von Watt), the humanist physician, and of John Kessler, and Appenzell anticipated both Bern and Basle in their acceptance of the Reformation.[5] In Schaffhausen it found an effective exponent in Sebastian Hofmeister, and his preaching led to its establishment in this Canton in 1529. About the same time it had made substantial progress in Glarus and the Grisons, and thus within five years of its triumph at Zürich it had asserted its supremacy in a large part of German-speaking Switzerland.[6]

Its rapid progress had, however, roused the bitter hostility of the Forest Cantons—Uri, Schwyz, Unterwalden, Luzern, and Zug. These not only adhered staunchly to the old faith, but refused toleration to the adherents of Zwingli and leagued themselves with Ferdinand of Austria against the Reformed Cantons, which were equally averse to tolerate Roman Catholics. The question of toleration was brought to a head by the burning of a Zwinglian preacher at Schwyz in May 1529. The practice of mercenary service, to which the Forest Cantons tenaciously adhered, and against which Zwingli urged forcible action, aggravated the dissension. The result was what is called the First War of Cappel. Happily it did not lead to bloodshed and ended almost as soon as it began in a treaty

[4] " Briefe und Akten zum Leben Oecolampads," ii. 280 f. (ed. by E. Staehelin, 1934).
[5] After the Second Cappel War the jurisdiction of the Abbot of St Gall was, however, restored. Schaff, i. 127.
[6] For the spread of the Reformation in German Switzerland see Schaff, i. 102-164; Oechsli, " History of Switzerland," 94 f.; Hadorn, " Die Reformation in der Deutschen Schweiz," 58 f. (1928).

which guaranteed mutual toleration, dissolved the alliance with Austria, recognised the right of the subject lands of the Cantons to accept or refuse the Reformation, bound the evangelical Cantons to renounce foreign pensions, but only recommended the Forest Cantons to do likewise, and exacted compensation to the children of the martyred Zwinglian preacher and to Bern and Zürich for the expenses of the war [7] (June 1529).

The acceptance of the principle of toleration was, however, but a makeshift on both sides, and Zwingli laboured, in association with the Landgrave of Hesse, to cement a great evangelical league, which should include France and possibly Venice, for the defence of the Reformation both in Switzerland and Germany against the Emperor Charles and his allies. Under pressure of necessity he thus, in the interest of the Reformation, involved himself in political complications against which he had formerly strenuously protested, though his policy was not marred by the corrupting influence of foreign gold. On the other hand, the Forest Cantons reverted to their alliance with Austria, and Bern and Zürich determined to bring them to submission by a blockade, instead of a renewal of active hostilities as Zwingli advocated. This expedient, which deprived them of grain and other necessaries, drove them to desperation, and resulted in the Second War of Cappel (October 1531) in which the Zürichers suffered a crushing defeat and Zwingli was slain (11th October 1531).

His aggressive policy thus led to disaster to himself and his cause, for though mutual toleration was again agreed to [8] as between the Protestant and Romanist Cantons, it was more to the advantage of the latter than the former, which lost some of the ground they had gained,[9] whilst the hope of reforming the Forest Cantons was blasted. As his attitude towards the Anabaptists and the Romanists shows, he as little as Luther, not to speak of the Romanist opponents of both, could systematically apply the Protestant principle of Toleration. This is all the

---

[7] " Buch der Reformation," 271 f. ; Ruchat, " Hist. de la Reformation de la Suisse," ii. 116 f., ed. by Vulliemin (1835).
[8] Zweite Landsfriede—Second Peace of Cappel, 20th November 1531. Zürich, in addition, was compelled to renounce her League with foreign cities and pay the expenses of the war. Schaff, i. 194 f.
[9] See the treaty in Ruchat, ii. 438 f.

more singular inasmuch as he was, as a theologian, in advance of his fellow-reformers. He refused to believe in the damnation of innocent children in spite of his own supralapsarian doctrine of predestination and election, which he worked out in his "Commentary on True and False Religion" (1525). He believed that there was a place in Heaven for all good men as well as for the Christian saints. But as a man of action his views were conditioned by what appeared the practical necessities of the situation, and on political and religious grounds he regarded the Forest Cantons as enemies to be fought and conquered in the interest of both the religious and the political welfare of the Confederation. His tragic end clouded his fame and weakened his subsequent influence. His place as the leader of the Reform movement on a larger scale in the west was taken by Calvin. With Calvin the centre of the movement passed from Zürich to Geneva.

CHAPTER II

EARLY LIFE OF CALVIN

EDUCATION

JOHN CALVIN or Cauvin was born on the 10th July 1509 in the episcopal city of Noyon in Picardy, where his father, whose legal ability had gained him many clients among the provincial nobility as well as the clergy, had attained an influential position as procurator.[1] He received his early education in the College Des Capettes, along with the sons of the lords De Montmor and De Genlis, who held his father in high esteem, and in whose homes he was a frequent guest. To this close association was due the refinement of manner which was afterwards to distinguish him from both Luther and Zwingli. At the age of eleven the Bishop of Noyon conferred on him the revenue of a small benefice, and before he was twenty he was the possessor of two others. He was an apt pupil,[2] and in 1523 his father sent him, along with the sons of De Montmor and De Genlis, to continue his education, under Maturin Cordier, in the College of La Marche at Paris, where he lived in the house of his uncle Richard.

Cordier was a humanist and, like John Colet, an educational reformer, though not as yet an adherent of the Reformation, and Calvin owed to him the command of an elegant Latin style, which distinguishes his writings from those of his fellow-

[1] Beza, "Vie de Calvin," 29, in "Calvini Opera," t. xxi. It was written immediately after Calvin's death and was prefixed to Calvin's "Commentary on Joshua." It was subsequently published in an enlarged form, and the author of this enlargement was Colladon, a friend of both Calvin and Beza, whose name, however, was not given, and it passed under the name of Beza. Beza later composed a life in Latin. All three are given in vol. xxi. of "Opera," ed. by Baum, Cunitz, and Reuss for the "Corpus Reformatorum." An English trans. by Beveridge of the Latin life is prefixed to vol. i. of the trans. of "Calvin's Tracts" relating to the Reformation, *Calvin Trans. Soc.* (1844). Additional biographical details in "Opera," v. xxxi.
[2] Lefranc, "La Jeunesse de Calvin," 13 (1888).

reformers.[3] In dedicating to him his " Commentary on First Thessalonians," he warmly acknowledges this indebtedness. When in 1537 he endeavoured to reorganise the college at Geneva, he succeeded in securing him as a member of its staff.[4]

From La Marche he passed to the College of Montaigu, which, under Noel Bedier, was a focus of obscurantism. Whilst its frugal fare and harsh discipline had been the butt of the satire of Erasmus, a former pupil, it at least drilled him in the dialectic art. His progress was rapid, for he was as studious as he was quick of apprehension. The religious bent of his mind is, too, already apparent. " He profited," says Beza, " so effectively from the instruction he received that in a few years he advanced to the study of philosophy. As to his morals, he was very conscientious, the enemy of vice, and very devoted to the service of God as then understood." [5] His father's original intention, and apparently his own inclination, was that he should proceed from the study of philosophy to that of theology.[6] But with the completion of his studies for the Master's degree in 1527 came a change of plan in favour of the law as a career.

This change of plan was due to his father, who, he tells us,[7] had by this time concluded that the profession of the law offered a more lucrative career to his son's ability. Like Luther, Calvin acquiesced in this change of plan, " in order to obey my father," rather than in accordance with his own inclination. At this period Orleans was the most famous law school in France, as well as a centre of humanist studies, where Erasmus, Reuchlin, and Aleander had respectively taught Latin, Hebrew, and Greek. Accordingly, early in 1528, he left Paris for Orleans to study under the celebrated jurist Pierre de l'Etoiles. As at Paris, he distinguished himself by

[3] Doumergue, " Jean Calvin, les Hommes et les Choses de son Temps," i. 66 (1899).
[4] Herminjard, " Correspondance des Réformateurs," iv. 456 (Statutes of the College, January 1538).
[5] " Vie de Calvin " (Colladon), " Opera," xxi. 54. Standonk, Bedier's predecessor, had introduced a very severe discipline and a very exacting course of study. See Renaudet's article on him in Bulletin de la Soc. de l'Hist. du Protestantisme Français, 1908, 69 f. On Erasmus' student days there, see Nichols, " Epistles of Erasmus," i. 104 f. (1901), cf. Allen, " Erasmi Epistolæ," i. 50.
[6] Preface to the " Commentary on Psalms," " Opera," xxxi. 21.
[7] Ibid., " Opera," xxxi. 21.

his quickness of acquisition and his intense application, which, in Beza's rather enthusiastic judgment, erelong put him on an equality with his teachers. Nevertheless, he was not the unsocial, querulous recluse of later tradition. On the contrary, a number of his fellow-students became his close friends, in whom he inspired a lasting affection.[8] His sojourn at Orleans lasted about eighteen months, when in the summer of 1529 he migrated to Bourges, the capital of the Duchy of Berry, which Francis I. had conferred on his sister Marguerite, Queen of Navarre. He was attracted thither by the fame of Alciati, the Italian jurist, who rendered Bourges the formidable rival of Orleans as a law school. Here, as well, probably, as at Orleans, he appears to have combined an interest in humanism with the study of jurisprudence. He began that of Greek under the German humanist, Melchior Wolmar,[9] an adherent of Luther, whom the Duchess invited from Orleans, where Calvin had, probably, already become acquainted with him, to teach the classics, and who from 1528 to 1534 acted as preceptor and guardian to the boy Theodore de Bèze, Calvin's future coadjutor and successor at Geneva. In warm acknowledgment of his indebtedness, he subsequently dedicated to him his " Commentary on Second Corinthians." [10]

With the death of his father in May 1531, whose relations with the Cathedral Chapter of Noyon had become strained over financial matters, and who had in consequence been excommunicated, came another change in his career. He was now free to devote himself to what was evidently his own predilection— the study of the classics, which his intercourse with Wolmar had quickened, and the life of the scholar. Though he erelong abandoned the law as a career, the time spent in these studies had by no means been wasted. They were, in truth, if as yet

---

[8] See Doumergue, i. 132 f. Iambart de la Tour makes him, without adducing his reasons, begin his sojourn at Orleans at the end of 1528 or beginning of 1529, " Calvin et l'Institution Chrétienne," 10 (1935).

[9] " Histoire Ecclesiastique des Églises Réformées," i. 19 f., ed. by Baum and Cunitz (1883). It is usually ascribed to Beza, but was very probably only supervised by him.

[10] " Opera," xii. 364 f. Beza afterwards (1560) dedicated to him his " Confession of the Christian Faith," in which he acknowledges his deep indebtedness to him both for his training in the classics and his instruction in the evangelical faith. This dedication, translated from the Latin into French by C. Martin, is given in " Almanach Jean Calvin," 1935. In it he makes no mention of having met Calvin.

unwittingly, a valuable preparation for what was to prove his permanent vocation as the legislator and organiser of the Reformation at Geneva and elsewhere. Meanwhile he prepared himself for that of the humanist scholar by attending the Greek lectures of Danès at Paris, and began the study of Hebrew under Vatable—both lecturers in the Royal College which Francis I. had just founded, and the protagonists of the critical study of the Scriptures against the obscurantists of the Sorbonne [11]—whilst working at his Commentary on the " De Clementia " of Seneca, which appeared in the following year, 1532.[12] It gave proof of extensive erudition and boded for its author a brilliant career as a humanist scholar, though it by no means attains the exacting standard of modern critical scholarship. It reveals, too, something of the spirit of his contemporary, Sir Thomas More, in the tendency to make the work the vehicle of its author's convictions. To a certain extent it does so. It emphasises, for instance, the insufficiency of philosophy as a guide to truth and a means of the formation of character. It lays marked stress on the supremacy of law in the State and the need for a strong but regulated authority, whatever its form, to enforce it. It reveals alike his dislike of political absolutism and his distrust of the influence of the people, who are but too prone to sedition, on Government which he shares with the humanists. " Cæsar without the republic is not Cæsar, the republic without Cæsar is not the republic." [13] Some [14] have even seen in it a set if veiled plea on behalf of the " Lutherans," as the adherents of the Reformation in France were termed at this period. This inference is, however, all too sanguine. Calvin is not yet the protagonist of the evangelical cause, but specifically a humanist of the school of Erasmus and Budé, and the work was evidently intended to establish its author's reputation as a scholar and, at most, a moralist. In it the future puritan reformer of Geneva appears in the rôle of the anti-Stoic, the champion of human sensibility, and this feature affords an additional reason for eschewing those

[11] See Doumergue, i. 201 f.
[12] " Opera," v. For an examination of its main ideas see Iambart de la Tour, " Calvin et l'Institution Chrétienne," 15 f. (1935).
[13] " Opera," v. 49.
[14] Guizot, Henry, and more recently Pannier, " Recherches sur l'Evolution religieuse de Calvin," 16 f. (1924).

preconceived generalisations about Calvin's character which historians have been too apt to make without due consideration of time and circumstance.

CONVERSION

After its publication in April 1532 he spent another year at Orleans as deputy Proctor (*Procureur*) of the Picard students who constituted one of the ten " nations " of the university (May 1532-33). It has been conjectured that after the completion of his official duties as Deputy Proctor he took the degree of Doctor of Law.[15] Some months later he had discovered that his life work was to be neither that of a humanist scholar nor a pundit of the law. By the autumn of 1533 the experience which he terms his " Conversion " had made him a convinced and ardent adherent of the evangelical faith and decided his destiny as an evangelical reformer. This experience and the change of destiny which it involved are reflected in the discourse which his friend and former fellow-student at Paris, Nicolas Cop, son of the royal physician, and Rector of the University for the year 1533-34, delivered on All Saints Day, 1st November. Whether Calvin actually wrote [16] the discourse or not, it is safe to say that he influenced its content, and the content is distinctively evangelical. It is nothing less than a manifesto on behalf of a reformation, not merely in the Erasmian but in the Lutheran sense, whilst reflecting in addition some characteristic traits of the Calvinist theology. Calvin, it is evident, was indebted to both Erasmus and Luther in his advance towards the evangelical standpoint.

[15] Pannier, " Recherches," 31 f.

[16] " Histoire Ecclesiastique," i. 25. A fragment of it in his handwriting was discovered at Geneva and a copy of the whole was found at Strassburg and published, " Opera," x^b. 30 f. The existence of the fragment in Calvin's handwriting gives weight to the contention of those who ascribe the composition of the discourse to him, though the Latin style is inferior to his. At all events, it shows his keen interest in it. His authorship of the discourse is accepted by Lefranc, " Jeunesse," 112 ; Lang, " Die Bekehrung Calvins " (1897); Doumergue; and more recently by Pannier, " Recherches," 39 f. It is rejected by K. Müller, " Calvin's Bekehrung," " Nachrichten von der Königl. Gesellschaft der Wiss. Göttingen," 1905, 188 f.; Wernle, " Zeitschrift f. Kirchengeschichte," xxvii. 97, who, however, in a later article, " Z.K.G.," xxxi. 569, seems to accept it; Baur-Weinsberg, " Johann Calvin," 7 (1909). It is doubted by Williston Walker, " Calvin," 101 (1906) ; Choisy, " Calvin," 25 (1925); Hunt, " Calvin," 39 (1933).

His description of the new theology as Christian philosophy
is taken from Erasmus. He borrows, as Lang has shown,[17]
from one of Luther's sermons on the same text (Mathew v. 3)
as that on which he bases the discourse in question. He proclaims, in a strain that is distinctly Calvinist, the certitude
of salvation, of which the believer is conscious. Throughout,
he emphasises, in contrast to the wretched sophists[18] of the
Sorbonne, the doctrine of salvation by the Grace of God in
virtue of faith alone, not of works, and the triumph of this
faith over doubt. He protests against the persecution of those
who are prepared to die for the Gospel and are denounced as
heretics, and thus stands forth as the apologist of the votaries
of the evangelical faith in the very presence of its inflexible
enemies, the doctors of the Sorbonne. The discourse was thus
not merely an exposition of this theology. It was a vindication
of it before the assembled university. Its boldness denotes
the man of conviction, who has unreservedly thrown in his lot
with the Lutheran Reformation, and is eager to take advantage
of the opportunity of advocating his cause. The situation at
Paris seemed at the moment highly favourable to the party of
reform. The obscurantists of the Sorbonne, under the leadership of Noel Bedier, had ventured to attack the sister of the
King, Marguerite of Navarre, the authoress of the obnoxious
" Miroir de l'âme pécheresse," as the patroness of heresy,
and had incurred the active hostility of the King in consequence. This fact, as well as his close association with the
obscure but active evangelical party at Paris,[19] probably
encouraged Calvin to write or inspire and Cop to deliver this
evangelical manifesto. At the same time, its intense conviction is that of one who is ready to venture all for the cause
he has at heart, though Cop apparently, in delivering it, toned
down some of its statements.[20]

Calvin had evidently before the composition of this discourse
experienced what he terms his " conversion." " God," he
tells us in the preface to his " Commentary on the Psalms,"
" by a sudden conversion tamed and made teachable my

---

[17] " Die Bekehrung Johannes Calvin's," 47 f.
[18] Perditissimi Sophistæ.
[19] He makes particular mention of Etienne de la Forge, the most earnest
of them, " Opera," vii. 185.
[20] Doumergue, i. 331.

mind." [21]   According to Beza, he had already, as a student at
Paris, been attracted to the evangelical faith through the
influence of his cousin, Pierre Robert Olivetan [22] (Olivier), its
ardent adherent, who was erelong forced to retire from Orleans
to Strassburg, and some years later translated the Bible, to
which Calvin contributed a preface in 1535,[23] into French,
in the solitude of the Vaudois valleys, where he sought a refuge
from persecution.   Beza further tells us of his intercourse with
Wolmar at Bourges, where he continued his study of the
Scriptures and was active in propagating a knowledge of them.
He is said even to have preached in the town to a small number
of believers and in the neighbouring villages (?).[24]   It is in itself
probable that he was already, as a student at Orleans and
Bourges, beginning to interest himself in the religious controversy which Lefèvre had roused in the schools in France
and Luther had intensified in those in Germany, and which
had brought on both of them the condemnation of the Sorbonne.
Besides Olivetan, two other fellow-students at Paris, Nicolas
and Michael Cop, whose father was a friend of Erasmus and
Reuchlin, were among his friends.   His interest in humanist
culture would of itself tend to beget a leaning towards the
reform movement, since this culture was in France, at this
period, associated with this movement, as represented at least
by Erasmus.

On the other hand, Beza, in representing him as already
in his student days at Paris contracting " in some measure a
taste for pure religion and beginning to withdraw himself from
papal superstition," was evidently outrunning the facts.   Calvin
himself tells us that " he was so obstinately addicted to the
papal superstition that it was by no means easy to extricate
himself from this quagmire," and that he was hardened in his
attachment to the traditional religion.[25]   There was evidently
a lengthy period of resistance before he could bring himself to
take the decisive step to the side of the evangelical reformers.

[21] " Opera," xxxi. 22, "animum meum . . . subita conversione ad
docilitatem subegit."
[22] " Opera," xxi. 29.
[23] See Gagnebin, " Almanach Jean Calvin," 1935.   The translation was
published at Neuchâtel in June 1535.
[24] Beza, " Opera," xxi. 55 ; " Hist. Eccles.," i. 20 ; Doumergue, i.
182 f.
[25] Pref. to Psalms, " Opera," xxxi. 22.

This decisive step he describes as " a sudden conversion," and in the Epistle to Sadolet in 1539 he both tells of the protracted process of self-examination and study which preceded it, and enables us to divine in what it actually consisted. It appears to have taken place during the eighteen months that elapsed between the publication of the " De Clementia " in the spring of 1532, when he is still the ardent votary of the new culture, and the composition of the Cop discourse in the autumn of 1533, when he has undoubtedly become the confirmed adherent of the reformed faith.

This experience has its intellectual and its psychic aspect. In its intellectual aspect, it is the culmination of the search for the truth in religion, of the intensive study of the Word of God in which He has revealed His will. The Word, not tradition or the authority of the Church, becomes for him the sole standard and test of true religion. He has learned to confide in its guidance alone and has thereby found his way to the evangelical faith. By its testimony, illumined by the Spirit of God, he has tested the traditional religion. He has found, he says, that they who were esteemed the authoritative exponents of the faith neither understand the Word nor give it its due place as the sole and authoritative divine revelation. They have deceived the people with strange doctrines, superstitions, absurdities. The papacy, he has discovered, is a usurpation, a travesty of pure Christianity, a tyrannic, corrupt institution. Error, superstition, idolatry have taken the place of true religion, the true worship of God ; trust in good works of trust in the righteousness of Christ. This system afforded him, indeed, transient intervals of spiritual tranquillity, and he was loath to abandon it. But, finally, he yielded to the convincing testimony of the Word and determined to renounce it.

The psychic aspect of this experience appears in the anxious quest for salvation which was interspersed with the quest for the true religion. As in the case of Luther, he had his periods of doubt about the efficacy of the ecclesiastical conception of salvation by way of penance and satisfaction for sin. It failed to give assurance in the presence of the divine judge at the bar of a reproving conscience. Conscience persisted in making its voice heard, and an extreme terror laid hold of him at times. " For when I descended into myself or raised my heart to Thee,

such a sense of horror gripped me that no purifications, no
satisfactions could assuage. And the more I examined myself,
the sharper became the stings of conscience, so much so that
there remained for me no other solace or comfort but to deceive
myself in forgetfulness. But as nothing better offered I went
on in the same train as I had commenced until there supervened a very different form of doctrine, not for the purpose of
turning us away from the Christian profession, but to bring it
back to its true source and restore it, purified from all filth,
in its purity." [26] Still he would not give in, but resisted strongly
the innovations put forward by the evangelical preachers
(apparently by his friends Gerard Roussel and Du Tillet,
among others, who subsequently lapsed from the evangelical
cause). Only with the utmost reluctance was he led to realise
that he had all his life been in ignorance and error. His reverence for the Church, the fear of schism, in particular, had held
him back until the insight that supervened on this long drawn-
out intellectual and psychic experience suddenly flashed on
his brooding and perturbed soul. With it came the conviction
that to reform the Church from the vices that contaminated it
was not to be guilty of schism, but to deliver it from this con-
tamination and restore " the true order of the Church " in
place of the papal distortion of it. This conversion was not,
however, equivalent to a full comprehension of the new theology,
of which he was to become the systematic expounder. He only
thereby attained " in some measure a taste of true piety." [27]

[26] " Épitre a Sadolet," " Trois Traités de Calvin," ed. by Schmidt,
88 (1934), and " Opera," v.
[27] Pref. to the " Commentary on the Psalms," " Opera," xxxi. 22. There has
been much discussion on the time and character of his conversion. Lefranc
holds strongly that it was a matter of intellectual enlightenment, " Jeunesse
de Calvin," 96 f. He thus ignores the psychic element. Lang contends
that it was a sudden and complete religious change, which took place shortly
before the composition of the Cop discourse, " Bekehrung," 37 f. This is
in accordance with Calvin's testimony, though it is evident that it was
preceded by a protracted search for truth in which an intellectual element is
present. Doumergue, whilst agreeing that it was religious in character,
places it as far back as 1528, and, following Beza, ascribes it to the influence
of Olivetan and Wolmar, though it was only completed after the publication
of the " De Clementia," i. 387 f. This does not take into sufficient account
the protracted resistance that preceded it. Holl agrees with Doumergue
in putting it as early as 1527-28, " Aufsätze," iii. 255 f. (1928). Wernle,
" Z.K.G.," xxxi., and Williston Walker agree with Lang as to its time and
character, though Walker thinks that it did not involve a conscious breach
with the Roman Church, and that this is not to be found in Cop's discourse,
" Calvin," 97 f. Similarly Hunt, " Calvin," 40 f. Pannier, on the other

EARLY EVANGELISM

His conversion proved to be an epoch-making event not only in Calvin's personal career, but in the history of the Reformation in Western Europe. In spite of his love of seclusion, due to his retiring disposition, he sprang at once into the position of a leader among the adherents of the evangelical movement. " Having thus been imbued with some taste of true piety (by ' the sudden conversion ' of which he tells in the previous sentence) I was straightway inflamed with so great a desire to profit from it that, although I did not altogether quit my other studies, I gave myself to them more slackly. Now I was completely astonished that, before a year passed, all those who had some desire for pure doctrine gathered themselves about me in order to learn, although I had made but a beginning myself." [28] He became, too, after the delivery of Cop's discourse, a marked man to its enemies. For the next two years his life was largely that of a fugitive who, under various pseudonyms, furtively wandered from place to place in constant danger of persecution, instructing on occasion his fellow-believers in the Word and striving to win converts for his new faith. The delivery of his rectorial discourse aroused the ire of the Sorbonne against Cop, who only saved himself from the inquisition of the Parliament of Paris by a hairsbreadth escape to Basle. Calvin, whose complicity was suspected and who had an equally narrow escape,[29] fled to Chaillot, whence, relying on the protection of the King's sister, he ventured back to Paris, only to withdraw, a second time, to Angoulême. Here he found a refuge in the house of his like-minded friend, the Canon Du Tillet, whose hospitality he repaid by teaching him Greek. From Augoulême he went to Nérac to visit the aged Lefèvre, Marguerite's protégé, who, according to Beza,

hand, sees in it a definite acceptance before the Cop discourse, and as the result of a gradual evolution of the evangelical faith, in opposition to the Roman Church, " Recherches," 46 f. Vienot places it as late as 1534, " Hist. de la Reforme Française," 188 (1926). So also I. de la Tour, " Calvin et l'Institution Chrétienne," 30.

[28] Pref. to " Commentary on the Psalms," " Opera," xxxi.

[29] He is said to have cheated the heresy hunters, who were on his track, by letting himself down from the window of the room by a rope made of the bedclothes. Beza, however, says that he owed his escape to the fact that he happened not to be at home when the police visited the College de Fortet, where he resided, but that his papers were seized, " Opera," xxi. 56.

divined the greatness of his future career. He next turns up at Noyon, whither he went to resign the benefices he could no longer hold. From Noyon, where he is wrongly said to have been imprisoned for a short time,[30] he paid a stealthy visit to Paris. It was during this visit that he came into contact for the first time with Servetus, whom he challenged to a theological discussion, which the anti-Trinitarian thought best not to accept.[31] Thereafter we find him once more at Angoulême, and then at Poitiers, where in a cave near the city he dispensed the Lord's Supper for the first time after the evangelical rite. Thence he flitted to Orleans and wrote a work against the Anabaptists.[32] The preface which he wrote in 1534 already reveals the consciousness of his mission as the protagonist of the evangelical faith. "When many are in danger of being ensnared by error, I do not see why I should not be called a betrayer of the truth, if in such necessity I keep silent and dissimulate." Nor will he be deterred from this defence by the reproach that he is breaking the unity of the Church and violating charity. "To these it may be answered that we recognise no unity except in Christ, no charity except that of which He is the bond. The fundamental thing in maintaining charity is that the faith should remain sacred and unimpaired among us." Finally, in view of the increasing risk of persecution, after what is called the affair of the Placards, which transformed Francis I. into a furious persecutor in January 1535, he sought a refuge, along with Du Tillet, beyond the frontier of France at Basle.

PLEA FOR TRUE RELIGION

At Basle, where he probably arrived in the beginning of 1535, he devoted himself to the further study of Hebrew and

---

[30] By Lefranc, "Jeunesse," 45 f. (May-June 1534), who confuses him with another John Calvin. This John had added to his name "Mudi" in order to distinguish himself from the Reformer. I. de la Tour repeats this mistake, "Calvin," 31.

[31] "Hist. Eccles.," i. 25. Perhaps he did not consider the then little-known Calvin of sufficient importance as an opponent.

[32] It was entitled "Psychopannychia" and was a plea for the continuous self-conscious existence of the soul after death in refutation of the Anabaptist contention that after death the soul sleeps till the resurrection. A first preface is dated Orleans, 1534; a second, Basel, 1536. But it was not published till 1542 at Strassburg, "Opera," v. 170 f. ; Wernle, "Calvin und Basel," 6-7 (1909). Latest ed. with Introduction and notes by Zimmerli (1932).

to the completion and publication of the first sketch of what ultimately developed into his theological *opus magnum*, the *Christianæ Religionis Institutio*, "Institutes of the Christian Religion." The object of its publication was partly apologetic. He had evidently begun it before leaving France,[33] for the purpose of instructing his co-religionists in the new theology. Meanwhile the persecution which drove him into exile had broken out. Not only so, but Francis I., in order to counteract the ill effects of this persecution on the minds of the German Protestant princes, whose alliance he was anxious, from political motives, to secure, represented the persecuted French Protestants, in a communication to the Imperial Diet, as violent sectaries of the Anabaptist type. It was this calumny that impelled Calvin to publish his work and to preface it with a dedicatory epistle to the French King, in which he sought to vindicate his co-religionists from the false charges brought against them. These charges he ascribes not to the King, but to the enemies of the faith who deceive him, and he appeals to the royal sense of justice to hear the other side before condemning his Protestant subjects in virtue of them. He boldly claims that the faith for which they are sent to the stake is the true religion, in contrast to the fabrications of the traditional Church, appeals to the Word of God in proof of his contention, and denies, in consequence, that it is something new or doubtful or incompatible with the doctrine of the ancient Fathers, as its adversaries assert. In short, he labours to make out that the new faith is the true faith, and that the traditional Church not only presents a travesty of it, but, in persecuting its professors, is persecuting Christ and doing the work of the devil.

In this argumentation he certainly succeeds in showing that his persecuted brethren are not the subverters of either religion or political and social order. They are neither heretics nor rebels. The plea is a very forcible one. Nevertheless, it is a plea on behalf of true religion, as he conceives it, not of religious liberty, of which he does not seem to have any adequate conception. It is the office of the King to maintain true religion, and heresy is apparently a crime which he may not suffer. At all events, Calvin, whilst nobly protesting against

[33] This appears from the dedication to Francis I. See also Introduction to vol. iii. of " Opera "; Autin, " L'Institution Chrétienne," 29 f. (1929).

the cruel persecution of his co-religionists, does not argue on behalf of toleration, but only of the recognition of his doctrine as the true religion. He has not risen to the full height of the cause he defends, and is, in fact, as dogmatic as those whom he attacks. In this respect he sees the question with mediæval eyes. Probably, however, his plea would have made no more impression on his bigoted opponents had he strengthened it by advocating the claims of true liberty as well as true religion. As it was, it fell upon deaf ears. It is indeed questionable whether Francis ever read it. At all events, it did not prevent him from developing in the sequel of his reign into the persistent persecutor, in spite of the humanist tolerance of the earlier part of it.[34]

[34] The dedicatory epistle to Francis is given in Latin in vol. i. of " Opera," in French in vol. iii. I reserve an examination of the contents of the " Institutio," in its more developed form, for a later chapter.

CHAPTER III

BEGINNINGS AS REFORMER

GENEVA AND ITS REFORMATION

THE citizens of Geneva were predisposed in favour of the Reformation by the struggle for political liberty which they maintained during the first three decades of the sixteenth century against their bishop and his ally, the Duke of Savoy. The constitution of Geneva was a curious combination of feudal and communal government. The bishop was sovereign superior of the city. The Duke of Savoy was his vassal under the title of Count or Vidomne,[1] whose office it was to watch over the security of the city and execute judicial sentences. The citizens had their part in the government through their Council and the General Assembly of the people or General Council, and their elected syndics or magistrates,[2] four in number. But the rights and privileges which the bishop, who since the middle of the fifteenth century was a scion or a dependent of the house of Savoy, swore, on his entry in office, to maintain were frequently ignored by him and the count, and the tendency was to transform the city into a dependency of Savoy. Against this tendency a party, under the leadership of Berthelier, Bonivard, and Hugues, in the beginning of the sixteenth century strove to vindicate the rights of the citizens and the independence of the State. In 1519 they sought and obtained the alliance of Freiburg as a preliminary step to joining the Swiss

---

[1] *Vice-dominus.* His deputy occupied the castle on an island in the Rhone.

[2] This Council was made up of two bodies—the Small Council of twenty-five, which had the right to co-opt thirty-five other citizens in certain cases, and thus became the Council of Sixty. As the result of the struggle with the bishop and the duke in the first third of the sixteenth century a Council of Two Hundred was established. On Geneva in the early sixteenth century see J. B. G. Galiffe, " Genève Historique et Archeologique " (1869), with valuable illustrations ; Doumergue, iii.

Confederation.[3] Whereupon Duke Charles III. forced them to renounce the alliance, and restored the bishop, John of Savoy, whom they had compelled to retire. The bishop put Berthelier to death and imprisoned Bonivard [4] in the castle of Grolée in Bugey. His successor, Pierre de la Baume, who was the pliant instrument of the ducal policy, drove Hugues into exile (1525).

The cause of Genevan liberty seemed irretrievably lost. But a year later (1526) the exiled Hugues succeeded not only in renewing the alliance with Freiburg, but in adding to it that of Bern. On the strength of this alliance the Government was reorganised on the model of that of its allies by adding a Council of Two Hundred to the lesser Council and the General Assembly of the people, which had hitherto performed the executive and legislative functions under the bishop. The attempt of the duke and the bishop once more to assert their régime was frustrated by the allies, who compelled their forces to retire and extorted the recognition of the rights of the citizens, whilst retaining their jurisdiction in a limited form [5] (January 1531).

The political struggle was erelong followed by the religious one. The chief agent in this struggle was William Farel, a native of Gap in Dauphiné, who had studied at Paris, and had come under the influence of Lefèvre. For some time he taught as Regent in the Collège of Le Moine, became a member of the reforming circle of Meaux, and evangelised furtively at Paris [6] and in other parts of France, until, in 1523, he was forced to quit the country and seek refuge at Basle. Three years later (1526) we find him established, as teacher and preacher,

---

[3] J. Fazy, " Précis de l'Histoire de la République de Genève," 126 f. (1838) ; Roget, " Les Suisses et Genève," i. 141 f. (1864). Hence the name Eidguenots=(Eidgenossen), applied to the patriotic party. A large number of historians assume that the term Huguenot, applied from about 1560 to the Protestants of France, was derived from this source. But this derivation has been questioned. For a discussion of the subject see Doumergue, vii. 379 f. (1927).

[4] Byron's " Prisoner of Chillon." But the episode of Byron's poem relates to a later imprisonment of Bonivard, 1530-36.

[5] The duke was to continue to exercise the office of Vidomne, the bishop to remain the superior of the city, with curtailed powers. See Ruchat, " Hist. de la Reformation de la Suisse," ii. 315 ; J. Fazy, " Précis," 180 ; Roget, " Les Suisses et Genève," i. 347 f. ; Doumergue, ii. 110.

[6] During his sojourn in Paris he probably founded the first Protestant congregation there. Doumergue, i. 89 f.

at Aigle, a dependency of Bern in the Pays de Vaud, which he successfully evangelised. In 1528 he took a powerful part in the disputation which resulted in the establishment of the Reformation at Bern, and during the next four years he extended his mission over a large part of French-speaking Switzerland with the assistance of Froment, Viret, and other young evangelists,[7] whom he inspired with his own missionary zeal. It was in October 1532 that, along with his fellow-evangelist Saunier, he directed his course to Geneva, where the tentative preaching of Olivetan, who had preceded him, gave promise of an effective mission. His preaching immediately aroused the hostility of the clergy, and during an altercation with the vicar-general of the bishop in the presence of a large number of clerics, he was repeatedly struck by some of the enraged priests and would have been drowned in the Rhone but for the intervention of the magistrates. The violent scene ended in his expulsion [8] along with Saunier and Olivetan. A like fate befell Froment whom he sent to take his place. Froment's return some months later produced another riot, which ended in his expulsion a second time. Nevertheless the number of those favourable to the Reformation went on increasing, and the intervention of Bern at length secured the return of both Farel and Froment, who were strengthened by the arrival of Viret shortly after, and persuaded the Council to permit their public preaching (March 1534).

An attempt by the bishop to restore his crumbling authority and suppress the movement by force, with the aid of the Duke of Savoy, at last decided the Council to hold the public disputation for which Bern had been pressing. As the result of this disputation, which took place in June 1535, and of the fiery preaching of Farel, the people smashed the images in the cathedral of St Peter in the following August, and the Small Council and that of Two Hundred ultimately adopted a resolution, which the General Assembly of the citizens confirmed

---

[7] Barnaud, " Pierre Virèt," 46 f. (1911).   For a detailed account of this mission, see Ruchat, i. 294 f.; ii. 174 f.; iii. 5 f.   See also Comité Farel, " Guil. Farel " (1930).
[8] Froment, " Les Actes et Gestes Merveilleux de la Cité de Genève," 6 f. (ed. by Revilliod, 1854) ; Jeanne de Jussie, " Le Levain du Calvinisme," 49 (ed. by Grivel, 1865).   On Olivetan's early evangelistic activity at Geneva, see Roget, ii. 21.

Geneva

(21st May 1536), to abolish the Mass and establish the reformed doctrine and worship and a system of compulsory education under Saunier as rector of the reconstituted municipal school. Before this consummation the army of Bern had advanced and compelled the army of the duke to retire, and thus Geneva, in adopting the Reformation under the protection of Bern, at the same time finally vindicated its independence as a self-governing republic of the old episcopal and ducal subjection. On its arms the city appropriately inscribed the adage " Post Tenebras Lux," as the motto of its newly won civil and religious liberty. The Council slips into the place of the bishop as the supreme ecclesiastical authority and proceeds to enforce the acceptance of the Reformed faith by the citizens, who must attend sermon under penalty of fine for neglect. Moreover, at the instigation of the preachers, it enforces discipline in the interest of religion and morality.

The Reformation was established, but it was neither organised nor consolidated, and the difficulties of the task of organising and consolidating it were very formidable. The old Church had still a considerable number of adherents. It had left a legacy of demoralisation, for the régime of a series of hireling bishops and the general profligacy of the clergy, which even the most ardent adherents of the old cult were fain to confess, had adversely affected the moral life of the people. Geneva needed moral regeneration as well as a new faith. This faith had to be maintained against a reactionary party and preserved from the licence for which it might be made to furnish a pretext. The new Church had to be organised and adjusted to the institutions of a republican government, which had assumed the supreme jurisdiction of the bishop as well as that of the duke. For this complicated and arduous task Farel was by no means fitted. He was an aggressive and powerful evangelist—fearless, uncompromising, even reckless in attack—but unfit to make due use of the victory which his daring had won. It was whilst struggling with the task which his success as an evangelist had thrust upon him that what seemed a mere chance threw a far stronger man in his way. In adjuring Calvin to share in this task, he secured the master mind which was not only to dominate Geneva, but to make it the citadel of the Reformation in Western Europe.

TENTATIVE ORGANISATION

Shortly before or after the publication of the " Institutes "
we find Calvin sojourning for a short time at the Court of the
Duchess of Ferrara, the daughter of Louis XII., who, like
Marguerite of Navarre, was a patroness of reform. His visit
seems to have been a furtive one, though some of his
biographers,[9] with more imagination than knowledge, have
represented him crossing the Alps as a sort of evangelical
crusader to attack the citadel of Romanism itself. All that he
evidently attempted was secretly to strengthen the evangelical
leanings of the duchess, whose husband, the Duke of Ferrara
(Hercules II.), was a staunch adherent of the Roman Church.
His visit was not without effect, for it paved the way to a life-
long correspondence in the interest of the Reformation. The
rest is largely legend.

Another furtive visit to Paris, after his return from Italy,
intervened before he at length found the vocation as an active
leader of the Reformation for which his studies, his rare
ability, and his religious experience had prepared him. It was
on the return journey from Paris that he touched at Geneva,[10]
in July 1536, with the intention of settling at Basle or Strassburg
to continue his theological studies. Reserved and even timid
by disposition, his aim was to serve the cause of the Reformation
as a student and a writer rather than as a man of action. Though
possessed in a rare degree of the qualities of a leader of men
and always hitherto appearing to take a directing part in the
little circle in which he moved, he had evidently not as yet
discovered these qualities, nor divined the great future that
awaited him. No one, in fact, ever entered on a great career
with less consciousness of his mission or less predilection for

---

[9] D'Aubigné, for instance. On his visit to the duchess, see Cornelius,
" Historische Arbeiten," 105 f. (1899). Two letters which he wrote during
this visit reveal his complete breach with the papal Church. One was
addressed to his Orleans friend Duchemin on the necessity of fleeing from
papal superstition ; the other to Gérard Roussel, who had accepted the
bishopric of Oloron, and whom he severely upbraids for his desertion of the
evangelical cause, " Opera," xxi. 60. They are given in " Opera," v. 239 f.
[10] The reason of his detour by Geneva was the outbreak of war between
Charles V. and Francis I. and the fact that the more direct routes to Strassburg were obstructed by the concentration of troops on the eastern frontier.
See Doumergue, ii. 175.

it. But at Geneva Farel laid hold of him. In spite of repeated protestations he summoned him, in the name of God, to assist him in his evangelical labours, and overcame his reluctance by threatening him with the divine judgment, if he persisted in his refusal. " In the evening," recounts Beza, " Farel hastened to the inn at which Calvin had taken a lodging for the night. He explained to him the situation of the Church and besought him to tarry and assist him. Calvin, startled by this unexpected appeal, adduced, in opposition, his plans, his desires, his tastes. The more Farel insisted, the more did his apprehension increase at the prospect which suddenly opened before him. Then Farel, trembling with a holy anger, rose to his feet. ' And I,' cried he, with a voice of thunder, ' declare it to you in the name of Almighty God. You adduce your studies as a pretext. If you refuse to devote yourself along with us to the work of the Lord, God will punish you, for you seek your own interest rather than that of Christ.' "[11] " This adjuration," adds Calvin, " so terrified and shook me that I desisted from the journey I had undertaken . . . as if God from on high had laid His hand on me to arrest me."[12] He would, however, only accept the function of " professor of the Holy Scriptures," as he henceforth entitled himself.[13] But under Farel's incisive influence, his diffidence disappeared, and in less than three months we find him taking part in the public disputation, under the auspices of the Government of Bern,[14] which resulted in the establishment of the Reformation at Lausanne and the appointment of Viret and Caroli as ministers of the Reformed Church.[15]

His first attempt as an organiser of the Genevan Church was, however, a failure. Though he had already, by the publication of " The Institutes," proved his powers as a theologian, he had yet to serve what he calls his " apprenticeship "[16] in the art of governing men. Farel had, it seems, introduced a reformed Order of baptism, marriage, communion,

[11] " Opera," xxi. 125.
[12] *Ibid.*, xxxi. 26 (" Commentary on the Psalms ").
[13] Sacrarum litterarum in ecclesia Genevensi professor, " Opera," v. 223.
[14] Bern had wrested Vaud from Savoy during the spring of 1536 and thus prepared the way for its evangelisation.
[15] Barnaud, " P. Viret," 138 f. ; Doumergue, ii. 214.
[16] So he afterwards wrote in his preface to his " Commentary on the Psalms," " Opera," xxxi. 26, " Inter prima rudimenta."

and public worship,[17] which he had printed at Serrières, near Neuchâtel, in 1533, for the use of the French-speaking evangelical churches. This Order Calvin materially supplemented in the Articles relative to the organisation, discipline, worship, and doctrine of the nascent Reformed Church, which the ministers presented in January 1537. According to this document the Lord's Supper, as instituted by Christ and observed in the ancient Church, shall be celebrated once a month,[18] and the unworthy debarred from partaking. If they persist in their sins, they shall be excommunicated in accordance with the New Testament usage, in contrast to that of the mediæval Church, which Calvin and his fellow-ministers denounce as a usurped tyranny over the Christian community. To this end the Council shall nominate certain reputable persons to watch over the morals of the community in the various quarters of the city and report delinquents to the ministers, who shall privately admonish them and, in case of non-amendment, publicly denounce them before the congregation. Failing repentance, they shall finally excommunicate them from the company of Christians, who are to cease intercourse with them until they give proof of penitence and amendment, although they may still attend the public preaching. "Beyond this correction the Church cannot go." It can only pronounce spiritual penalties. If, nevertheless, they make no account of its excommunication, it will be for the Council to judge whether it shall suffer such contempt of God and His Gospel to go unpunished. Moreover, in order to distinguish between the adherents and the enemies of the Reformation, all the inhabitants shall make confession of their faith, and the members of the Council are requested to show them an example by making such confession. There follow recommendations for the congregational singing of Psalms in public worship, for the instruction of the young in the faith by means of a Catechism and the periodical examination of the children by the ministers, and for the revision of the laws

---

[17] " La Manière et Fasson qu'on tient es lieux lesquels Dieu de sa Grâce a visités."

[18] The Supper ought to be celebrated once a week, but as the people are not ripe for this innovation, a monthly celebration will meanwhile suffice.

relating to marriage, which have been arbitrarily imposed by the Pope.[19]

The Articles are an attempt to combine the autonomy of the Church with the sanction and co-operation of the State. The Church formulates its doctrine, discipline, and worship. The State sanctions them and co-operates in their maintenance. In thus submitting the Articles for the sanction of the State and accepting its co-operation in their enforcement, Calvin was following the procedure of Zwingli and other reformers in the organisation of the Swiss Reformed Churches. But, unlike them, he strove, at the same time, to safeguard the autonomy of the Church by investing in the ministers the power of excommunicating unworthy members, who persisted in conduct inconsistent with their Christian profession. In view of the abuse of the power of excommunication in the mediæval Church, Zwingli and most of the Swiss reformers were prepared to vest the maintenance of discipline in the civil government, which had hitherto exercised supervision over public morals by means of sumptuary and other social legislation. Whilst Calvin also recognised this traditional function of the mediæval municipality, he held strongly that in spiritual things, especially the maintenance of the purity of the Lord's Table, the right of maintaining discipline by means of excommunication inhered in the Church itself. In claiming this right he went back to the model of the early Church, in which it undoubtedly inhered, though, in drawing up the article relative to excommunication, he appears to have taken his cue from the similar but ultimately unsuccessful attempt of Oecolampadius at Basle and Bucer at Strassburg to adopt this expedient.[20] Whether the quick-witted, contentious, and freedom-loving Geneva would prove more amenable to this tentative ecclesiastical régime remained to be seen.

[19] "Opera," x². 6 f.; Herminjard, "Correspondance des Réformateurs," iv. 154 f. Calvin was the author of the Catechism, Lang, "Introduction to "Der Heidelberger Katechismus," 35 (1907), "Quellenschriften zur Geschichte des Protestantismus," ed. by Kunze and Stange. See also Courvoisier, "Les Catechismes de Genève et de Strasbourg," *Bull. Soc. Hist. du Prot. Français*, 1935, 105 f.

[20] See "Briefe und Akten zum Leben Oecolampads," ii. 448 f.; Wernle, "Calvin und Basel," 10 f. (1909). For Bucer see Strohl, *Bull. Soc. Hist. du Prot. Français*, 1935, 131 f.

Meanwhile both Councils approved generally of the Articles, with the modification that the communion should be celebrated quarterly instead of monthly, and issued decrees in reference to baptism and marriage, the shutting of shops during divine service on Sunday, and for the repression of vice and the surrender of images [21] (16th January 1537). Three months later the Small Council directed the Confession of Faith, which Calvin or Farel drew up in accordance with the Articles, to be distributed among the inhabitants of the various divisions of the city, preparatory to their declaring on oath their adhesion to it [22] (April 1537). The demand to swear adhesion aroused protest and resistance on the part of both Romanists and Reformed. Romanists could not, of course, honestly swear, whilst many of the Reformed objected to the demand as an unwarrantable infringement of personal liberty. The dissension over the Confession was aggravated by dissension over the question of ecclesiastical discipline, which the ministers were urging the Council to enforce and to which many of the citizens were by no means disposed to submit.

At the end of July the Council of Two Hundred resolved to put an end to the contention over the Confession by ordering all the captains of the various districts to swear on pain of being deprived of their office, and to march the inhabitants, district by district, to the Cathedral of St Peter to do likewise.[23] Even so, there were still many dissentients, in spite of the fact that the Small Council threatened them with expulsion from the city if they persisted in their refusal [24] (19th September). Both Councils repeated the threat in November, and on the 25th of this month the opposition challenged their tyrannic procedure in the course of a violent scene in the Assembly of the People. It was emboldened in its resistance by the Bernese Commissioners at Geneva, whose attitude was, however, disavowed by their Government as the result of a visit to Bern by

---

[21] " Registres du Conseil," " Opera," xxi. 206 f. This volume of the " Opera " contains extracts from the Registers relative to the Reformation at Geneva. It is invaluable for the study of the work of the Reformer.

[22] " Opera," xxi. 210 f. The confession is given in ix. 693 f. It is debatable whether the Confession was written by Calvin or Farel. See the discussion in Doumergue, ii. 237 f. He ascribes it to Calvin. Lang, on the other hand, to Farel. Introduction to " Der Heidelberger Katechismus," 35 f. In any case it was evidently strongly influenced by Calvin.

[23] " Opera," xxi. 213.   [24] Ibid., xxi. 215 f.

Calvin and Farel. Ultimately, in deference to a pacific missive of the Bernese Government approving the Confession, its leaders were induced to swear their adhesion [25] (4th January 1538). It is impossible not to sympathise with it as far as it was actuated by conscientious scruples or the claims of individual liberty. To Calvin such public confession on oath might seem a necessary expedient in the circumstances, as a means of distinguishing friend from foe and frustrating the machinations of the enemies of reform. It was none the less a questionable policy to overrule, in the name of expediency, conscientious scruples and individual liberty, and to punish the opposition on such grounds by civil penalties. It was really fitted to make more enemies than it thwarted. It was all the more objectionable in view of the fact that Calvin himself laid such stress on the rights of conscience and on the necessity of sincerity in matters of faith.

There remained the question of excommunication. The authorities, in accordance with usage, were ready enough to abet the preachers in the work of practical reformation by punishing evildoers with imprisonment or the stocks, even if the delinquent was guilty of nothing more serious than playing at cards or coquettishly curling the hair.[26] They hesitated to carry into effect the reiterated demands of the preachers for the enforcement of excommunication, and their hesitation was increased by the explosion of popular feeling against the ministers and their abettors in the Councils in the General Assembly on the 25th November 1537. Ultimately on the 4th January 1538 the Council of Two Hundred decided that no one should be debarred from partaking of the Lord's Supper who wished to do so, whilst prohibiting the recurring mockery by the populace of the preachers in the streets and taverns.[27] This was a distinct setback for the ministers. It was all the more serious inasmuch as it was due to the pressure of an increasing opposition to them. Still more ominous, the

[25] " Opera," xxi. 215 f. ; Herminjard, iv. 330 f.
[26] " Opera," xxi. 216. Kampschulte, " Calvin," i. 291 (1869). This work by an old Catholic is the fruit of careful research, and is still serviceable to the student. It is critical and fairly objective, though it suffers from the fact that it was written under the influence of the works of J. B. G. Galiffe (1862-63), which are strongly adverse to Calvin.
[27] " Opera," xxi. 220.

annual election of magistrates and members of the Councils resulted in a triumph for the opposition. The four syndics or magistrates elected were anticlerical and the majority of the Councils were on the same side (3rd February 1538). It is not necessary to regard this opposition as springing merely from moral perverseness. It was a legitimate protest against a régime which threatened to subject the citizens to a puritanic and prying inquisition, backed by temporal penalties, and might well seem to endanger the liberty which they had won in the struggle with their oppressors. It was, too, partly at least, a revolt against the interference, the domination of foreigners in the affairs of the community. Farel, Calvin, and Corauld, their associate in the ministry, were Frenchmen. They were, in addition, ill-fitted to appreciate the spirit and institutions of a free community. They had grown to manhood in a country where absolutism was rampant, and they appear to have brought with them to Geneva something of the dictatorial spirit which was transforming France into an absolute monarchy at the expense of its constitutional and local liberties. They were, besides, too doctrinaire, too hasty, too uncompromising in their demands, and made unstinted use of the pulpit to denounce their opponents. Their lack of prudence, their predilection for drastic methods were, in fact, fitted to defeat their well-meant aims.

The situation was, moreover, rendered more difficult by doctrinal quarrels with Anabaptist sectaries with whom Farel insisted on publicly disputing, and with Pierre Caroli, evangelical preacher at Lausanne, who was called to account for advocating prayers for the dead, and in turn accused Farel and Calvin, as well as his colleague Viret, of Arianism before the Bernese Commissioners at Lausanne,[28] then under the jurisdiction of Bern (February 1537). Calvin protested their belief in the doctrine of the Trinity, and adduced the chapter in the Confession on the subject in proof of their orthodoxy, even if, as Caroli noted, he had avoided the use of this technical term as unsuitable in a document meant for popular instruction. Of his Trinitarian belief there is not the least doubt, as his teaching on the subject in the " Institutes " conclusively proves. Caroli retorted by asking them to join with him in

[28] Herminjard, iv. 183 f.

assenting to the Apostles', the Nicene, and the Athanasian Creeds. Calvin refused. For him the Word of God, not the Nicene and Athanasian Creeds, was the compelling authority for faith. " We have sworn the faith in the one God, not in Athanasius, whose Creed no true Church has ever approved." [29] The Commissioners referred the case to the Bern Consistory, and ultimately Calvin succeeded in securing the convocation of a synod of ministers of French-speaking Switzerland at Lausanne to deal with the contention on the 14th May 1537. At this synod he passionately denounced his accuser, who, he said, had no more faith than a dog or a pig, and was an epicurean and a hypocrite. He had an irascible strain in him, and in this mood too often allowed his passion to run away with his judgment and his good taste. He defended his orthodoxy so forcibly, however, that Caroli was fain to withdraw his charge against him, if not against Farel. He reiterated his refusal to sign the Nicene and Athanasian Creeds, whilst disclaiming any desire to repudiate these Creeds. The faith ought not to be tied to mere words or syllables. Neither he nor his fellow-ministers were prepared to impose a tyranny of this kind on the Church and regard a man as a heretic merely because he refused to repeat the formulas dictated by another. Truly a remarkable as well as a forcible vindication of freedom in matters of theological controversy. However forcible, his reasoning was certainly rather inconsistent with his insistence on the enforced acceptance of his own Confession at Geneva, even with the plausible contention in support of it that this Confession was based on the Word of God. The synod, nevertheless, supported him and declared against his opponent. A second synod, convened at Bern in the beginning of June, came to the same conclusion, and the Council of Bern gave him and his fellow-preachers a certificate of orthodoxy.[30] But the episode did not tend to enhance their authority at Geneva, where people were remarking that the ministers should first agree among themselves before seeking to constrain others.[31] It excited no little perturbation in the Swiss

[29] Herminjard, iv. 185.
[30] For these proceedings see " Opera," vii. 294 f., in which he gives a detailed account of the controversy entitled " Adversus P. Caroli calumnias." See also Herminjard, iv. 235 f.
[31] Herminjard, iv. 187.

churches, whose leaders were not satisfied with his attitude and were fain to declare their formal approval of the Athanasian doctrine, thus indirectly censuring what appeared to them his rather compromising attitude.[32]

CONFLICT AND BANISHMENT

After the election in February 1538 the position at Geneva became very precarious. In vain Calvin renewed the demand for the enforcement of excommunication.[33] The tension on the score of ecclesiastical policy erelong reached a critical stage through the action of Bern in proposing uniformity of ecclesiastical usages between the two Churches. In making this proposal the Bernese Government was mainly actuated by political motives. It was eager to establish its influence over Geneva in opposition to France, which cherished a similar design, and it regarded an ecclesiastical union as a means to the attainment of this end. It accordingly submitted a scheme for the introduction of the ecclesiastical usages prevailing at Bern relative to the rites of baptism and the Lord's Supper, and the observance of the chief Christian festivals.[34] In its apprehension at the designs of France against the independence of the Republic, which it suspected the clerical party, without substantial reason, of abetting, the Council accepted the proposal, and at the same time forbade Calvin and Farel, who had criticised its ecclesiastical policy, to mix in politics [35] (11th to 12th March 1538). It directed them to attend a synod summoned by Bern to Lausanne to discuss the question, and to support a policy on which it had not consulted them, and which the Bernese Government also stipulated that they should support.[36] This was certainly a high-handed encroachment on the autonomy in spiritual things for which Calvin contended. Both he and Farel, nevertheless, obeyed so far as

[32] Herminjard, iv. 239 f. ; Doumergue, ii. 267.

[33] " Opera," x[b]. 154 ; Herminjard, iv. 367 ; Calvin to Bullinger, 21st February 1538.

[34] Bern retained the use of the font in baptism, unleavened bread in the Supper, and the observance of Christmas, Easter, Ascension, and Pentecost, whereas Farel had discarded these usages on the establishment of the Reformation at Geneva.

[35] " Opera," xxi. 222.

[36] Ibid., x[b]. 179 ; Herminjard, iv. 403.

to attend the synod, which adopted the scheme for the French-speaking territories under the jurisdiction of Bern.[37] But they were not prepared to carry it out at the bidding of the Council, which resolved to accept it. Whilst not disposed to lay much stress on such ceremonial points or sacrifice unity to form, and ready enough to make use of the co-operation of the State in the maintenance of discipline and the true faith, Calvin, as we have noted, held strongly that the Church itself should be free to decide, and should not take its orders from the civil authority in things spiritual. He advocated the plan of referring the decision on the question to the synod of the Swiss churches, which was to convene towards the end of April at Zürich to deliberate a general understanding apart from State interference.

Accordingly, when on the 19th April he and Farel were summoned before the Council and asked whether they would observe the new ecclesiastical order, which at the request of Bern it had accepted,[38] they asked for delay, pending the meeting of the synod at Zürich. After their withdrawal the Council sent its usher to demand whether they would preach and dispense the Communion in accordance with the Bernese rite on the following Sunday, the 21st. They refused to do either. Meanwhile it resolved to forbid Corauld, who had earlier in the month attacked the authorities in a violent sermon, to preach further on pain of imprisonment in case of non-compliance. Preach he nevertheless did on the following day (20th April) in defiance of this prohibition, and was promptly lodged in prison. Calvin and Farel, accompanied by Ami Perrin and a number of their influential supporters, immediately repaired to the Council to protest and demand a meeting of the Two Hundred. A heated altercation ensued, during which Farel angrily reminded its members of his services to the Republic. " Without me," thundered he, " you would not be here." Corauld, he was told, had used outrageous language against the citizens and their rulers, and had justly been placed

---

[37] Herminjard, iv. 410 f. Whether they voted for this resolution is uncertain, though the Bernese Government declared that it had been carried unanimously (iv. 413). It seems unlikely that they did, and they probably reserved judgment till a representative assembly of all the Seven Churches should finally decide.

[38] " Opera," xxi. 223 f. ; Herminjard, iv. 415 f.

in durance for his violence and disobedience. Their offer to give surety for his future good conduct was emphatically refused. When again asked whether they would comply with the Bernese rite in the celebration of the Communion on the morrow, they replied that they would act as God should command them. Ultimately in the evening the usher was sent to forbid them to preach unless they undertook to do so. They had already made up their minds not to comply and now resolved to disregard the prohibition.[39] Preach they did accordingly—Calvin in St Peter's, Farel in St Gervais'—in denunciation of the wickedness of the citizens and the slackness of their rulers in repressing the contempt of such mockers of the Gospel, who were unfit to receive the Communion at their hands.[40]

Their sermons were interrupted by angry shouts and the preachers owed their escape from threatened violence to the protection of their friends, who escorted them to and from the services. In the afternoon the smaller Council resolved to refer the matter to the Two Hundred and the General Assembly of the people. As the result of their deliberations on the following two days, it was resolved by a large majority in the latter to order them to quit the city within three days. "Very well," returned Calvin, when the sentence was communicated to him, "the sooner the better. If we had served man, this would have been a poor recompense. But we serve a great Master who will know how to reward us." [41] He confesses, however, that the excitement and danger of these tumultuous days were no small trial to one of his naturally timid disposition. The people threatened to throw him into the Rhone. At night they sang derisive songs and fired shots before his dwelling, and the memory of these demonstrations haunted him to his dying day. "You may imagine," said he to his colleagues on his deathbed, "how these things astonished a poor, timid scholar such as I am and always have been." [42]

They had provoked their fate by their inexperience and their lack of prudence and self-restraint in the face of an

[39] " Opera," xxi. 223 f.
[40] Herminjard, iv. 422. Calvin and Farel's account of these events to the Council of Bern. See also Doumergue, ii. 269 f.
[41] Beza, " Vita "; " Opera," xxi. 128.
[42] " Opera," ix. 892; cf. xxi. 102.

opposition which was by no means purely perverse and which they could only obviate by hastening slowly. They showed a lack of insight into human nature in seeking to exact a mechanical change of faith and dragoon the citizens into compliance with a strict disciplinary system, without taking time to educate them up to their own moral standard. They presumed too much on the power of a dictatorial pulpit oratory to overawe or transform human nature. Nor did they understand the art of speaking the truth in love, and forgot that people would not be badgered into accepting it, especially in a free community like Geneva. On the other hand, the Councils were equally inconsiderate and aggressive in hurrying on the changes in ecclesiastical usages, without consulting them or listening to their plea on behalf of independent judgment, and without any consideration for their legitimate objections. They had taken exception not so much to the administration of the Communion after a certain order, which was after all of little importance, but to the arbitrary method of forcing it on them, and especially to the command to dispense the Communion to all and sundry without regard to moral character. They complained, not without reason, in their statement to the Council of Bern, that they had not been allowed sufficient opportunity to state their case, and that they had been condemned without being sufficiently heard.[43] Even the Bernese Government felt that the authorities of Geneva had been too precipitate and dictatorial. In response to the appeal of the ministers, it admonished them to moderate their rigour for the sake of peace, especially in matters which were after all things indifferent in themselves.[44] The synod of the Swiss churches, which met at Zürich in the end of April, and to which they submitted fourteen Articles relative to the dispute, likewise espoused their cause. In the Articles they expressed their willingness to accept the Bernese usages with slight modifications, reiterated their demand concerning the moral supervision of the people, excommunication, and the monthly celebration of Communion, and claimed that the ministers should have a voice in the calling and ordination of pastors and should be allowed to exonerate themselves from the

---

[43] Herminjard, iv. 425.
[44] *Ibid.*, iv. 428.

calumnies and indignities heaped upon them.[45] At the same
time, they admitted that they had perhaps been too " severe,"
and professed their readiness to receive instruction and advice.[46]
The synod expressed its approval of these Articles,[47] whilst
exhorting them to moderate their harshness and observe
Christian gentleness in their treatment of an unruly people.
It wrote to the Council of Geneva on their behalf, and remitted
to the Bernese Government the task of bringing about an
accommodation on the basis of the Articles. To this end the
Council of Bern sent an embassy to Geneva, which was accompanied by Calvin and Farel as far as the frontier village of
Nyon. The embassy was unsuccessful. The General Assembly,
to which the final decision was referred, refused by an overwhelming majority to allow them to enter the city and resume
their ministry [48] (26th May 1538).

At Strassburg

Along with Farel, Calvin retraced his steps with characteristic bitterness of heart against his persecutors. He
retired to Basle with the intention to withdraw from public
work and devote himself to the life of the scholar. He shrank
from the prospect of again carrying such a burden, which, as
he wrote to Du Tillet,[49] who had by this time resolved to
return to the Roman Church, appeared to him "unsupportable."
He was not left long to cherish this illusion. He received
a pressing invitation from Bucer, Capito, and John Sturm to
come to Strassburg [50] to minister to the French congregation
there. The invitation did not include Farel, since it appeared
to Bucer advisable that they should separate instead of nursing
their grievances by their continued association. He hesitated
on this ground to accept, and it was only after renewed solicitations that he consented. With the call of Farel to Neuchâtel

[45] Herminjard, v. 3 f. ; " Opera," x[b]. 190 f.
[46] " Opera," x[b]. 193.
[47] Quæ Tiguri magno omnium consensu nobis concessa fuerant. Herminjard, v. 17; cf. 22; v. 13 f. ; " Opera," x[b]. 193.
[48] " Opera," xxi. 229 f.
[49] Herminjard, v. 44. For Du Tillet Calvin had become by this time
too rash and precipitate, too much given to rely on his own judgment to
make sufficient allowance for the opinions of others. Herminjard, v. 103 f.
[50] Herminjard, v. 64.

to fill the place of Marcourt, who had been transferred to Geneva, his hesitation disappeared. He accordingly yielded, and spent the next three years (September 1538 to September 1541) as minister of the French congregation, lecturer in the theological school, and ecclesiastical statesman at Strassburg, where he found a helpmeet and a happy marriage in Idelette de Bure, whom he married in 1540.

With the goodwill of the city authorities, to whose jurisdiction the congregation was subject, he organised it on the model which he had failed fully to realise in Geneva. He instituted monthly Communion, from which the unworthy were debarred, and subjected communicants to an examination *closed* of their personal worthiness to partake of the Supper. He introduced a reformed order of worship, based on Bucer's modification of that of Diebold Schwarz, who had translated the Roman Mass into German and adapted it for the use of the Reformed Church at Strassburg in 1524.[51] In addition to his pastoral labours, he lectured on the Gospel of John and the Epistles to the Romans and Corinthians in the college which John Sturm had organised on humanist lines. As the first-fruits of his great series of Commentaries, he published that on Romans in 1540. His fertile literary activity during this period included an amplified edition of the " Institutes " and an irenic tract on the burning question of the Sacrament of the Lord's Supper, which divided the Lutheran and the Swiss Reformed Churches so sharply.[52]

As an ecclesiastical statesman he took part in the Conferences in 1539-41 at Frankfurt, Hagenau, Worms, and Regensburg on the question of an accommodation between the German Protestants and the Roman Church, which Charles V. initiated in the pursuit of his plan of securing a settlement of the religious question in Germany. In this capacity he made his influence felt in stiffening the attitude of Melanchthon, with whom he contracted a warm friendship, as the chief protagonist of the Protestant cause. At Regensburg he strove to bring about an alliance between the Protestant League of Schmalkald and

---

[51] See Erichson, " Die Calvinische und die altstrassburgische Gottesdienstordnung " (1894) ; Doumergue, ii. 488 f. ; Maxwell, " John Knox's Genevan Service Book," 25 f. (1931).
[52] " Trois Traités de Calvin " (1934), ed. by A. M. Schmidt.

Francis I. in the hope, which erelong proved visionary, of thereby securing toleration for his French fellow-Protestants, though he received, through Francis' sister, Margaret, his thanks for this service to France. During these protracted negotiations he obtained an insight into the issues of the Reformation as a religious and political movement, enlarged his personal acquaintance with its leaders, and received an invaluable training in the conduct of affairs on a large scale.

REPLY TO SADOLET

More effective was his defence of the Reformation in his brilliant epistle to Cardinal Sadolet, Bishop of Carpentras in Dauphiné, who took advantage of the contention at Geneva to write a letter to the Council and people exhorting them to return to the Roman Church. In this missive he strove to discredit the Reformers as crafty and seditious men, who were actuated by motives of personal ambition in their revolt against the Church, whilst lauding the institutions and virtues of the Genevese, whose disunion was the inevitable fruit of their teaching. He attacked the doctrine of justification by faith alone and exalted the teaching and authority of the Church, in which alone salvation is to be found. Which, he asks, is more likely to possess the truth and assure salvation—the Catholic Church with its ancient faith, or these innovators who have started up during the last twenty-five years, who stir up the people against the Church and wrest the Scriptures in support of their seditious and perverse teaching? He pictures two persons appearing before the judgment seat of God and representing the Romanist and Protestant standpoint respectively in their defence. Though he does not actually mention Calvin, the second is evidently meant to impersonate him. One of the pleas that he urges before the Sovereign Judge in defence of his hostility to the Church is the fact that his merits had not received their due recognition, whilst unworthy persons had been preferred to honours and offices. Naturally judgment goes in favour of the Romanist, and the Protestant is consigned to hell. Their crowning crime, on which he dwells at the close of the epistle, is that they have broken the unity of the Church and substituted for it a medley of quarrelling sects.

The epistle is skilfully conceived, though not very formidable in argument, and in the circumstances it was fitted to work mischief to the cause of the Reformation at Geneva. Calvin, therefore, though rather reluctantly, entered the arena with a reply in the beginning of September 1539.[53] He writes in a courteous but firm tone, and happily avoids, on this occasion, the personalities and scurrilities usual on both sides in such polemics. He disposes of the insinuation of unworthy personal motives by saying that, if he had consulted his personal interest, he would never have left the Church. He appeals to facts to prove that the Reformers have, on the other hand, gained neither honour nor wealth, but only a bare subsistence by their adherence to the Reformation, and that they have not reformed the Church in order to seize, but to deliver it from, its ill-used power and property. He denies that the Reformation means defection from the truth and desertion from the Church. Is it defection from the truth to ground it on the Word of God, which Sadolet, in his exaltation of the Church, ignores ? With the Church as the society of all the saints in all the world and in all the ages, he denies that he and his brethren are in disagreement. All that they have attempted is to restore the form of the ancient Church, which has been mangled and almost x destroyed by the Roman pontiff and his faction. He will not confine himself to the Apostolic Church, though he is of opinion that it is the only model of a true Church. He asks him to compare the Roman with the Church of the Fathers— of Chrysostom and Basil among the Greeks, of Cyprian, Ambrose, and Augustine among the Latins. Only the ruins of this Church remain in the Roman mediæval distortion of it. He seeks to prove this in reference to doctrine, ceremonies, and discipline. He arraigns the ridiculous subtleties with which the scholastics have obscured the teaching of God's Word, and the miserable rubbish which the preachers proffer from Roman Catholic pulpits. He explains and defends the Reformed doctrine of justification by faith alone, and denies that it leaves no room for works. Justification involves regeneration and sanctification as its fruits, and he attacks, from this point of view, the Church's doctrine of penance and satisfaction for sin

[53] Sadolet's epistle was presented to the Council of Geneva on the 26th March 1539. " Opera," xxi. 245.

as incompatible with the one sacrifice of Christ, which it robs of its unique significance. He arraigns the gross superstitions, such as transubstantiation, auricular confession, the intercession of saints, purgatory, which have grown around its practices and beliefs, and have falsified Christianity. He refuses to accept such practices and beliefs merely because the Church sanctions them, and confronts the degenerate papal hierarchical Church with that of the more primitive time, which, he claims, the Reformed Church truly represents. He will not go the length of denying the title Church to the Roman Catholic communion. But he maintains that the actual papal Church is largely anti-Christian, is a Church of ravening wolves and tyrants who have abused the legitimate power conferred by Christ on His ministers, and have exercised a bloody tyranny over the conscience. Even if the Pope were what he claims to be—the successor of Peter—this only entitles him to the obedience of the Christian people as long as he maintains fidelity to Christ and the purity of the Gospel. Mere ecclesiastical authority can never take the place of the Word of God and the individual conscience, which alone can enable the Christian to be certain of the truth. This he cannot be if he is dependent on a mere external authority like the Roman hierarchy. Hence the ascription by the Reformers to the Church (in the Reformed sense) of the power of judging, in contrast to the arrogant assumption of authority and inerrancy on the part of the Pope and the hierarchy. This power of judging is not infallible, since even truly religious minds do not always attain to the mysteries of God. But if it takes its stand on the Word of God, the conviction of the truth is so clear and certain that it cannot be overthrown by either men or angels. Nor does he claim a monopoly of righteousness for the Reformed Church, since its members are sinful and fallible. But he challenges comparison between its discipline and that of Rome—that fountain-head of unspeakable abominations— and is ready to abide the trial at the great judgment seat to which Sadolet had appealed and before which he, in conclusion, presents the cause of the Reformation in a very different light.

Comparatively brief and restrained in spirit, the reply is the most forceful plea of its kind which the age produced and convincingly shows that the Reformation had gained a champion hardly second in intellectual power to Luther and of more refinement of spirit.[54]

HIS RECALL

Sadolet did not venture a rejoinder and his effusion seems to have had little effect on Geneva, where the influence of Calvin's friends was beginning to make itself felt in the party strife which rent the city. That the antagonism of the authorities to the preachers was not actuated by lack of zeal for the reformed cause is apparent from the fact that they vigorously repressed the Romanists. They made as unstinted use of their power against those who refused to conform as they had done against Farel and Calvin. They gave these nonconformists the option of attending Church and partaking of the Lord's Supper or banishment.[55] They were equally active in maintaining a rigid morality by punishing such crimes as dancing and card-playing, as well as the singing of indecent songs, blasphemy, and absenteeism from worship. They vigorously applied the system of informing against offenders, which Calvin had only sought to organise more effectively, and the fact conclusively proves that he was the organiser rather than the author of this inquisitorial régime. In view of their puritan zeal, they hardly deserved the opprobrious epithets (agents of Satan, etc.) which he and Farel had hurled against them in their communications with their friends at Bern, Basel, and Zürich.

The opposition on religious grounds was, however, by no means quiescent. In a letter written on the 1st October 1538 Calvin in vain exhorted his adherents to patience and moderation.[56] The ministers Marcourt and Morand, who had taken the place of the exiles, are found frequently complaining to the Council of the slanders and insults of which they were the objects.[57] The party of the Guillermins, as Farel's adherents were called, openly boasted that the day of their triumph was not far off.[58] At the quarterly celebration of the Communion

---

[54] The epistle of Sadolet and Calvin's reply are in " Opera," v. 365 f. English translation by Beveridge in vol. i. of Calvin's " Tracts," published by the Calvin Translation Society. The latest edition of it is that of A. M. Schmidt, " Trois Traités."

[55] " Opera," xxi. 235.

[56] Herminjard, v. 121 f.

[57] " Opera," xxi. 236 f.

[58] *Ibid.*, xxi. 238. They were so named after Farel's Christian name Guillaume.

at Christmas 1538 there were not a few absentees, among them Saunier, the rector of the college, Cordier, and his other assistants, who refused to receive it in the approved fashion, and were punished with banishment.[59]   The ministers were denounced as hirelings, deceivers of the people, and corrupters of Scripture, and threatened to resign.[60]   In response, the Council arraigned two of the leaders of the Guillermins, Ami Porral and Claude Pertemps, who had likewise refused to communicate, and forced them to conform by the threat of banishment.   Their compliance was apparently, in part, due to the fact that Calvin strongly advised against schism.[61]   The strain was further eased by a public reconciliation of the Genevese ministers with their predecessors at a meeting held at Morges, in March 1539, at which Farel was present,[62] and of which Calvin, though absent, warmly approved.   The soothing effect of this reconciliation was, however, nullified by Sadolet's letter and the Council's courteous acknowledgment of it.[63]   The Guillermins professed to see in this act of courtesy the confirmation of their suspicions of the fidelity of the Council to the Reformation, and though their suspicions were unfounded, they served the purpose of discrediting the dominant party.   In vain the Council redoubled its efforts against the Romanists by compelling them to declare against the Mass, under pain of banishment, and carrying out a visitation in quest of images, which it ordered to be destroyed.[64]   Political blundering in the negotiations of their deputies with Bern, relative to the disputed jurisdiction over certain territories, which gravely compromised the independence of the Republic, augmented its unpopularity and led to violent dissension and even bloodshed between the " Articulants," [65] as the dominant party was called, and their opponents, led by Sept, Perrin, and Pertemps.   The struggle ended with the execution of Jean Philippe, its leader (10th June 1540), and the overthrow of the party.

The retirement of Marcourt and Morand followed some weeks later and the way was cleared for the return of Calvin,

---

[59] " Opera," xxi. 240-242.
[60] Herminjard, v. 208-210.
[61] *Ibid.*, v. 211 f.
[62] *Ibid.*, v. 243 f; *cf.* 336 f.
[63] " Opera," xxi. 245 f.
[64] *Ibid.*, xxi. 253 f.
[65] So named in reference to the articles of the obnoxious treaty.   They were also nicknamed " Artichauts."

to whom the two Councils and the General Assembly of the people sent invitations to resume his labours in their midst [66] (October 1540). He was by no means enamoured of the prospect, and would fain have remained in a sphere more congenial to his retiring disposition and his scholarly tastes. Nearly a year elapsed, during which Viret acted as *locum tenens*, before he at last yielded to the pressure of his friends and re-entered Geneva (13th September 1541). He had now completed the " apprenticeship " in leadership which he had begun there five years earlier. He was more mature in mind, richer in experience and knowledge for his three years of varied activity at Strassburg in association with Bucer and his fellow-theologians. He was thus far better fitted for the renewal of the arduous task for which his previous inexperience had proved insufficient. His return was a most momentous event in Reformation history, for the pale, thin figure, with the piercing eyes, though infirm body, that once more appeared in the pulpit of St Peter's was not merely to dominate the little Republic on the shores of Lake Leman for the next quarter of a century, but to make it the capital of a spiritual dominion whose boundaries extended to the northern seas and ultimately beyond the Atlantic.

[66] " Opera," xxi. 265 f.

CHAPTER IV

REORGANISATION OF THE GENEVAN CHURCH

THE MINISTRY AND DISCIPLINE

ON the day of Calvin's return the Little Council at his request nominated four of its members and two members of the Council of Two Hundred to draft, along with him and his fellow-ministers, ecclesiastical ordinances to be submitted to the two Councils and the General Assembly of the people.[1] During their passage through these bodies they were subjected to much discussion and underwent some modification before they were finally adopted by the General Assembly on the 20th November 1541. They distinguish four classes of office-bearers in the Church—pastors, doctors, elders, and deacons. The office of pastor is to preach the Word of God, administer the sacraments, and along with the elders to maintain a brotherly supervision over the community. No one shall take upon himself the pastoral office without being duly called thereto by means of examination, institution, and ordination by the ministers. He must give proof of his knowledge of the Scriptures and his aptness to expound them, of his orthodoxy and the purity of his life. Having passed this examination, the ministers present him to the Little Council, which, if satisfied as to his qualifications, direct him to preach before the congregation " in order that he may be received with the common consent of the faithful." In the draft the election was vested in the ministers and subject only to the consent of the people, the Council merely accepting the ministers' nomination. With this limitation of its power it was, however, not satisfied, and it added a claim conferring on it the right to accept or refuse him if it should deem it expedient to do so. The judgment of the ministers was thus liable to be reversed by the

[1] " Opera," xxi. 282.

Council, and Calvin was fain to acquiesce in this important restriction of the ecclesiastical by the civil authority. In the ordination which followed, the ancient practice of laying on of hands was discarded by reason of the superstitions connected with it and " the infirmity of the time," though Calvin would otherwise have preferred to introduce it. The ceremony was, therefore, limited to a declaration of the nature of the pastoral office and to special prayers on behalf of the new pastor.[2] Finally he takes an oath of fidelity to God and the State in the discharge of his office.

For the study of the Scriptures the ministers of the city and the villages under the jurisdiction of the Republic meet once a week (the congregation). In case of irreconcilable doctrinal contention, they are to request the elders to help to bring about concord, and if they fail, the question is to be referred to the Council, who shall decide the quarrel. The Government is thus the final judge of doctrine as well as exercising a controlling voice in judging the qualifications of candidates for the ministry. For the maintenance of clerical discipline the ministers shall meet every three months for mutual exhortation and correction, and to the ministers thus convened for these various purposes was later applied the title, " the Venerable Company."

A lengthy list of offences of a religious and moral nature is added relative to the maintenance of clerical discipline. Some of these, such as heresy, schism, rebellion against ecclesiastical order, simony, drunkenness, are absolutely incompatible with the ministerial office and are to be severely punished. Others, such as neglect of the study of the Scriptures or of pastoral duty, are to be dealt with by way of brotherly admonition. In the case of those in the first category, the punishment is reserved to the magistrates, who, in addition to inflicting the civil penalty incurred, deposes the culprit from the ministry.

For ecclesiastical purposes the city is divided into the three parishes of St Peter's, St Gervais, and the Madeleine, and the number of ministers fixed at five, with three assistants, the number being gradually increased as the circumstances demanded. Calvin believed in the efficacy of the sermon, and it

---

[2] It does not appear that Calvin himself was ever ordained, though he thus introduced ordination as indispensable for entering on the ministry.

was certainly not his fault if Geneva was not amply instructed in the Word. On Sundays at daybreak the ministers are to preach in St Peter's and St Gervais, and again at nine o'clock in all three churches. At midday there is catechising of the children of each parish, and in the afternoon sermons again. Sermons, too, on Monday, Wednesday, and Friday in each of the churches—in all, seventeen sermons per week in a town of about 13,000 inhabitants. Calvin would have introduced frequent Communion, as in the primitive Church, but was fain once more to be content with the quarterly celebration of it. The young may not be admitted before receiving proper instruction in the Catechism and making profession of the faith therein contained. Marriages and baptisms are to be performed in church before the sermon.

The office of the doctor is " to teach the faithful in sound doctrine in order that the purity of the Gospel may not be corrupted by ignorance or false opinions." Theological instruction is of the utmost importance. But in order that such instruction may be profitably followed, a preliminary knowledge of languages and other sciences is indispensable. Hence the necessity of a system of primary and secondary education in the interest of both the Church and the State—for the provision of an educated ministry and the training of the young for civic life. Accordingly " a learned man " shall be appointed to take charge of this important work with a staff of lecturers in languages and dialectic for the more advanced students, and elementary teachers for the children of both sexes. The doctor and his assistants are subject, like the ministers, to ecclesiastical discipline, and are to be examined and approved by the ministers, though they are not ordained. As in the case of candidates for the ministry, the Council limited the power of the ministers by adding the stipulation that they must be presented to it and be examined in presence of two of its members before appointment.

The office of the elders is " to watch over the life of each individual, to admonish amicably those who shall be found to be at fault and lead a disorderly life, and, if need be, to report to the body which shall be entrusted with the task of making fraternal corrections." To this end the Small Council shall, after consultation with the ministers, elect twelve persons of

approved life and piety—two from its own membership, four
from the Council of Sixty, and six from the Council of Two
Hundred — for the approval of the Two Hundred.   If
approved, they shall take an oath similar to that prescribed
for the ministers.   For the better supervision of the people
each quarter of the city is to be represented.   At the end
of each year they are to present themselves to the magistrates who are to decide whether they have faithfully performed
their duties and shall be continued in office.   To the deacons,
who were elected in the same manner as the elders, is assigned
the care of the poor and the sick, and the administration of the
city hospital, in which separate accommodation is provided for
those unable to work and for widows and orphans.   Begging
at the church doors is strictly prohibited.

In conjunction with the ministers the elders compose the
Consistory, which meets once a week to consider disorders in
the church and the remedies to be applied.   It has no coercive
jurisdiction, which resides in the Council.   But the Council
places at its disposal its officers, who summon delinquents
before it, and in case of refusal to appear, the Council enforces
compliance.   If the offence refers to doctrine and if the accused
proves recalcitrant after repeated admonition, he is to be excommunicated and denounced to the magistrates.   The same
procedure is followed in case of refusal to attend church and
of offences against morality.   Whilst contumacy and rebellion
incur excommunication in such cases, there is to be no unnecessary rigour, and the object to be kept in view is not to
cause justifiable soreness, but to apply correction as a medicine
" to restore sinners to the Lord."   In spite of some opposition,
Calvin succeeded in vindicating for the Consistory the right of
excommunication of persistent offenders.   He did not seek to
arrogate to it the right to impose civil penalties, and agreed to
add an article explicitly denying to the ministers civil jurisdiction and limiting their power to matters spiritual, in accordance with the Word of God.   " The Consistory," the article
continues, " is not in anything derogatory to the authority of
the State, or to ordinary justice.   The civil power remains
intact.   When it is necessary to inflict punishment and constrain parties, the ministers with the elders, having heard the
parties and made such remonstrances and admonitions as they

shall consider necessary, must represent the whole case to the Council, which will consider their report, ordain, and judge according to the merits of the case." The spiritual and the civil power have thus each its distinct jurisdiction, and Calvin was all the more ready to recognise the fact inasmuch as he could now count on the co-operation of the civil authority in the maintenance of discipline.[3]

For his model of the ministry he goes back to the Church of the early second century rather than to that of the strictly apostolic age. In the apostolic age the local Christian community was under the charge not of a single pastor, but of a number of functionaries known interchangeably, as he notes,[4] as presbyters (elders) and bishops. It was only in the early second century that the single bishop or pastor of the Christian community came into existence, as in the Epistles of Ignatius, and was differentiated from the presbyters or elders, whilst the teacher or doctor and the deacons, as in the apostolic age,

[3] The Ordinances are given in " Opera," x^a. 15 f. Calvin took a leading part, as a member of a commission, in revising and systematising the laws and constitution of Geneva during 1541-43. " Opera," x^a. 125 f., which gives the fragments in his own handwriting of his proposals. An examination of his contribution to this reform of the Genevan laws is given by Bohatec, " Calvin und das Recht," 211 f. (1934). The tendency of this revision is to augment the power of the Executive Council and diminish that of the Assembly of the People. It modifies the constitution in an aristocratic direction. See also Kampschulte, i. 415 f.; H. Fazy, " Les Constitutions de la République de Genève " (1890); Goyau, " Une Ville-Église " (1919), and " Jean Calvin," Revue des Deux Mondes, 1914. F. F. Roget denies that Calvin exercised any influence on the constitution of Geneva. " On it (the political framework) Calvin has not even left the impress of his little finger," " A Criticism of Current Ideas on Calvin," 22. Surely an extreme statement.

[4] " Opera," x^a. 17. Lang thinks that Calvin's ecclesiastical organisation owed not a little to the Anabaptists of Strassburg with whom he came in contact. " The ecclesiastical idea of Calvin had its historic cradle not so much in Geneva as in Strassburg, the citadel of Anabaptism on the upper Rhine," " Reformirte Kirchenzeitung," 1908, 252 f. In their organisation of their communities the Anabaptists instituted the threefold ministry of pastors, elders, and deacons. See my " Luther and the Reformation," iv. 46. Calvin may have taken a cue from this organisation, though he could quite well have found it in the early second-century constitution, and may have been influenced by the Anabaptist differentiation between the Church and the State which in their case, however, was absolute. On the early second-century ministry see my " From Christ to Constantine " (1936). Courvoisier maintains with no little force that Calvin's conception of the ministry was influenced by Bucer, who in his sketch of a constitution for the Church at Strassburg advocated the fourfold ministry. Bull. Soc. Hist. du Prot. Français, 1935, 108 f. See also his " La Notion d'Église chez Bucer," 37 f., and Strohl, " La Théorie et la Pratique des Quatre Ministères à Strasbourg avant l'Arrivée de Calvin," ibid., 123 f.

remained distinct from both. It was this stage of the development of the ministerial office in the early second-century Church that Calvin took as his model. At the same time, he modified this model in accordance with the exigencies of the Genevan Republic. The elder is not ministerially ordained to his office as in the early Church. He is a layman who is nominated by the Council and is purely a member of one or other of the Councils, who performs certain ecclesiastical functions. Similarly the deacons differ from the early model in being laymen. Ordination is given only to the pastor, and even in the case of the pastor the laying on of hands is, at first at least, for reasons of expediency, not considered an essential of holding ministerial office, though Calvin would have preferred to revive at once this apostolic practice. For him the distinctive feature of the true ministry lies in the effective preaching of the Word, the right administration of the Sacraments, an adequate knowledge of the Scriptures, aptitude for preaching, and holiness of life. In this respect he shows a marked reaction from the mediæval hierarchical conception of the ministry.

RELATION OF STATE AND CHURCH

For Calvin the Church, as we have already noted, is autonomous in spiritual things. In its own sphere it is distinct from the State, whilst accepting the co-operation of the State in the performance of its function in asserting and maintaining the Rule or Kingdom of God. Though he succeeded to a certain extent in asserting this distinction, he did not succeed, in the meantime at least, in fully vindicating the Church's autonomy in spiritual things. He had to accommodate theory to the actual political constitution of the Republic, and was fain to compromise accordingly and submit to the encroachment of the State on its autonomy.

The civil authority insists, for instance, on approving or rejecting any candidate for ministerial office presented to it by the ministers. It assumes the right to decide finally in any theological dispute between the ministers. It vindicates the right to approve the qualifications of the doctor. It really controls the administration of discipline in virtue of the fact that the elders are its deputies as much as ecclesiastical officials and form a majority of the Consistory, over which one of the magistrates, who bears his baton as the emblem of the civil authority, presides, and are paid by it for their services,[5] though it leaves the excommunication of offenders to it as an ecclesiastical body. In the exercise of its authority it is closely mixed up with the ecclesiastical administration. On the whole, however, the spiritual power, in the essentials of preaching, the administration of the sacraments, excommunication, receives fairly generous recognition, and with goodwill on the part of the Councils, the arrangement was quite a workable one. " Although it is not perfect it is tolerable, considering the difficulty of the times," wrote Calvin.[6] On the one hand, he departs from the mediæval ecclesiastical tendency to exalt the Church above the State and interfere in the civil jurisdiction. On the other, the civil authority recognises to a considerable extent the spiritual jurisdiction of the Church. Unfortunately, neither repudiated the vicious mediæval idea of visiting spiritual offences with civil pains and penalties. The Church excommunicates, and formally its function ceases at this point. But the State requires the delinquent to be handed over to it for punishment—in a civil capacity, indeed—and the Church acquiesces and reports the case to the magistrates. Calvin, apparently, had no difficulty in approving this questionable course. Nay, he seems to have only too thoroughly shared the common view of the age that such co-operation in carrying out the disciplinary measures of the Church was necessary and salutary.

Public Worship

Besides revising and simplifying the Catechism for the instruction of the young, which he had composed in 1537,[7] he drew up a formulary for the conduct of public worship and the administration of the sacraments. It was based on that which he had introduced at Strassburg, but adapted to the simpler liturgy of Farel already in use at Geneva. His aim, as he tells us in the preface, was to make worship intelligible and edifying. He strenuously controverts the traditional and superficial view that the worshipper can be truly devotional

---

[5] " Opera," xxi. 289.   [6] Herminjard, vii. 409.
[7] " Opera," v. 313 f. The revision is in vi. 1 f.

without understanding the prayers, or in merely beholding a certain ritual. Worship is not a dead thing, but a living act of the heart and the intelligence, touched and enlightened by the Holy Spirit. Does not St Paul forbid to speak in an unknown tongue which does not tend to edification ? Prayer must, therefore, be offered in the common language in order that the people may intelligently and profitably participate, and no amount of subtlety can excuse the Roman practice of using the Latin tongue as the language of worship. This holds also of the sacraments. They are not mere spectacles or ceremonies to be celebrated without a due understanding of their significance. For lack of this understanding they have degenerated into superstitious magical performances. Hence, in view of the prevailing ignorance, the composition of the formulary as an aid to an intelligent and edifying worship. Special emphasis is laid, in addition to ordinary prayer, on praise as a medium of devotion. From the beginnings of the Church praise as well as prayer has formed part of public worship, and Calvin, like Luther, and in contrast to Zwingli, extols its devotional value. " We know by experience that singing is fitted powerfully to move and inflame the hearts of men as a means of invoking and praising God with a more vehement and ardent zeal." This advocacy of song in the service of the sanctuary pleasingly reflects a side of Calvin's nature, which the conventional conception of the Reformer as a hard and unemotional personality tends all too much to obscure. He evidently felt the power and charm of music, and though he denounces its misuse as an expression of the lower as well as the higher feelings, he is alive to its elevating influence and in particular its utility in worship. He had emphasised the fact in the Articles of 1537, but had been unable for lack of material to introduce the singing of Psalms. He had found the means of doing so at Strassburg with the help of Marot's translations, which he supplemented by some of his own, and of the musical gift of some of his friends, who composed tunes for them. He would, however, ñot hear of instrumental accompaniments, which he regarded as a papist device and for which he found no warrant in the primitive Church.

The liturgy opens with an exhortation to prayer, after which follow confession, the singing of a Psalm, a prayer for enlighten-

ment by the Spirit in the preaching of the Word, which is left
to the discretion of the minister. The absolution pronounced
by the minister and the chanting of the Commandments, with
relative prayers, in the Strassburg liturgy are omitted—the
former apparently in deference to the anti-Romanist scruples
which Calvin, in this respect, did not share. After the sermon
there follows a long intercessory and general prayer, and the
service is concluded with the benediction. Special prayers are
added for use in time of affliction, such as pestilence and war,
and forms are given for the administration of baptism, the
celebration of the Lord's Supper, and the performance of the
ceremony of marriage.[8]

The service is characterised by its simplicity, its reverence,
its devotional feeling. It represents a radical simplification of
worship in comparison with that of the mediæval Church. It
is not, however, original, for Calvin made use, in its composition,
of the liturgy which he had drawn up for his Strassburg congregation, and which, as has been noted, was based on the
German Mass introduced at Strassburg by Diebold Schwarz
in 1524 and subsequently modified under Bucer's influence.
The Geneva liturgy was an adaptation, in the direction of
ancient simplicity, of this composition, as already adapted for
the use of the French congregation at Strassburg. It was
intended to edify as well as give expression to devotional
feeling. The prayers accordingly reflect the Reformed theology
and have in this respect in certain parts a rather pronounced
confessional character. They are, too, rather lacking in the
element of thanksgiving, except in the case of the celebration
of the Lord's Supper. The liturgy proves that Calvin was
conscious of the desirability of a common form of worship
in the Reformed churches, if only because of its utility in
helping towards an intelligent participation in divine service,
on the part of the worshippers, and affording a clear
differentiation between the Reformed and the Roman Catholic
service. He leaves, however, considerable latitude to the
minister.

<hr>

[8] " Opera," vi. 166 f.

CHAPTER V

THE CALVINIST RÉGIME

Its Theocratic Tendency

CALVIN'S supremacy at Geneva was by no means established by his recall and his organisation of the Genevan Church. The party which had effected his exile, though overthrown, still existed, and the experience of the full-fledged Calvinist discipline erelong materially added to the number of its adherents. These erelong included even Ami Perrin, the former leader of the Guillermins, who had been charged by his party to secure his return.[1] Calvin's ideal of government was practically, if not formally, a theocracy. He sharply differentiated, indeed, between the civil and the spiritual powers, and he had no desire to revolutionise the political institutions of Geneva in a theocratic direction. He was, and remained simply the most influential minister of the Genevan Church and exercised no official authority outside the ministerial sphere. The political constitution remained what it had been— that of a free republic with its executive and legislative organs as embodied in the Councils and the General Assembly of the people. Calvin was simply a member of the community charged with the ministry of the Word and limited in the exercise of his office by ordinances which, while they recognised and secured the rights of the ministerial function, subordinated the Church in important respects to the State. From this point of view the republic was no theocracy in the sense that the ecclesiastical usurped the rights and function of the civil power. The Government, in fact, tended to subordinate the Church to the State, not the State to the Church. On the other hand, in virtue of his ability, his strength of character, and his consuming zeal as a minister of the Word, Calvin exercised an immense, if not always a decisive influence on the executive power. His aim, his striving was to mould the life of the

[1] " Opera," xxi. 265.

85

community by the Word in subjection to the divine law as expressed in the Old Testament as well as the New. This law, as he understood it—embodied in a rigid system of ecclesiastical discipline and backed by the State—should govern the community. Thereby the Kingdom or Rule of God on earth should be established. In this sense the Calvinist régime is theocratic, or if we prefer the term clerocratic, in so far as it gave scope, under clerical influence, to the Word or Will of God, as interpreted and applied by the ministers.

In itself the theocratic conception—the Rule of God on earth—is a legitimate one. Since the Christian State has an ethical as well as a political basis and is invested with an ethical function, it is, or ought to be, bound in its action by the ethical principles applicable to the life of the individual Christian. It, as well as the Church, may, nay ought, to make its contribution, in its own sphere, to the realisation of the ideal of the Kingdom of God. In striving for the realisation of this ideal by the exemplification of Christian ethics in the action of both the community and the individual, Calvin was only discharging one of the most important functions of the Christian minister. All government ought to be theocratic in this sense—in the sense of the application of the principles of probity, justice, humanity, in accordance with the Nature and Will of God and the ethical capacity and obligation of man, in national and social life and in international relations. It is, moreover, in the real interest of the State that it should be so. To ignore its ethical character and function, to exalt the State above morality, to divorce politics from ethics means, as history has so often tragically proved, ultimate calamity for the nations and for humanity. In the age of Calvin this was the dominant conception in spite of the plausible and often hypocritical parade of zeal for the old Church or the new on the part of too many of the Governments of the day. The age of Calvin was also the age of Machiavelli and Machiavelli, not Christ, was the ruler of those who ruled. Moreover, in judging his disciplinary system, we must bear in mind the widespread demoralisation of the Church as well as the State in the early sixteenth century. His discipline was a natural and a very needful reaction from the prevalent moral declension of both. It is, in fact, to his honour that he should have set himself to effect a radical reform of morals as well as of doctrine, and should have so resolutely insisted on its realisation. For him the return to primitive Christianity involved the revival of the primitive Christian ideal of life—complete consecration to God in accordance with the moral teaching of Christ and the apostles, as well as the revival of primitive institutions and doctrine. The fact does him the utmost credit in view of the long and widely prevalent degeneration of the Church and the world.

On the other hand, the spirit and method of this otherwise laudable and necessary régime are open to grave objection. Its spirit is unduly puritanic. It tended to nurture a narrow formalism, to ascribe an artificial religious value to things indifferent or innocent in themselves, to cramp individual liberty by a rigid legalism, to narrow it to the measure of the puritan formalist and breed the Pharisee. Calvin is, in this respect, the mediæval monk in the guise of the evangelical Reformer, with this difference that, whilst the choice of the monastic profession was voluntary, his puritanism is obligatory on all as an essential of the Christian life. We miss in him the larger and freer spirit of Luther, who emphasised the freedom as well as the servitude of the Christian man. We miss, too, the Pauline emphasis on " the liberty of the Gospel," which the apostle defended so stoutly against its legalist opponents, and which Calvin himself in theory recognised. In method he carries over to the Reformation the mediæval spirit of regulation in religion and morality at the expense of individual liberty. He makes use of a harsh penal code in the interest of both, and visits offences against discipline with civil pains and penalties, in glaring violation of the Gospel, which makes the religious life the spontaneous fruit of faith and love. For this principle the Calvinist régime substitutes an inquisitorial, harsh, tyrannical system of legally enforced obedience. It takes advantage of the barbarous and abhorrent practice of torture to extort confession of moral and even doctrinal delinquencies. Let us do Calvin the justice to say that he did not originate the system of regulating the life of the individual in accordance with the methods of a harsh and inhuman legalism. This was an inherent feature of mediæval municipal law and practice. At the same time, justice requires us also to

say that he approved of it and made use of it in the maintenance
of discipline, if he also sometimes deprecated its abuse.[2] In
this respect—and this may serve as an excuse, if not an exonera-
tion—he was a man of his time. In these matters he was as
unenlightened as the generality of his contemporaries, equally
unable to apprehend aright the Gospel he professed and
preached. " The Calvinist discipline was not inspired by
the charity, the patience distinctive of the Gospel. It was
impressed by a legalist and juridical spirit, which is more the
spirit of Moses than the spirit of Jesus Christ, more the spirit
of the Old Testament than that of the New Covenant." [3] It
is, in verity, a strange aberration from the Gospel to see in
such methods a legitimate adjunct of Christian discipline. In
principle it is akin to the mediæval method of burning heretics
for the glory of God and the salvation of the heretic's soul or
inflicting lesser penalties for religious offences. It is, in fact,
the same aberration projected into the Reformation. Sin, or
what was regarded as sin, is criminal in the view of the Church
as well as the State, and must be punished as such. Hence
the punishment of extreme cases of heresy and blasphemy
with death, as Servetus and Gruet experienced to their cost.
To neglect to attend sermon or sacrament (and sermons were
both numerous and lengthy) is a crime. To swear or even to
jest is criminal, and woe to the sinner who joked at Calvin's
expense. To criticise a preacher is blasphemy—the preachers
reserving a monopoly of criticism to themselves. To dance
or wear forbidden finery, to sing a worldly song, to break the
Sabbath is to make one liable to both ecclesiastical and civil
proceedings. Granted that Geneva, as the result of the old
degenerate clerical régime, was an immoral city, though,
according to M. Roget, its immorality has been exaggerated,
and that Calvin needed all the help he could get in his fight
against immorality. Was it necessary in combating it to
magnify petty misdemeanours into gross sins and punish them
as crimes against God and society ? Was not such fussy and
unwarrantable rigour likely to defeat itself by engendering
legitimate opposition, or only begetting formal compliance
as well as breeding the Pharisee ? Conformity in such matters

[2] See, for instance, " Opera," xxi. 348.
[3] Choisy, " Calvin," 87.

does not mean moral transformation. In denouncing petty faults or mere deviations from ecclesiastical prescription as heinous sins, Calvin and his fellow-preachers could only appear to the more sane as well as the vicious section of the community as dictatorial doctrinaires.

THE CONSISTORY AT WORK

The instrument for maintaining this disciplinary system is the Consistory. The Registers of both Consistory and Council are full of characteristic details of the working of this politico-ecclesiastical régime. There are numerous examinations [4] by the former and prosecution by the latter for offences of varying degrees of culpability. Taking them as they occur in the record, we find among them charges of playing at cards,[5] papistical opinions,[6] using charms for healing purposes,[7] criticising the ministers.[8] Absence from sermon and the Lord's Supper, inability to repeat the Lord's Prayer and the Creed, addiction to popish practices frequently recur.[9] Others deal with family quarrels,[10] frequenting taverns and gambling, frequent defamation of Calvin,[11] superstitious practices,[12] drunkenness,[13] promiscuous bathing and prostitution,[14] swearing,[15] dancing,[16] praying to the virgin and the saints,[17] buying and selling crosses and other emblems of idolatry, marriages between Protestants and Catholics,[18] hostility to the French refugees,[19] kneeling at the grave of a deceased husband and saying *Requiescat in pace*,[20] mocking of God's Word,[21] etc. In the less serious cases the Consistory contents itself with an admonition and prescribing a course of sermons or of the Catechism. In other cases it sends the delinquent to the Council for due punishment. On the whole the accused proffer explanation and profess repentance. Occasionally, however, they show an independent spirit, question the authority of the Consistory, even stand up to Calvin and freely tell him what they think of him and his

[4] For certain years the Register is lacking.
[5] " Opera," xxi. 289.
[6] *Ibid.*, 291.
[7] *Ibid.*, 294-297
[8] *Ibid.*, 301.
[9] *Ibid.*, 303-310.
[10] *Ibid.*, 322-323.
[11] *Ibid.*, 327 *passim*.
[12] *Ibid.*, 334, 366.
[13] *Ibid.*, 366.
[14] *Ibid.*, 367.
[15] *Ibid.*, 370.
[16] *Ibid.*, 377-378.
[17] *Ibid.*, 387.
[18] *Ibid.*, 406.
[19] *Ibid.*, 410, 420.
[20] *Ibid.*, 422.
[21] *Ibid.*, 422.

inquisitorial régime. Such "insolences" are duly reported to the Council and the defiant party usually gets the worst of it. Not seldom we get the impression that the Consistory is disposed to be overbearing and tyrannical in its effort to maintain conformity to the minutiæ of discipline. On the other hand, the all too-frequent accusations of sins of the flesh, of fornication and prostitution, especially in connection with the public baths (*éstuves*) and the taverns, prove that its disciplinary activity was by no means superfluous and that it performed a necessary and serviceable function in the interest of social morality. An effort to stem immorality was, indeed, urgent, and the object aimed at was altogether laudable, however dubious, in some respects, the method of accomplishing it. Calvin and his fellow-inquisitors had, it is evident, an uphill task in fighting this immorality, and in their striving to bring the ethical teaching of the pulpit to bear on practical life, the Consistory, in this part of its activity, was rendering an important practical service to the State as well as the Church. A vigorous oversight of the community was a necessity of the situation, and this could only be effectively carried out by an organised and vigilant body in addition to preaching and pastoral supervision. The Consistory was an attempt to energise the Reformation as a means of moral regeneration, to curb the antinomian tendency which it tended to some extent to foster, to meet the reproach of its enemies that it exalted faith at the expense of works. From this point of view, there is not a little to be said for it as a practical expedient suited to the times, for fighting the impurity, licence, and cynicism which threatened to paralyse the work of the Reformers. At the same time, the records of its proceedings show some very objectionable features. It encourages the busybody and pays far too much attention to mere gossip. It is the happy hunting ground of Mr and Mrs Grundy. It maintains a regular system of espionage and breeds the informer, who makes it his business to sniff out ecclesiastical and other offences among his neighbours. It is too much actuated by a petty persecuting spirit and shows an inordinate zeal about trifles. It is altogether lacking in the saving virtue of humour. Most objectionable, it is harshly intolerant of religious convictions that differ from its own. It compels Jean

Balard, for instance, to renounce his papistical opinions and profess " the verity of the Gospel." [22]   It is all too ready to denounce such convictions as " blasphemy " and to identify the Word of God exclusively with its own views.   It resents criticism as " insolence," though the criticism appears at times by no means unwarrantable, and Calvin in particular shows a vindictive spirit in pursuing his critics.[23]

ABETMENT BY THE COUNCIL

In the maintenance of discipline it acts in the closest co-operation with the Council.   It refers to it ecclesiastical offences which, in its judgment, merit more than Consistorial remonstrance and admonition, and in cases of refusal to submit to its authority it invariably does so.   The Council, indeed, takes action on its own initiative against criminal offences which are also ecclesiastical offences.   But indirectly as well as directly the Consistory makes its influence felt in the administration of a widely ramified criminal law.   Calvin's vigilance and authority are constantly in evidence in its proceedings and usually in the direction of intensifying their rigour.   He is the driving force both in public and behind the scenes.   The following examples taken from its Registers here and there serve to illustrate the Council's activity under his vigilant auspices.   It institutes proceedings against those whom the ministers accuse of opposition to the Word of God which often means apparently criticism of their sermons and their actions.[24] It dismisses Castellion for dissenting from Calvin's teaching and suspends, or deposes, or imprisons, or removes to the country parishes those of his fellow-ministers who, on various grounds, become obnoxious to him.[25]   It orders the inhabitants of town and country to attend sermons and punishes refusal, after three warnings, with banishment.[26]   It sentences to death a large number of persons, principally women, accused of conspiring to spread the pest and devoting themselves to the devil, and orders them to have their hands cut off and to be burned at the stake [27] (March 1545).   It does not appear that

[22] " Opera," xxi. 291.
[23] *Ibid.*, xxi. 451 *passim.*
[24] *Ibid.*, xxi. 337, 342, etc.
[25] *Ibid.*, 361-364, 374-375, 451, etc.
[26] *Ibid.*, 345, 348-349.
[27] *Ibid.*, 349.

Calvin and his fellow-ministers were responsible for this atrocity. But they do not seem to have protested against it, and in November of the same year Calvin and the minister Bernard " demand a legal inquisition against heretics (sorcerers) in order to extirpate this race." [28]   Unfortunately, like everybody else, they believed in witchcraft, and this may explain, though it does not justify, the matter of fact tone in which Calvin mentions this tragic incident in a letter to Myconius.[29] It repeatedly takes action against those who indulge in witticisms at his expense. It banishes Millon D'Auvergne, for instance, whom he charged with " making ballads and farces against him to the dishonour of God and the Word." [30]   Ridicule Calvin could not stand, though he certainly gave the wits considerable provocation to subject him to this kind of attack.   When, for instance, he gravely prayed the Council to decree that no name savouring of idolatry should be conferred at baptism and the Council put on trial one recalcitrant father, who refused, at the dictation of the minister, to discard the name Claude for Abraham.[31]   Or when it sent another to prison for insisting that the child should be baptized Balthazar, and created a disturbance when the minister insisted on calling him John.[32] It suspends the theatrical representation of sacred subjects (a relic of the passion play) after a lengthy controversy with the ministers on the subject.[33]   It goes the length even of shutting the taverns and substituting for them puritanic clubs or casinos (*abbayes*), which speedily proved a complete failure.

[28] " Opera," 365.
[29] *Ibid.*, xii. 55.
[30] *Ibid.*, xxi. 422.
[31] *Ibid.*, 387.
[32] *Ibid.*, 426-427 ; *cf.* 390-391.
[33] *Ibid.*, 385.

CHAPTER VI

RENEWED OPPOSITION

CALVIN'S SENSE OF AUTHORITY

OPPOSITION to this tutorial régime, necessary and salutary in some essential respects though it might be, was inevitable, and the opposition grew in strength up to 1555, when Calvin finally gained a decisive victory over the party that had striven for years to overthrow him. More than once he was in danger of losing the support of the Council, in which his enemies became powerful as time went on. The struggle became a pitched battle of long duration and tested to the utmost his rare powers of will and mind and his strength of character. What carried him through it to ultimate triumph was his supreme belief in himself as God's instrument. Naturally a timid man and the victim of frequent illness, he knew neither fear nor hesitation when what he held to be the cause of God was at stake. Hence the commanding sense of his authority as God's minister, the implacable, relentless pursuit of opponents which, unfortunately, was aggravated by a vindictive temperament. Opposition to him is opposition to God and His Word. It was not permissible to doubt that his interpretation of the Word as preacher and theologian was inerrant and must be received as the truth of God. This implied belief in himself was an indispensable adjunct of his mission. But it could not fail to excite antagonism in a high-spirited community accustomed to fighting for its liberties, and containing a governing aristocratic class jealous of its power and not inclined to share Calvin's pessimistic doctrine of the utter corruption of human nature.

CHARACTER OF THE OPPOSITION

It was not merely a question of reforming an immoral city. The opposition to Calvin sprang by no means solely from

libertinism in thought and life, as some historians have represented. The term Libertine which later came to designate this
opposition was not applied to it in his lifetime. The Libertines
of his day were a sect of Spirituals, which, originating at Lille
and spreading in France, held pantheistic and antinomian
views, and which Calvin attacked in 1545 in a philippic " Against
the fantastic and furious sect of the Libertines, who call themselves Spirituals." [1] His polemic against them was all the more
bitter inasmuch as they dared—not, indeed, without some show
of logic—to make use of his dogma of predestination in support
of their teaching. If God has ordained everything by His
decree, the evil as well as the good is ascribable to Him. To
their pantheistic way of thinking there is, therefore, no radical
distinction between them, and responsibility and guilt do not
really exist. God is the all, the only energising power who
works in us, and sin is a mere imagination. The spiritual
man has emancipated himself from this illusion and lives his
natural life in childlike communion with God's Spirit in perfect
freedom from the law and without consciousness of guilt.
Such an immoral interpretation and application of the dogma
of predestination was not, however, professed by the anti-
Calvinist party in Geneva, and there is nothing in Calvin's
philippic against the sect to warrant the assumption that in
writing against it he had this party in mind. His attack is
directed against a movement which was active in France and
the Netherlands and was fitted to discredit the Gospel and
hinder its spread. If it had taken any considerable hold in
Geneva there is nothing in his anti-Libertine writings [2] or in
the Registers of the Council and the Consistory to lead us to

---

[1] " Opera," vii. 148 f. ; cf. " Épitre contre un certain Cordelier, suppost
de la Secte des Libertins," ibid., 341 f. (1547). Niesel (" Calvin und Die
Libertiner ") controverts K. Müller's contention that Calvin misunderstood
and, therefore, misrepresented the sect, " Zeitschrift f. Kirchengeschichte,"
1929, 58 f. According to Müller, it was quietistic, not pantheistic, and was
not Libertine in morals, " Z.K.G.," 1922, 83 f. Niesel makes out that
Calvin had a personal and accurate knowledge of their tenets, whilst
not hazarding a definite judgment whether, on the ground of their
pantheism, he was justified in ascribing to them a consequent immorality,
ibid., 74.

[2] He controverts in his philippic against the sect the opinions of Antoine
Pocque, one of its leaders, with whom he had some controversy in Geneva,
but who seems to have made only a flying visit to the city. His anti-
Libertine writings are directed against the propaganda of the sect in
France.

infer the fact. At most there are in the Registers only slight traces of its influence.[3]

Some of the leaders of the anti-Calvinist party like Favre and Berthelier were, indeed, men of licentious habits, and it of course attracted those to whom, on this ground, the Calvinist régime was obnoxious. But it is an error to represent it as essentially the champion of Libertinism in the moral and religious sense. It was, in fact, largely actuated by political motives. It revolted against the encroachment of the Calvinist régime on personal liberty and its influence in the government of the Republic. It strove to vindicate this liberty by depriving the Consistory of the right of excommunication and to counteract this influence by intensifying the subordination of the Church to the State. In this respect, it revived the earlier opposition to Calvin, and the experience of the full-blown Calvinist puritanism added not a few of the former adherents of the Guillermin party to its ranks. It focussed in addition the old antagonism to the influence of foreigners, who found in Calvin and his fellow-ministers of French nationality their active patrons, and whom persecution in France was driving in ever larger numbers to seek a refuge at Geneva. For the patriotism, to which this growing foreign influence was obnoxious, Calvin had no appreciation. For him Geneva was not a second fatherland, but a stronghold in which to wage the battle for the Gospel and from which to carry on a mighty propaganda in the lands in Western Europe, particularly in his native France. With such political motives was combined, in many cases, dislike of the Calvinist theology, especially the dogma of absolute predestination. The intolerance which suffered none with impunity to differ, even by a hairsbreadth, from his dogmatic interpretation of Christianity kept alive the old antagonism to an enforced Confession.

---

[3] See, for instance, xxi. 469, 481. Kampschulte gives a good account of the sect and Calvin's relation to it, ii. 13 f. Staehelin asserts the older view of the influence of the Libertine sect on the opposition, Herzog-Hauck, "Encyclopedie," iii. 669. Similarly Henry, "Life of Calvin," ii. 41 f., English translation by Stebbing (1849). Their views are treated at large by Schmidt, "Les Libertins Spirituels" (1876); Jundt, "Hist. du Pantheisme Populaire du Moyen Age et au Seizième Siècle" (1885).

RENEWAL OF CONFLICT

For the first five years, *i.e.*, up to 1546, the opposition was furtive rather than public. There was only one concerted attempt to undermine Calvin's position and this attempt failed. In March 1543 the Council of Sixty proposed to deprive the Consistory of the right of excommunication and to transfer it to the Small Council.[4] The proposal called forth the strenuous opposition of Calvin, who declared that he would suffer death or exile rather than yield, and the Small Council declined to accept it.[5] The real struggle began with the prosecution of Pierre Ameaux in 1546, a former adherent of the Guillermin party and a member of the Little Council, who expressed his opinion of Calvin too freely at a supper party, calling him a wicked man, a Picard, a preacher of false doctrine, an ambitious intriguer who had managed to dominate the Government, etc.[6] For this rash utterance he was arrested at the end of January 1546 and tried a month later by the Council, which was divided in opinion as to the punishment of his offence and referred the case to the Two Hundred.[7] The Two Hundred decided in favour of mildness and merely directed him to ask pardon of God, the magistrates, and Calvin [8] (2nd March 1546). The sentence was a triumph for the Calvinist opposition, and Calvin resented it as a blow to his influence. Thus to question his teaching and asperse his character was a sin against God, and demanded a stern atonement if he was to retain his authority. He brought the matter before the Consistory, which supported him in his demand for exemplary punishment. Thus supported, he refused to be present at the carrying out of the sentence or to appear in the pulpit unless such blasphemy against God was punished with the severity it merited. Accompanied by the Consistory and his fellow-ministers, he repeated the demand before the various Councils with the result that the Two Hundred directed the retrial of the case. Ultimately the Small Council was fain to decree the sentence proposed by the party in favour of severity and order the unfortunate culprit to make the tour of the city,

---

[4] " Opera," xxi. 309.
[5] *Ibid.*, xi. 521.
[6] *Ibid.*, xxi. 368-369.
[7] *Ibid.*, 370.
[8] *Ibid.*, 371.

clad in his shirt and carrying a lighted torch, and on his knees implore the mercy of God and the magistrates as well as pay the expenses of the suit [9] (8th April).

Besides the growing tendency to criticise Calvin, the opposition manifests itself in rebellion against the authority of the Consistory. At a wedding party some of the guests had the temerity to dance, and for this enormity the Council sent the whole company to prison, despite the fact that it included Corne, one of the syndics and president of the Consistory itself, Ami Perrin, his wife Francisca Favre, and other notable citizens. The Consistory also summoned the delinquents to appear before it for discipline. Corne received its admonition in a submissive spirit. Perrin was at first recalcitrant, but also ultimately gave way. Some of the others denied the offence or adopted a defiant attitude, and Francisca Favre accused Calvin of carrying on a vendetta against her father François Favre, and her brother Gaspard, against whom the Consistory had instituted proceedings for immorality. She called him a wicked and bloodthirsty man and threatened him with expulsion from the city. Calvin told her that the Consistory could make no distinction of persons, and that it was bound to vindicate the cause of God [10] (April to May 1546).

The incident, which created a great sensation, increased the number of his enemies, and henceforth Perrin and his friend Pierre Vandel, as well as the Favres, became the active leaders of the antagonism to the petty tyranny of the Consistorial régime. The elections of the following year (February 1547) added to the number of their supporters in the Council, and François Favre, having been convicted of adultery, angrily refused to confess his sins to the Consistory or recognise its right to subject him to further penalty. A violent altercation ensued, Favre repeatedly aspersing the presumption of the ministers in sitting in judgment on him, and the minister Poupin, in the absence of Calvin, retorting by calling him a dog and excommunicate.[11] The Consistory reported his defiance to the Council and demanded reparation for his contempt of its authority. It found the new Council more critical of its demands and less prompt in conceding them.[12] It

[9] "Opera," 371-378.
[10] Ibid., xxi. 377 f. ; xii. 334 f.
[11] Ibid., xxi. 395-396.
[12] Ibid., 399.

not only delayed a decision of the case, but debated the question whether the Consistory, in insisting on subjecting delinquents, whose offences had been punished by the civil court, to further proceedings, had not exceeded the powers conferred on it by the Ordinances. There was, indeed, some force in Favre's contention that, having suffered punishment by the civil authority for an offence against the criminal law, he was not liable to further prosecution by an ecclesiastical court, if he did not freely choose to submit himself to its jurisdiction. The Council so far sympathised with his contention as to resolve that only in cases of obdurate sinners was the Consistory entitled to take further proceedings, and that it " should leave those who were repentant in peace." It urged the contending parties to show a conciliatory spirit, severely rebuked the minister Poupin for his violent language in the Consistory and the pulpit, enjoined the members of the Consistory to admonish delinquents in a courteous spirit (*gracieusement*), and arrogated to the Council the right to send such to the Consistory or not at its discretion.[13] Calvin regarded this decision as a virtual vote of censure and a blow to the Consistorial régime and the maintenance of discipline.[14]

On the 29th March he accordingly appeared before the Council to parry the threatened attack. Whilst disclaiming on behalf of the Consistory any desire to encroach on the rights of the sovereign authority, he insisted on the necessity, in the interest of discipline, of maintaining Consistorial authority and the impossibility of doing so if all delinquents were not subject to its jurisdiction. In deference to his arguments the Council yielded on this point, whilst maintaining the distinction in the treatment of obstinate and repentant sinners, and admonishing the Consistory to be more circumspect in its judgment of evidence and more restrained in its censures. At the same time, it directed Favre to acknowledge its authority. On this understanding a formal reconciliation took place,[15] Favre thereafter retiring to the country.

The truce was of short duration. A few weeks later Perrin

---

[13] " Opera," 399-401.
[14] *Ibid.*, xii. 505, "non video in toto numero cui fidam. Video certe neminem illic esse cordatum. Si desistam totum Consistorium ruat necesse est."
[15] *Ibid.*, xxi. 399 f. ; xii. 508.

and Calvin again appear at variance over the tremendous question of allowing the city militia, of which he was captain-general, to celebrate, as of yore, their annual festival in slashed breeches, which the Consistory had vetoed as too great a concession to youthful vanity, and the Council had prohibited. In deference to Calvin's opposition, the Two Hundred, to whom the Small Council referred the question, refused the request. The refusal excited the ire of the gallant arquebusiers, who failed to appreciate the sinfulness of arraying themselves in the traditional uniform, in spite of Calvin's fussy insistence on the danger of thereby encouraging human pride and perversity.[16] Some weeks later Perrin's wife, the irrepressible and outspoken Francisca Favre, again appears in the Registers as guilty of dancing during her husband's absence on a mission to the French Court, and of using scurrilous language against the minister Poupin in the Consistory. For this conduct the Council ordered her arrest (24th June 1547), and kept her under lock and key for some weeks, when she managed to escape and followed her father into retirement.[17]

PROSECUTION OF GRUET

The bitter ill-will against Calvin and his fellow-ministers, intensified by these petty prosecutions, found vent in an anonymous placard, which some malcontent had placed in the pulpit of St Peter's. It threatened to make them rue the day that they had left their monkery to play the masters over a free city. " When one endures too much, one takes revenge. We will not have so many masters. Mark my words." [18] On the complaint of Calvin, the Council arrested Jacques Gruet on suspicion of being the author of this truculent outburst, though it could not be proved to be in his handwriting. Gruet was a secret free-thinker and a minor poet, a member of the Favre circle, and at the same time a friend of Calvin's protégé, the refugee Maigret. Calvin himself appears to have suspected his free-thinking tendency and to have contracted a special aversion to him, and the examination of the papers found in his house revealed what seemed to him and also to the Council

16 " Opera," xxi. 405 f.
17 *Ibid.*, 407-409 ; xii. 545 f.   18 *Ibid.*, xii. 546 ; xxi. 407 f.

a criminal degradation of mind. They showed not only antipathy to Calvin as a domineering, ambitious zealot, but what
was to him a still more deadly crime, a flippant, sceptical
tendency to mock at the Scriptures, at Moses, at Christ, at the
doctrine of immortality. Among them was an intended appeal
to the General Assembly to overthrow the puritanic Government
of the city, and a letter to one of the ministers of the King of
France soliciting his intervention for the same purpose. They
contained, in addition, evidence of Libertinism of thought
and morals as well as of what must have appeared to the Calvinist
party a revolutionary radicalism. All laws, human and Divine,
are, for instance, declared to be mere inventions of men, and
similar " execrable allegations." [19] The Government saw in
these private documents not only diabolic perversity of mind,
but a conspiracy against religion and the State—treason as
well as blasphemy. A conspiracy involves accomplices and
therefore Gruet was subjected to repeated torture to force him
to reveal their names. Not even the most excruciating torments
could extract from him this admission. In the midst of his
agony he admitted the authorship of the placard, which he had
hitherto denied, confessed, too, that his life was worthy of
death and begged his tormentors to end his sufferings by
inflicting this penalty forthwith. But he steadfastly refused to
incriminate others and it seems that there was no conspiracy
to reveal. Gruet was evidently nothing more than a superficial
free-thinker and a free-liver, with a dangerous predilection to
scribble his thoughts, as the impulse seized him, but without
the gift or perhaps the desire to play the part of an active
revolutionary. The stubborn and even heroic refusal to evade
the most horrible ordeals by bearing false witness shows, in
spite of the laxity of his morals and the cynical scepticism of
his views, a highly creditable respect for truth. This alone is
sufficient to condemn the fiendish methods by which his judges
strove to shake his constancy. These methods were, unfortunately, in accordance with the practice of the age, despite its
zeal for the Gospel, and the fact that Calvin, whilst emphasising
the enormity of such sins as dancing and sporting slashed hose,
could find nothing to denounce in the fiendish torment of

[19] See summary of the process in " Opera," xii. 565 f., and Calvin's letter
to Viret, *ibid.*, 546-547.

18368

a shallow and comparatively insignificant free-thinker, who refused to tell a lie, throws a doleful light on the warping influence of conventional ideas and inhuman practice on the ardent disciple of Christ. The editors of his letters say that he took little part in the proceedings, and a recent biographer [20] asserts that he took none. The fact seems to be that he did his best to get him condemned, and Kampschulte traces his hand in the second series of articles presented against him.[21] At the same time, he was only performing what even the opposition party esteemed a duty to the State and religion. Such a cynical critic of the religious and moral order, who cherished views akin to, or even worse than, those of the Libertine sect, was anathema to even the opponents of Calvinist puritanism. The anti-Calvinist members of the Council accordingly voted for the death sentence, which was carried out on the 26th July, and the fact is an additional proof that their opposition was by no means actuated by sympathy with Libertine ideas. Despite this unanimity in the face of the cynicism of his general cast of thought, the charge of conspiracy had not been made out, and Gruet, though a sceptic and a moral reprobate, may be reckoned among the many victims of judicial bias, legalised barbarity, and religious intolerance.

THE RÉGIME IN DANGER

The revelation of Gruet's ultra-radical anti-Calvinism seemed to accentuate the necessity of Calvin's puritanic system, and, in spite of some compunction on the part of several members of the Council over his barbarous fate, served to discredit and paralyse the opposition for the time being. The effect was seen in the arrest of Favre and his daughter who had ventured back to the city, and of Perrin who had likewise returned from his embassy to France [22] (September 1547). Favre and his daughter secured their release by professing submission to the Consistory.[23] Perrin's case was complicated by the discovery that, during his mission to France, he had discussed with Cardinal Du Bellay the plan of sending a small French force to Geneva as a precaution against the danger of

[20] Reyburn, " Calvin," 141 (1914).
[21] Ibid., ii. 62 (ed. by Goetz, 1899).
[22] " Opera," xxi. 413.
[23] Ibid., 414 f.

an attack by the Emperor Charles, who had succeeded for the
time being in overthrowing the Protestant cause in Germany.
The discovery of a project which, on the part of the French
minister, was merely a move in the interest of France and
touched patriotic susceptibilities, promised finally to rid Calvin
of his ablest enemy, who was deprived of his office of captain-
general and retained in prison. Unfortunately for him, it
involved his friend the refugee Maigret, who had obtained
information of the project and had denounced it to the Council,
but who was himself denounced by the Bernese ambassador
as a dangerous plotter in the interest of France, and was placed
under arrest. To condemn Perrin, Calvin's enemy, was to
condemn Maigret, his friend, and even to compromise Calvin
himself. When the Two Hundred met on the 16th December
to deliberate on the situation, the approaches to the Council
Chamber were crowded with excited factions, who threatened
to come to blows, whilst inside the two parties—Perrinists
and Calvinists—engaged in violent altercation. In this emer-
gency only the energetic intervention of Calvin prevented the
uproar from ending in bloodshed. At the head of the ministers
he made his way through the hustling, yelling crowd into the
senate house and ultimately succeeded in making his voice
heard above the tumult and arguing the infuriated disputants
into a calmer mood.[24] It was an act of superlative courage
and it had its reward in bringing about at least a temporary
cessation of the strife. The proceedings against both Perrin
and Maigret were quashed and a formal reconciliation of the
contending parties followed.[25] But Calvin's association with
the questionable Maigret had seriously undermined his influence. In seeking to overthrow Perrin, he had narrowly
escaped being overthrown himself and had learned how precarious was his power. " I am broken," wrote he to Viret,
" unless God stretches forth His hand." [26]

Whilst he felt his weakness, the Perrinists came out of the
encounter conscious of their strength. It was, however, only
four years later that they succeeded in securing a decisive

    [24] " Opera," xii. 633 f.; xxi. 418.
    [25] Ibid., xxi. 418 f.
    [26] " Opera," xii. 633, 17th December 1547; cf. ibid., 653. Letter to the
same, 19th January 1548. " Et tamen fervent non minus quam antehac
fractiones . . . Vix lætum augurium expecto."

majority in the Council and attempted a final trial of strength
with their hated enemy. For Calvin this interval was a period
of severe strain which was intensified, as we shall see in the
next chapter, by conflicts with theological opponents. His
infirm body suffered more frequently from attacks of illness.
In March 1549 he lost the wife whom he calls " the best com-
panion of my life " and " the faithful helper of my ministry." [27]
His affliction was intensified by the fact that the wife of his
brother Antoine, one of the ministers of Geneva, had to appear
before the Consistory on a charge of adultery.[28] There were
quarrels in the Venerable Company and even scandals, involving
Ferron, Megret, D'Ecclesia, and other ministers, to try his
temper and make sport for his enemies. There was recurring
friction with the Council, which took every opportunity of
tightening its grip on the ministers. It sought, for instance, to
curb the tendency to use outrageous language in their sermons
in criticism of individuals and even those in authority, directing
them to refrain from abusing the liberty of the pulpit and
confine themselves to the preaching of the Word of God.[29]
It called Calvin to account for the strictures on its doings
which he had written in a letter to Viret, and which came to
its knowledge. Only after the personal intervention of Farel
on his behalf did it agree to waive further proceedings and
accept his disclaimer of evil intention and his profession of
regret, on condition that " he should do his duty better another
time." [30] Perrin, one of the syndics for the year 1549, Favre,
and many others carried their antipathy the length of abstain-
ing from Communion. Some called him Cain, and gave the
name Calvin to their dogs.[31] The Registers of these years
bear ample evidence of a persistent and ever bolder antagonism
to the Calvinist régime. The Government, indeed, professes
zeal for the Gospel, for the repression of all manner of vice,
for the maintenance of the Calvinist Reformation in doctrine
and life, under threat of severe proceedings against evildoers.[32]
It even, for instance, takes measures, in the spirit of Calvin,
to give practical effect to its professions. It directs the ministers
to preach every morning and to repeat oftener the Lord's

[27] " Opera," xiii. 230.
[28] *Ibid.*, xxi. 435 f.
[29] *Ibid.*, 426, 429 f.
[30] *Ibid.*, 435 f.
[31] *Ibid.*, 442 f.
[32] See the proclamation of January 1549, " Opera," xiii. 158 f.

Prayer and the Commandments during worship. Even Calvin found it necessary to protest against this multiplication of sermons as beyond the capacity of the ministers, whilst refusing to agree to the more frequent repetition of the Lord's Prayer and the Commandments as savouring of " sorcery and enchant-ment." [33]   It abolishes the Church festivals as tending to " scandal," [34] and stiffens the laws against cursing, swearing, and blasphemy.[35] It ordains the visitation of every family by the ministers twice a year.[36] These facts are an additional proof that the Perrinist party, despite the moral laxity of adherents like Berthelier, was by no means Libertine in the invidious sense. Liberal is, in fact, rather the term that would properly designate its character. At the same time, the old deference to Calvin disappears from the Registers and the change of attitude is amply apparent in the tendency to exercise over him and the ministers a more critical control. The diminution of his former dominating influence appears, too, in the weakening of the Consistorial régime and in the increas-ing antagonism to the French refugees. Berthelier and his band, "the Children of Geneva," as the roystering young bloods, of whom he was the leader, were called, insulted Calvin and the ministers in the streets and carried on a regular vendetta against the refugees. Hence the oft-recurring complaints in the Registers of this period of the " insolences " against the ministers, of the open contempt and defiance of the Consistory on the part of men like Berthelier, Bonna, Sept, and other influential Perrinists, of slackness on the part of the authorities in repressing the rebels, of abstention from sermons and Supper, etc.

The growing spirit of insubordination culminated in the attempt to deprive the Consistory of its power of excommunica-tion in 1553 when, as the result of the February elections, the anti-Calvinist party secured a decided majority in the Council.[37] Perrin, Vandel, Berthelier, Bonna, Sept, saw in this decisive swing of the pendulum their chance of settling accounts with a body with which they had long been at daggers drawn. Berthelier was chosen to open the attack. It was a question-

[33] " Opera," xxi. 457.   [35] Ibid., xᵃ. 59 f.
[34] Ibid., 470 f.   [36] Ibid., xxi. 468.
[37] Three of the four syndics, including Perrin, belonged to the opposition party.

able move in tactics in view of his worthless character, which had brought him into frequent collision with the Consistory during the previous ten years and only too well merited its censures. But he enjoyed no small prestige as the son of the man who had given his life for the republic in the early days of its struggle for independence. He was the hero of young Geneva and fitted by his reckless predilection for a fight to lead the attack which more politic heads had planned. He accordingly appeared in the Council on the 1st September to profess a desire to partake of the Lord's Supper and petition for permission to do so, despite the fact that he was under the bann of the Consistory. The Council sent for Calvin, who vigorously protested against the request in the interest of ecclesiastical discipline, and controverted the right of the Council to grant it. After his withdrawal the majority nevertheless empowered Berthelier to communicate if he felt free in his conscience so to do. Burning with indignation, Calvin again appeared and appealed to the Ordinances in proof that the Council had usurped a function that belonged to the Consistory, expatiated on the iniquity of profaning the holy Supper by the admission of so worthless a person, and swore [38] that he would rather die than be a party to this profanation. The Council insisted on keeping to its decision, and next day, Communion Sunday, the 3rd September, he boldly proclaimed to a crowded congregation in St Peter's his determination to resist the intruder should he dare to present himself at the Lord's Table. " We celebrate to-day the Supper," he thundered at the end of an impassioned discourse. " Should any one to whom access has been forbidden by the Consistory presume to force his way to the Table of the Lord, I herewith testify that I shall do what my duty requires of me, even at the risk of my life." Happily he was not called on to put his threat to the test. The Council had given Berthelier a hint to stay away, and Calvin's moral strength had triumphed once more over the political finesse of his enemies.[39]

He had, too, the best of it in the lengthy investigation which ensued. He seems, however, to have expected that his defiance would once more end in his expulsion, and in the

[38] " Juravi etiam, etc.," " Opera," xiv. 606.
[39] " Opera," xxi. 551 f. ; xiv. 605 f. ; Kampschulte, ii. 203 f.

afternoon preached what was virtually a farewell sermon on Paul's address to the Ephesian elders. " He was," he said, " ever ready to serve the Church in public and private. But things had come to such a pass that he did not know whether this would not be his last sermon in Geneva, seeing that those who were in power sought to constrain him to do a thing which it was not lawful for him to do in accordance with the will of God. He exhorted the people to make no account of his person, but to cherish the Word of God which he had preached to them. Therefore he said to them as St Paul said to the Ephesians, ' Brethren, I commend you to God and the Word of His Grace.' " [40]

THE TURNING POINT

The episode proved to be the turning point in his long struggle with the opposition. The worthless character of Berthelier, whom they had foolishly presumed to measure against a moral personality like that of Calvin, tended to discredit the whole manœuvre. They had not the courage even to abide by their assumption of the power to override the action of the Consistory in such matters, and agreed, at the demand of the ministers, to decide the question of their respective powers by an examination of the Ordinances. Ultimately, after protracted and at times stormy negotiations, they resolved " to observe the Ordinances as hitherto practised " [41] (18th September 1553). Calvin had good reason for writing to Bullinger that " the good cause had proved the superior one." [42] A further attempt to reopen the question in November led, indeed, to a discussion in the Council of Two Hundred, which reverted to the position taken up by the Little Council on the 1st September, and ultimately, after another uncompromising declaration on the part of Calvin, to a resolution to invite an expression of opinion on it from the chief Swiss Churches.[43] But this resolution was a further proof that the Perrinists were not really as formidable as might appear, and were losing rather than gaining ground in their efforts to subject the Church

[40] Colladon, " Vie de Calvin," " Opera," xxi. 78; cf. Beza, " Vita," ibid., 147.
[41] " Opera," xxi. 554.
[42] " Superior esset bona causa," " Opera," xiv. 655.
[43] " Opera," xxi. 559 f. ; xiv. 678 f.

to the State. Zürich and Schaffhausen, whilst stating their own method of maintaining discipline, expressed their approval of the Genevan Consistorial system.[44] Basle was less favourable and Bern was hostile.[45] But the balance of opinion was on the whole favourable to Calvin. The opposition thereupon dropped Berthelier and a general reconciliation ensued. In January 1554 the members of both parties solemnly bound themselves "to obey God and the Government and to keep the Word of God," and dined amicably together as a sign of peace.[46] No mention was made of the Ordinances and Calvin's triumph was in this sense incomplete. But he had succeeded in thwarting the attempt of the Perrinists to discredit and paralyse the Consistorial system, and their impotence as well as the reaction in his favour, which their tactics had provoked, appeared in the reversal of the balance to their disadvantage in the elections in February. Finally, in January of the following year, 1555, he succeeded in obtaining from all three Councils the formal recognition of the right of excommunication by the Consistory in accordance with the Ordinances.[47] "At length," wrote Calvin to Bullinger, "after long struggles the right of excommunication has been confirmed to us"[48] (February 1555).

The elections of this year resulted in the total rout of the Perrinist party. Despite years of bitter antagonism, Calvin's iron resolution and ceaseless activity had begun to tell in the moral training of a new generation, which appreciated the regenerating tendency of his work and his devotion to a high, if withal narrow ideal of social life. He could now pit against the young Geneva of Berthelier a young Geneva of ardent disciples, ready to back him up in his determination to root out him and his licentious crew. He had, too, in the colony of refugees from England, Scotland, Italy, as well as from France, which included many men of rank, culture, and weight of character, a strong battalion of devoted supporters. Their presence, if it had excited discontent and dislike, of which the opposition had sought to avail themselves, shed lustre on the city, and helped materially to enhance the reputation in foreign

[44] "Opera," xiv. 699 f.
[45] *Ibid.*, 691.
[46] *Ibid.*, xxi. 567.
[47] *Ibid.*, 580 f.
[48] *Ibid.*, xv. 449.

lands which Calvin's activity had conferred on it. The success of his struggle with his enemies was accompanied by a diminution of this antipathy, and resulted in their admission in much larger numbers to the rights of citizenship. Between the middle of April and the middle of May 1555, for instance, as many as sixty of French nationality were thus admitted. These weighty accessions to the strength of the Calvinist party re-animated the hostility of its old opponents, who realised its significance for the future consolidation of the Calvinist régime. They revived the old cry of the refugee danger and repeatedly protested against the policy of the Council. The Council paid no heed to their protests.[49] The result was a street brawl on the night of the 16th May, in which some blows were exchanged between the two parties before the syndic Aubert succeeded in restoring order. The riot does not seem to have been pre-meditated, except perhaps on the part of the more impulsive and irresponsible members of the Perrinist party. Perrin himself and Vandel came to the aid of the magistrates in the attempt to quell the tumult. Two of the actual law-breakers — the brothers Comparet — were arrested. Several more arrests followed during the next few days. The Council pro-fessed to see in the riot a premeditated attempt to thwart its policy by force, and even to massacre the syndics and the members of the Council and their French protégés.[50]   It resolved to make use of the incident to crush the Perrinist opposition once for all. Perrin, Sept, and several other leaders saved themselves from arrest by flight. Refusing to obey the summons to return for trial, without a safe-conduct, they were on the 3rd June sentenced to death, in spite of the efforts of Bern on their behalf.[51] Those who had been arrested were arraigned on a charge of treason, refused Counsel, and tortured in order to extract the confession of conspiracy. Others whom, in the agony of torture, they incriminated and who, unlike Vandel and Berthelier, did not succeed in making their escape, swelled the number of the accused. On the 6th August Berthelier and Vandel were sentenced to death *in absentia*. To four of the prisoners, including Berthelier's brother, François

[49] " Opera," xxi. 604 f.
[50] Calvin to Bullinger, " Opera," xv. 641.
[51] " Opera," xxi. 608.

Daniel, the same fate was assigned and the sentences were duly executed. Others were punished with perpetual banishment, the remainder with lesser penalties. A cruel and ruthless retribution had overtaken the Perrinist opposition and Calvin was at length master of Geneva.

Unfortunately he displayed, as usual, his lack of moderation in the pursuit of his enemies. He believed implicitly in a conspiracy against him and his cause, and he shrank from no barbarity in order to get at the truth and punish such miscreants. "We shall see in a couple of days," wrote he grimly to Farel, "what the torture can extort from them." [52] It was evidently a judgment of God of which he and his associates were the instruments, and there was apparently no incongruity to his mind in thus associating God with the torment of his fellow-creatures who opposed his adamantine will. Calvin's God on such occasions, it must be said, is not exactly the God of the Gospel, which he professed to preach and of which he claimed a monopoly of true knowledge.

SIGNIFICANCE OF CONFLICT

His long struggle with his enemies is important in its far-reaching effects. What was at stake was not merely the maintenance of his disciplinary régime in a small republic numbering about 13,000 inhabitants. From this point of view the struggle seems parochial. One becomes weary of the ceaseless bickerings between the Consistory and its opponents over the minutiæ of personal conduct, of which the Registers are full. Much of what they record is of the nature of the local *Chronique Scandaleuse* of very limited interest. They constantly display on the part of Calvin and his fellow-preachers the tendency to magnify trifles into grave offences, a lack of moral perspective, a zeal which appears to the larger conception of human action and personal liberty not according to knowledge. From this point of view, the long drawn-out quarrel seems often enough to be a storm in a teapot. It is concerned with the personal doings of a series of individuals not one of whom, with the exception of Calvin himself, is a great historic personality. The subject-matter of it seldom rises above the status of much

[52] "Opera," xv. 693.

ado about little or nothing. The Consistory too frequently
appears as a petty-minded, prying inquisition into the thoughts
and doings of people guilty of nothing more heinous than a
tendency to criticise Calvin and his sermons, to dance or play
cards or sing a song which he pronounces to be *déshonnête*, to
dare to have an opinion different from his, to prefer a game
of bowls to going to church, and so forth. All this, gravely
recorded in the Registers for nearly fifteen years running,
becomes wearisome to the historian accustomed to deal with
large questions and impatient of the triviality of much of it
and the misjudged zeal expended on it.

On the other hand, the pettiness of much of the drama is
relieved by the personality of the chief actor in it. In Calvin
we feel in the presence of a big man amid the smaller men
among whom his lot is cast. The conflict which he wages
has, accordingly, its larger aspect, which the pettiness of a great
deal of it cannot belittle. He is engaged in a warfare which is
the same all the world over, whether the arena is large or small
—a warfare with sin in the form of personal and public evils,
with licence of thought and life which sap the foundations of
morality and weaken and degrade the State as well as the individual. To establish the kingdom of God in a community all
too morally lax, to make the Church a real moral influence by
demanding of its members a life in accordance with the profession of the Gospel, to uproot the canker of Libertinism and
prostitution from public and private life—this is the fact that,
taken along with the great intellectual and moral qualities of
the Reformer, redeems this otherwise petty struggle with the
Genevan opposition. Calvin judged that he could only thus
establish the kingdom of God in the community by means of
an institution which should supervise and regulate its life in
accordance with his conception of the kingdom. The supervision and the regulation were apt to be petty and tyrannical
and vitiated by a puritanic formalism incompatible with the
liberty of the Gospel and the individual. Its weakness is obvious
in the effort to impress on the religious and social life of Geneva
the stamp of Calvin's legal mind and intolerant spirit as well
as of the Gospel. Its strength in nurturing an earnest, God-
fearing, if all too formal and narrow type of Christian character
is equally patent. It is this conflict on which, despite its petty

elements, large issues depended, which Calvin waged during these years of stress. It is, in fact, the birth throes of that Puritan movement which was to wield such a moulding influence in the history of the Western lands, of which Calvin became in a large measure the spiritual director—of France, Holland, England, Scotland, and North America. In the Puritan principles, the conception of life, the cast of thought which he succeeded in stamping on the little republic on the shore of Lake Leman were the makings of great things in a far wider area in the religious and even the political sphere. Immersed though he was in this local conflict, he was fighting for a far larger end than that of merely establishing his moral mastery of a small republic. For him Geneva was the capital of the far wider spiritual Empire which he conceived, and to the establishment of which in the Western lands he devoted, as we shall see, no small part of his activity.

CHAPTER VII

CALVIN AND HIS THEOLOGICAL OPPONENTS

CASTELLION

SÉBASTIEN CASTELLION or Chatillon was a native of St Martin du Fresne in Brigey, where he was born in 1515. His parents were peasants and he probably shared in his father's toil before he was enabled, at the age of twenty, to become a pupil of the College of the Trinity at Lyons. Lyons was at this period the chief nursery of the new culture in France. Its numerous printing presses attracted literary men of distinction like Dolet, Marot, and Rabelais, who found employment as correctors for the press or superintended the printing of their works. The college was imbued with the humanist spirit and some of its teachers like Raynal, Aneau, and the Scot Florence Wilson (Volusenus) were men of some literary mark as well as enthusiastic pædagogues of the new type. Castellion appears to have been one of their most distinguished pupils. His proficiency as a Greek scholar gained him the post of tutor in an aristocratic and rich family and a considerable reputation among the poets and scholars of the literary circle, of which, as M. Buisson has shown,[1] he appears as one of the ornaments. Lyons was a nursery of the reformed doctrine as well as of the new culture, and it is certain that, during his sojourn here, Castellion, like many another ardent young humanist, was led by way of his humanist training and sympathies to the study of the new theology. A contemporary testimony ascribes this transition to the influence of his teacher Aneau. M. Buisson thinks it was due mainly to the perusal of Calvin's " Institutes," the publication of which, in 1536, made a deep impression on the cultured society of Lyons. Certain it is that, when he quitted Lyons in 1540, it was to Strassburg that he turned his

[1] " Sébastien Castellion," i. 30 f. (1892).

steps and in the house of Calvin that he found a lodging with a view to his training as a minister of the evangelical faith.[2]

At the instance of Farel he was invited, a couple of months before Calvin's return, to become regent of the school at Geneva. In March 1542 his appointment as principal regent was confirmed, with the additional duty of preaching at the village of Vaudœuvres.[3] For the instruction of his pupils he composed a series of Latin Dialogues on the Biblical history, which served the double purpose of imparting religious knowledge as well as a graduated training in the Latin language, and became for two centuries an educational classic. During the pestilence of 1542-43 he bravely offered to act as chaplain to the hospital in place of the heroic minister Blanchet, whose colleagues, with the exception of Calvin, refused to face the risk of the deadly infection to which he had fallen a victim. For some reason that does not appear in the Registers of the Council, his offer was refused, and Beza, in his biography of Calvin,[4] accuses him of having withdrawn it from motives of fear. As M. Buisson has shown, the accusation is entirely unfounded, though it long remained to enshadow his memory. By this time his relations with both Calvin and the Council had become strained. Calvin irritated him by pointing out some errors in the translation of the New Testament, which he had undertaken, and declining to revise the manuscript owing to pressure of work. In consequence of the famine and enhanced prices following on the pestilence he had requested a rise in salary for himself and his assistants, which Calvin supported, but which the Council refused. He thereupon intimated his intention to resign his post and the Council, in view of his learning and zeal, proposed that he should be received into the ministry (17th December 1543). Calvin objected on the ground that his theological views rendered him unfit for the office. Castellion, it appears, questioned the canonicity of the Song of Solomon, which Calvin regarded as divinely inspired, and the received interpretation of the clause in the Creed, "He descended into hell." He demanded to be heard in defence of his opinions, and a debate took place between him and Calvin before the Council. The Council tried in vain to hush up the quarrel and Castellion took steps

[2] Buisson, i. 102 f.   [3] " Opera," xxi. 280, 294.   [4] Ibid., xxi. 134.

to secure an appointment elsewhere.[5]　To this end he sought
and obtained a testimonial signed by Calvin in the name of the
ministers of Geneva, certifying the integrity of his life and
explaining the nature of the theological dispute which prevented
them from receiving him into the ministry.[6]　The dispute,
inconsiderable in itself, is important as marking two divergent
tendencies in the Reformed movement.　On the one hand, the
tendency to accept without question a preconceived dogmatic
view of the inspiration of all the books contained in the canon ;
on the other, to exercise the right of critical judgment and
refrain, in deference to conscientious objections, from subscribing to the accepted view of certain of these books or even
of an article of the Creed.　The reconciliation of these divergent
tendencies proved impossible, and the impossibility was
heightened by an unconscionable and bitter attack made by
Castellion on the personal character of the ministers as a body
at their weekly meeting at the end of May 1544.[7]　Calvin
complained to the Council of his intemperate language,[8]
though his personal correspondence amply shows that he
himself was far from satisfied with the conduct of some of his
colleagues.　The Council called in the intervention of Viret
from Lausanne.　With his assistance it found that Castellion,
who had certainly shown himself to be impulsive and rather
opinionated, had been guilty of evil speaking and deprived
him of his office of preacher at Vaudœuvres.　He therefore
resigned his office as headmaster and left Geneva.[9]

To Calvin the issue appeared a vital one.　To him the
absolute authority of the whole Bible was a fundamental
doctrine, with which the case for the Reformation seemed to
stand or fall.　To admit the contention of Castellion seemed
to endanger the whole evangelical movement, which opposed to
the infallible authority of the Roman Church that of the inspired and infallible Word as contained in the traditional canon.
It was a narrow and mistaken, if, from the standpoint of the

---

[5] For these proceedings see the Registers of the Council in " Calvini
Opera," xxi. 312, 326 f. ; xi. 673 f. ; Herminjard, viii. 78 *passim* ; ix. 115
passim ; Buisson, i. 186 f.
[6] " Opera," xi. 674 f.
[7] *Ibid.*, xi. 720 f. ; Herminjard, ix. 265.
[8] " Opera," xxi. 336.
[9] *Ibid.*, xxi. 337 f.　For Calvin against Castellion, see Doumergue,
vi. 8 f. (1926).

time, an explicable judgment. It ignored what was an equally essential doctrine of the evangelical Reformation—the right of individual judgment and freedom of speech, which Luther had so forcibly enunciated and so heroically maintained against his Romanist opponents in the earlier stage of the movement.[10] Castellion was only exercising this right as a critical scholar, and even if his criticism of the ministers was provocative, it was far from being unmerited in the case of some of them. He had no little reason for feeling aggrieved against the theological dictator of Geneva and continuing, on occasion, the fight against his intolerant dogmatism.

In this deeply aggrieved mood he betook himself to Basle, where he ultimately found a penurious employment as corrector to the printer Oporin. The next eight years were for him years of extreme misery. Oporin could pay him only a small wage and this little irregularly. He tried in addition various expedients to maintain his wife and young family—literary work which brought him little or nothing, poorly paid lessons in Greek at the Pædagogium, even manual labour. He devoted the time he could snatch from these harassing occupations to the task of translating the Bible from the original languages into Latin and French, which he had begun at Geneva. It was only in 1553 that this struggle with want was alleviated for the time being on his appointment, through the influence of his friend, the celebrated jurist Boniface Amerbach, to the chair of Greek in the University. In this position he resumed, under the thin guise of anonymity, the struggle with evangelical intolerance, as represented by Calvin, which he had begun at Geneva. The preface to the Latin translation of the Bible, published in 1551, and dedicated to Edward VI., already contains a noble plea for toleration in a larger sense than that of Calvin addressed to Francis I. in the preface to the "Institutes." It is a heroic protest against the spirit of the age which, in spite of all the emphasis on the knowledge of the Bible, all the zeal for doctrine, distorts and dishonours the religion of Christ. This religion, he proclaims, consists in the love of God and in a true and living piety. It alone can lead us to a true knowledge of God. Instead of it, what do we find ? Strife, intolerance, persecution—the striving to

[10] See my " Luther and the Reformation," ii. 241 ; iv. 299 f.

shed the blood of those who differ from us, were it only on a single point of theology. And this in the name of Christ who commanded us to offer the other cheek to the striker, to render good for evil, to leave the tares among the wheat till the harvest. The principle of using earthly weapons in a spiritual battle is a total perversion of the Christian religion, which teaches us to conquer error by patience and clemency—the true weapons in Christian warfare and the only ones which lead to victory. There are so many obscurities in theology that there is ample room for the exercise of charity, and there is nothing to be feared from the exercise of this charity towards those who act from conscientious conviction.[11]

Equally remarkable is the independence with which he treats the Scriptures. He rejects the theory of mechanical inspiration. He distinguishes between the letter and the spirit of the Bible, the spirit only being of God. The right understanding of them is the work of God's spirit in the individual believer. This sounds in agreement with Calvin. But for Castellion it does not mean, as for Calvin, the illumination of the believer by the Holy Spirit by means of an infallible Bible. It means illumination in accordance with the moral and religious intuitions of the individual, and it assumes the right to use the individual judgment in accordance with critical scholarship and enlightened reason. Hence the frank recognition of the imperfection of revelation resulting from the difficulty of knowing the exact meaning of many words and phrases and even of the thought of the writer. At most, we can only give the probable meaning in such cases. " Castellion," says M. Buisson, " treats the Bible not as a human book, but as a book of which the letter is human and the thought divine." [12]

BOLSEC

In the year in which Castellion published his Latin translation of the Bible, Calvin was once more engaged in the intolerant pursuit of a theological enemy. In this case the enemy was Bolsec and the quarrel centred in the doctrine of predestination. Bolsec was a native of Paris and had been a member of the Carmelite Order before his sympathy with the

[11] Buisson, i. 306 f.   [12] Ibid., i. 316.

Reformation brought upon him the persecution of his fellow-monks, which ended in his flight to the court of the Duchess of Ferrara. From Ferrara he found his way to the village of Veigy near Geneva where (having since his breach with Romanism taken up the study of medicine) he became the physician of the Sieur de Falais, an influential refugee and a warm friend of Calvin, though he does not appear to have had a regular medical training. He combined with his new profession a keen interest in theological questions, and took an active part in the weekly discussions of the ministers. Whilst adhering to the Calvinist doctrinal system as a whole, he found it difficult to accept the doctrine of absolute predestination. He ventured to express his doubts on the subject, and at a meeting of the Venerable Company on the 16th October 1551 dissented, in outspoken fashion, from the views of the minister St André. To ascribe the eternal election and reprobation of the sinner to God was, he contended, to make God a tyrant, and to ignore the presence or lack of faith in deciding his fate. The doctrine was based on the perversion of Scripture as well as on a false interpretation of the teaching of Augustine. It was, in fact, heresy. Calvin, who had arrived during the discussion, rebutted the accusation in a vehement speech, and adduced passages from the Scriptures and Augustine in support of the impugned doctrine. Bolsec seems to have been over-whelmed for the moment by the angry torrent of argument and did not venture to reply. His temerity, nevertheless, cost him dear. He was immediately arrested by an ardent Calvinist police agent, who happened to be present and consigned to prison.[13] Instead of resenting, the Council approved of the arbitrary action of its official, and at the instance of Calvin and Farel, who happened to be in Geneva and had been present at the meeting, ordered Bolsec's trial on a charge of blasphemy and false doctrine, on the basis of a series of articles which the ministers presented against him[14] (19th October 1551).

Despite Calvin's onslaught and his arrest, Bolsec had recovered courage. His objections to the Calvinist view of predestination were evidently based on sincere conviction, and

---

[13] " Procès de Bolsec," " Opera," viii. 145 f. ; Beza, " Vita Calvini," xxi. 143 f. The " Procès de Bolsec " is reproduced in " Opera," viii., with some additions from H. Fazy, " Procès de Bolsec " (1865).

[14] " Opera," viii. 147 f. ; xxi. 489.

during the proceedings of the next few days he calmly and
firmly maintained these objections both by word of mouth and
in a formal written statement, without any attempt to explain
them away. He professed his firm adhesion to the teaching of
Calvin in every other particular. But he held stoutly by his
contention that the dogma in question was contrary to the
Word of God, which teaches the free offer of salvation to all
who believe, unconditioned by any eternal divine decree of
election and reprobation. It is imperative to abide by its
teaching and eschew all reasonings which tend to trouble and
confound simple people. On their side, the ministers handed
in a formal refutation of his written statement, in which Calvin,
whilst adducing the usual arguments in favour of his own view,
accused him of calumny, prevarication, ignorance, imprudence.
Bolsec's statements do not, however, bear out these charges
and they certainly contrast, in point of moderation and good
taste, with those of his opponent, who was only too ready to
impute evil motives to those who ventured to contradict his
theology.

The Council thereupon invited the two parties to debate
the question before it. According to the scribe, Bolsec was
hard pressed by the superior debating power of his antagonist
and ultimately took refuge in the expedient of referring it to
the judgment of the Churches of Bern, Basle, and Zürich.[15]
The Council, still more bewildered, welcomed the proposal,
but, in view of his failure to find the necessary bail, refused
his repeated request to be meanwhile liberated from prison.
This, in spite of the fact that as a citizen of Bern (Veigy being
situated in Bernese territory), he was not subject to its jurisdiction, and of the protests on his behalf of M. de Falais, who
reminded it that every Christian ought in justice to be allowed
freely to express an opinion on such a subject, without being
thrown into and kept in prison like a common criminal. The
Council was at this period not too favourable to Calvin and the
ministers. But if some of its members resented his dictatorial
attitude in matters of discipline, they were not disposed to
question his doctrinal system, or to resile from the right of the
civil authority to enforce conformity to it, especially as Bolsec,

[15] " Opera," viii. 172.

as a foreigner, shared in the growing dislike of which the refugees were the object.[16]

Pending the reply of the Swiss Churches, Calvin attempted to prejudice these Churches against the culprit in letters intended to influence their judgment. More legitimately, he strove to strengthen his position by bringing forward a number of witnesses to testify against him before the Council, and the investigation dragged on throughout the month of November. In the beginning of December came the replies of the Churches. That of Basle declared Bolsec's assertion that his teaching was in accordance with its confession to be untrue. It adhered to the doctrine of election, but emphasised faith as a condition of salvation and the lack of faith as the cause of condemnation, and preferred to eschew such disputation and abide by " the simplicity " of the Gospel. Whilst refusing to associate themselves with Bolsec's views, the Basle ministers practically agreed with him in laying stress on faith rather than on predestination as the important element in the preaching of the Gospel.[17] Calvin could certainly not claim the reply as a declaration in his favour. That of Zürich, whilst stating the doctrine of election, on the ground of Scripture, with dogmatic emphasis and vindicating Zwingli from the aspersions of Bolsec, reproached both parties for their intemperate zeal and added a strong plea for moderation and conciliation.[18] The Bernese ministers similarly deplored the spirit of strife and severity in their Genevan brethren and exhorted them to charity and mildness, especially in view of the difficulty of the doctrine, so hard to reconcile with the Scripture passages which represent God as not willing the death of a sinner, but that all should turn to Him and live. Though Bolsec is unknown to them, they have heard from others that " he is not so bad a man." The Bernese magistrates, in a separate note, wrote in the same strain, emphatically advised the Council to eschew such oppressive methods of dealing with the accused, and reminded it and the ministers of the discredit which their violence was tending to throw on the evangelical cause in France and elsewhere.[19]

[16] There is nothing in the evidence to show that Bolsec was merely the cat's-paw of the anti-clerical party in Geneva.
[17] " Opera," viii. 235-237.
[18] Ibid., viii. 229-233.   [19] Ibid., viii. 238 f.

The replies were thus on the whole more favourable to Bolsec than to Calvin. They agreed that undue dogmatism on such a question was more likely to be harmful than advantageous to religion. In the opinion of Zürich and Bern at least, Calvin's uncompromising and persecuting zeal was plainly unchristian, injudicious, and unjust. He was greatly chagrined [20] and showed his chagrin by proposing that the replies should be withheld from Bolsec. The Council fortunately had a juster sense of controversial fairness and refused the request. It professed, however, to see in them the condemnation of his views, but in deference to the representation of the Bernese magistrates and in view of his long detention in prison, " graciously " limited his punishment to perpetual banishment from the republic. The gravity of the offence merited, indeed, in its opinion, a capital penalty, and the accused might, it would seem, be thankful for the magnanimity shown him (22nd to 23rd December 1551) ! The sentence against him seems to have been actuated by apprehension lest, if they let him off, Calvin and his fellow-ministers would resign.[21]

The magnanimity was not so apparent to Bolsec, who regarded himself as the victim of Calvin's persecuting and intolerant spirit. He kept up the attack from the safe refuge of Bernese territory until he was driven away by his influence. His subsequent career does not reveal the strength of conviction which he displayed throughout the trial. Repairing to France, he was admitted by a Reformed Synod at Orleans to the ministry on recanting his errors (1562) and shortly afterwards deposed as " an apostate." He ultimately reverted to Romanism and in 1577 revenged himself by publishing a grossly libellous biography of his former arch-enemy.[22] We can understand his resentment, though we may not admire his subsequent vacillations, and certainly cannot approve of his mendacious distortion of Calvin's character and career.

Happily for the reputation of Swiss Protestantism, Calvin's persecuting spirit, if it had succeeded in ridding Geneva of an

---

[20] See letter to Farel, " Opera," xiv. 218.
[21] " Opera," viii. 245 f. See also the notices of the trial in the Registers of the Council, " Opera," xxi. 489 f. ; Hunt, " Calvin," 193 (1933).
[22] " Histoire de la Vie de Jean Calvin " (1577), Cimber et Danjou, " Archives Curieuses," v. See the account of his life by Choisy in Herzog-Hauck, " Encyclopedie," iii. (1897).

obnoxious theological opponent, had incurred the disapproval
of the chief Swiss Churches, with the exception of that of
Neufchâtel, which, without being asked, sent an emphatic
condemnation of Bolsec.[23] In Geneva itself the solemn
proclamation of the sentence evoked popular protests. It
excited the sarcasm of Melanchthon, and the reaction in
favour of moderation in a case of this kind appears in the
different treatment accorded to Trolliet in the following year.
Like Bolsec, Trolliet was an ex-monk whose request to be
admitted to the ministry some years before had been frustrated
by Calvin. He found a livelihood as a lawyer and signalised
his antagonism to Calvin not only by joining the anti-Calvinist
party, but in attacking the doctrine of predestination, as set
forth in the " Institutes " and in the treatise which Calvin
wrote on the subject after Bolsec's trial.[24] He roundly declared
his teaching to be heretical. Calvin complained of his audacity
to the Council (June 1552), and as the Council hesitated to
undertake a new trial over this thorny subject, threatened to
resign and leave the city. Faced by this dilemma the Council
was fain once more to sit in judgment whilst the disputants
argued the pros and cons of God's eternal decree. On this
occasion, however, it refrained from concluding against either
party in the quarrel, and got out of the difficulty by declaring
that the " Institutes " was a sound book and was not to be
called in question in future, and that Calvin was a good and
true minister. On the other hand, it pronounced Trolliet to
be a good citizen and a good man [25] (9th November 1552).

[23] " Opera," xiv. 221 f., " Totum profanum hominem, qui in sacris non
secus versatur quam immundissimus porcus."
[24] " De Aeterna Dei Prædestinatione," " Opera," viii. 257 f., January
1552.
[25] " Opera," xxi. 354 f., 360 f., 434, 510 f. ; xiv. 334 f., 371 f.

CHAPTER VIII

SERVETUS

EARLY CAREER

THE quarrel with Bolsec and Trolliet was a mere skirmish compared with the trial which in the following year ended with the burning of Servetus.

Michael Servetus was probably a native of Tudela in Spanish Navarre whither his father had removed from Villanueva in Aragon.[1] The year of his birth was either 1509 or 1511—the latter being the more probable date. His father, who was a lawyer, intended him to follow his own profession, and to this end, after spending some time at the University of Saragossa, he studied law at Toulouse about 1527-28. He became secretary to Quintana, chaplain and later confessor to Charles V. What is more important, in view of his future eminence in theological controversy, he learned at Toulouse to prize the Scriptures, of which, though a Christian after the traditional fashion, he had hitherto been ignorant. They produced on his ardent mind an impression which remained the decisive influence throughout his versatile intellectual life. This experience can only be described as a conversion to Christ, though it was not, except in its intense reality, identical with that of Luther or Calvin. He was present with his master at the coronation of Charles V. at Bologna in December 1529 and accompanied him to the Diet of Augsburg in June 1530. In the autumn he turned up at Basle and got into touch with Oecolampadius, who appears to have been impressed

---

[1] In 1538 the father also appears under the name of Hernando Villanueva and the son, in later adopting the name Villeneuve, by which he was known during his sojourn in France, was only following the paternal example. On the title-page of his first book on the Trinity he adds to the name Servetus that of Reues. This was supposed by Tollin to indicate the name of his mother. But such a combination was not uncommon, and in Mr Gordon's opinion, " probably appertained to a considerable branch of the Serveto tree," " The Personality of Servetus," 8 (1910).

by his keen interest in theological questions. He was, however, startled to find that he rejected the orthodox doctrine of the Trinity. After striving in vain to convince him of his error he told him that he could not recognise him as a Christian if he would not confess the consubstantiality and the co-eternity of the Son with the Father.[2] Servetus was not the man to be silenced by such an ultimatum, or weaned from his opinions by the conventional statement of the orthodox doctrine. He was certainly not of a docile disposition and even at the age of twenty had made up his mind that the doctrine was an utterly untenable one and, layman though he was, that it was his mission to teach the theologians its falsity. He was already conscious of the intellectual powers which stamp him as an independent thinker in theology as well as science. But while actuated by an earnest search for truth he was apt to be impatient and arrogant towards men of more conventional mind.

From Basle he moved to Strassburg and received a sympathetic reception from Bucer and Capito. Both discussed the Trinitarian question with him, and Bucer even addresses him as " Michael dilecte " in one of the letters, in which he controverts his views.[3] They were, however, as unsuccessful as their Basle colleague in disarming his criticisms of the doctrine in question, and of that of justification by faith, to which he also took exception. The startling proof of their failure erelong appeared in the work " On the Errors of the Trinity," [4] which was published at Hagenau in 1531. Its publication excited a storm of protest on the part of the Reformed theologians from Zürich to Wittenberg. Zwingli wrote to Oecolampadius strongly condemning it and exhorting him to do all in his power to prevent the mischief which threatened the cause of Christianity. Oecolampadius passed the exhortation on to Bucer, with the request to write to Luther disclaiming any complicity on the part of the South German and Swiss theologians with the blasphemy of " this beast," as he now termed Servetus.[5] Bucer fulminated against him in most

[2] See his letter to Servetus in " Opera Calvini," viii. 857 f. ; " Briefe und Akten zum Leben Oecolampads," ii. 472 f.
[3] " Opera," viii. 869 f.
[4] " De Trinitatis Erroribus Libri Septem." The title-page contained the author's name, " Serveto, alias Reues, a Spaniard of Aragon," but not that of the printer or the place of issue.
[5] " Opera," viii. 866 f. ; " Briefe und Akten," 638 f.

violent language from the pulpit, and Luther called it "a horrible, wicked book." Melanchthon was less explicit, and while condemning its immaturity, was not so sure that the orthodox notion of three persons was above question. It alarmed the papal nuncio Aleander, who wrote to Rome about it, but was apparently unable to get up a Romanist heresy hunt against the author. At all events the Roman Catholic theologians took no part in the controversy over it.[6] In Spain, however, it attracted the notice of the Inquisition which sought to inveigle the heretic back to his native country, and thus "conduce to the service of God and the well-being and advancement of our holy Catholic faith." [7] Despite this outcry, Servetus ventured to return to Basle and attempted to renew relations with Oecolampadius. He reminded him of the doctrinal differences prevailing among the Reformers themselves and of the enormity of putting a man to death for an error in the interpretation of the Scriptures. He begged him not to oppose the sending of a parcel of the objectionable work, on which the Basle authorities had requested his judgment, to the Lyons fair, and seems to have promised, on their demand, to retract his errors.[8] He professed, indeed, in the preface to a new work on the subject—"Two Dialogues concerning the Trinity "—which he published in 1532, through the printer of the previous one, to retract what he had written. In reality he reaffirmed it with some modification, which meant no essential change of view and aggravated his offence by denouncing in the conclusion the theologians as "tyrants of the Church." He had, however, lost all hope of either winning the Reformers for his views or securing even toleration for them. He had argued at Basle and Strassburg with all the sanguine fervour of the young man of genius with a mission, and he had been disillusioned. He did not, indeed, renounce his beliefs. But he gave up the idea of finding a field for their propaganda in Germany and German Switzerland, and moved on to Paris [9] in search of a new sphere of activity.

[6] Gordon, " The Personality of Servetus," 14 f.
[7] Gordon, " Servetus and the Spanish Inquisition," 2 f. (1925). Based on Bataillon's " Michel Servet poursuivi par l'inquisition espanole," *Bulletin Hispanique*, January to March 1925.
[8] " Opera," viii. 861 f. ; " Briefe und Akten," ii. 629 f.
[9] Apparently by way of Lyons. He mentioned in the course of his trial at Geneva a sojourn at Lyons after he left Quintana at Augsburg.

ATTACK ON THE DOCTRINE OF THE TRINITY.

His failure is not surprising. The Reformers in attacking
and renouncing the mediæval ecclesiastical system and the
mediæval conception of salvation, and professing allegiance to
the Bible as the supreme authority, retained the patristic
theology as developed by the General Councils of the fourth
to the sixth centuries. Servetus, on the other hand, saw in this
development from the Council of Nicæa onwards a corruption
of Christianity. His significance consists in the fact that he
discarded the metaphysical christology of the Councils as a
perversion of Scriptural teaching and regarded the evangelical
Reformation as, in this respect, a case of arrested development,
which it was necessary to carry further. The Reformers
have only imperfectly restored Christianity. He will show
them how to complete the process. Hence the two youthful
compositions launched from the Hagenau press, the thesis of
which he set forth in more mature fashion twenty years later
in the work which led to his martyrdom at Geneva—the
"*Christianismi Restitutio*," or "Restitution of Christianity." The
tendency thus to advance on the teaching of the Reformers was
not peculiar to him. It was finding expression in the anti-
Trinitarian agitation of the time, and it is interesting as an
anticipation, in its own way, of the trend of modern progressive
theological thought away from the metaphysical Christ of the
Councils to the historic Jesus. It is interesting, too, as a
revival of that of the Monarchians of the third century—of a
Praxeas, a Sabellius, a Paul of Samosata—who, in the interest
of the unity of God, repudiated the current doctrine of the
Trinity, which they regarded as teaching Tritheism, or belief
in three Gods. Servetus does not, however, merely repeat
their specific conceptions of Christ, though he is at one with
their anti-Trinitarian attitude.

If immature, these early works reveal both independence
and boldness of thought and no inconsiderable learning. He is
familiar with the Old and New Testaments in the original
languages. He knows Arabic as well as Hebrew, Greek, and
Latin. He shows some knowledge of the patristic and scholastic
theology. He shows, too, considerable skill in applying the
historical and exegetical method in order to test by its means

the validity of the orthodox conception of Christ, and establish his own conception in opposition to it. At the same time, his critical treatment of the Scriptures would not satisfy the exacting demands of modern scholarship, and in spite of his scientific method, he is inclined to regard them from the standpoint of his own preconceived theory. He shares the traditional application of the Logos theory to Jesus as the Word of God, the Divine medium of revelation, without pausing to consider whether this application was in keeping with the historic reality. He has no adequate historical knowledge of the evolution of this conception of the historic Jesus under the influence of Greek on later Christian thought, though he treats the conception in his own independent fashion. He is somewhat of a doctrinaire, of remarkable ability indeed, but with a strong dash of the self-confidence and the superiority of the extemely clever young man of twenty.

God, he maintains in these early works, is, in Himself, unknowable and incomprehensible. He can only be known in so far as He reveals or manifests Himself. This He does in a series of self-revelations, in various forms, in accordance with a determined plan, or " economy," or " disposition." [10] In the first instance He created the world by His Word.[11] " And God said, Let there be light," etc. (Gen. i. 3 f.). The Word in this self-revealing, creative act is God Himself, who speaks and thereby brings into existence the heavens and the earth and all things therein. In the second instance, He manifests Himself more fully in Jesus Christ, who was potentially contained in His creative Word, whose appearance was dimly adumbrated in the Old Testament, and in whom the self-revealing God, the creative Word ultimately took concrete form for the further enlightenment and the redemption of mankind. To this end Jesus was divinely generated in the womb of the Virgin Mary.[12] As thus generated, He is " the true, real, natural Son of God," [13] who embodies Deity itself.[14] In the Son, who derives His being from God through the virgin

---

[10] Per οἰκονομίαν variis Deitatis formis.
[11] *Oraculum, Vox, Logos.*
[12] Being Divinely generated He is of the same substance as God. *Consubstantialiter,* ὁμοούσιος.
[13] " De Erroribus," 93.
[14] *Res ipsa.*

and embodies Deity, the one God thus manifests Himself in visible, concrete, human form. In the third instance, the self-revelation of God is completed in the activity of the Spirit—the vitalising, divine effluence, which operates the sanctification of the soul.

Servetus himself thus professes a doctrine of the Trinity of Father, Son, and Spirit, as unfolded in creation, redemption, and sanctification, in accordance with the divine " disposition," or " economy." [15] But his Trinity is a purely " economic," not a metaphysical one. It stands in sharp antagonism to the metaphysical Trinity of the orthodox theologians, who posit three eternal, distinct, consubstantial persons or hypostases in the Godhead. For Servetus, on the other hand, according to his reading of Scripture, there are not three eternal, coexisting, and consubstantial persons in the Godhead, but three manifestations of the one indivisible God, who has successively revealed Himself in His creative Word, in His Son Jesus Christ, and in His sanctifying Spirit. These manifestations do not connote any actual distinction [16] in the Godhead. They are only the various forms or aspects of the one self-revealing God in the realisation of the divine economy or disposition. The Trinity in the orthodox sense, which the theologians since the Council of Nicæa have foisted on the Church, he utterly rejects as unscriptural, irrational, and incompatible with the belief in one God. " This philosophic pest " is derived, not from the Scriptures, but from Greek philosophy.[17] It has given rise to a crowd of heresies.[18] Metaphysics have perverted and ruined Scripture truth. It is absolutely impossible to form an intelligible or credible idea of how three eternally distinct hypostases in the Godhead can constitute one God. It will not do to say that it is sufficient to believe, even if what we believe is unintelligible, or to try to solve the enigma by saying that the three have one essence, nature, etc. This is metaphysical verbiage, logomachy.[19] It really involves Tritheism, three Gods. It has been a stumbling-block to many sincere Christians, and an impassable bar to the conversion of Jews

[15] For his own statement of it, see " De Erroribus," 29.
[16] Aliqua verum in Deo distinctione.
[17] " De Erroribus," 43. Hæc philosophica pestis.
[18] *Ibid.*, 38 f., 112.
[19] *Ibid.*, 32.

and Mahometans, who ridicule our stupidity in cherishing such a belief and making it the test of orthodoxy.[20]

In attacking the traditional doctrine of the Trinity it was far from his intention to devaluate or belittle Christ. If for him Christ is the Son of the eternal God, not the eternal Son of God, his conviction of His divinity as the embodiment of Deity is as whole-hearted as that of his opponents, though he disbelieved in their metaphysical conception of it. For him God is seen in Christ, who is His image, as the sun is seen through the ray.[21] In Him is embodied the manifestation of God, which was formerly contained in the Word spoken by God Himself. He is the concrete revelation of the one God, who speaks to man with a human voice and seeks to reconcile him to Himself. He even goes the length of saying that without Him we could have no knowledge of God at all, and seems in his passionate evaluation of Him to ignore the natural revelation of God in the mind and conscience of man and in nature.[22] With Him and Him alone we enter into the sphere of God. His advent is the unlocking of the great secret. " Such great things has the advent of Jesus Christ operated that everything is changed. There is a new heaven and a new earth. He enables us to ascend into heaven. Heaven is opened and by His own revealed Word God has disclosed Himself to us. We have entered the portals of God and see those things which are hid in Him." [23] To Him is given all power in order that the divine economy, or plan, or disposition may be realised in the redemption and reconciliation of man. For Servetus He is God, Master, Lord. He and the Father are one as the sun and the ray are one. As the incarnation of God He is to be worshipped, for in worshipping Him we worship God. " Wonderful is the sacrament which joins God to man, and also man to God, so that in a marvellous fashion God appropriated the body of Christ to Himself that it might be a peculiar tabernacle of His own habitation." [24]

To this Christ he shows the most passionate devotion. " Christ," he declared, " is my unique Master." He is an extraordinary combination of the scientific mind with the ardent

[20] " De Erroribus," 43.
[21] Ibid., 46.
[22] " Dialogus," i. A 5.
[23] " De Erroribus," 109.
[24] Ibid., 59.

religious temperament. " The key of his history," rightly says Tollin, " is his piety." [25]

That such an ardent Christian should have been burned by his orthodox opponents as a renegade from Christianity passes comprehension. That he was burned at all merely for his theological beliefs is bad enough. That he should have been burned in spite of his passionate devotion to Christ is a deplorable example of human stupidity and brutality.[26]

His Later Career

Nevertheless, this was the fate that awaited him twenty years later. Meanwhile he shook the dust of Reformed Germany off his feet and withdrew to Paris, where for the next two years he studied mathematics and physics in one of the colleges of the university under the name of Villeneuve or Villanovanus. This name he assumed as a precaution against detection as the author of the attack on the Trinity, which would certainly have cost him his life if he had refused to recant. He evidently had no desire for martyrdom, and though he seems to have discussed theology with Calvin, who was already at this period a leader of the evangelical party of Paris, he avoided, apparently for the same reason, keeping an engagement to dispute with him the points at issue between them.[27] From 1534 to 1537 we find him, still under the name of Villeneuve, at Lyons earning a livelihood as reader for the press of the Trechsels, and editing and annotating for them an edition of Ptolemy's Geography, which shows considerable geographical knowledge. He probably became acquainted with Pagnini, who sojourned at Lyons at this time, and whose Latin Bible

[25] " Servetus," 12, trans. by Dardier (1879); cf. his " Charakterbild M. Servet's," 21 (1876).

[26] I have taken my account of his anti-Trinitarian views from a copy of the " De Trinitatis Erroribus " and the " Dialogorum De Trinitate Libri Duo " in the library of the University of Edinburgh. It is evidently a later reprint of the works published in 1531 and 1532. See Cuthbertson, " A Tragedy of the Reformation," 17. His teaching is treated in greater detail by Trechsel, " Die Protestantischen Antitrinitarier vor Socin," i. 67 f. (1839); Dorner, " Doctrine of the Person of Christ," Div. II., vol. ii. 161 f. (Eng. trans., 1862); Tollin, " Lehrsystem M. Servets " (1876-78).

[27] " Histoire Ecclésiastique des Eglises Réformées," i. 25; Colladon, " Vie de Calvin," " Opera," xxi. 57; Beza, " Vita Calvini," " Opera," xxi. 123.

he later edited at Vienne.[28]   He became acquainted, too, with the famous Lyons physician Champier, whose works on medicine and astrology imbued him with an engrossing interest in these subjects. Returning to Paris, he devoted himself to the study of medicine under Guinterus (Günther), Fernelius, and other leading teachers, and is said to have taken the degrees of M.A. and M.D., though his name does not appear in the register of graduates. He lectured on Ptolemy's Geography and on Astrology, wrote his treatise on Syrups, which attracted widespread attention, attacked the doctors in his astrological lectures for their ignorance of this science, was attacked by them in turn for his presumption, and at their instigation ordered by the Parliament of Paris to confine his lectures to the astronomical side of the subject and own himself to be in the wrong (March 1538). Smarting under this rebuff, he again started on his travels [29] and ultimately in 1540 settled as a physician at Vienne, whose archbishop, Pierre Paumier, had been one of his auditors at Paris. Whilst erelong acquiring, under the archbishop's patronage, a large practice as a physician, he found time to continue his literary work and brought out an improved edition of Ptolemy in 1541, and in the following year one of Pagnini's Latin Bible, based on the edition of Novesianus, with annotations by himself. These reveal the striving to interpret the Bible in the light of contemporary history, though this scientific principle of interpretation is only imperfectly applied. But the application was sufficiently daring to lead the writer, not too honestly, to pass off his own comments as those of Pagnini himself ! Even so, the commentary was condemned by the ecclesiastical authorities of Lyons, Rome, and Madrid, though the tolerant Archbishop of Vienne apparently found no offence in it, and seems not to have withdrawn his patronage from the editor.

CORRESPONDENCE WITH CALVIN

Its publication shows his continued interest in theology and the fact is further evidenced by his correspondence with Calvin,

---

[28] Gordon, " Personality of Servetus," 16. He thinks that he was taught Hebrew by him.

[29] He was at Louvain in June 1538, as we learn from a letter to his father, which is in the Record Office. Gordon, " Personality of Servetus," 4.

begun in 1545 and continued into the year 1547. The inter-
mediary to whom he owed this revival of relations with Calvin
was the Lyons bookseller Jean Frellon, for whom he had edited
a number of works and who was a friend of the Genevan
Reformer.[30] From Calvin's letter to Frellon on February 1546,
it appears that he had attempted in vain to persuade Servetus
to renounce his theological views, and was not minded to waste
further his time in corresponding with him unless he showed
a more docile spirit. He had opened the correspondence by
asking information in reply to three questions on the Sonship
of Jesus, regeneration, and baptism, and Calvin had explained
to him the orthodox Reformed doctrine on these subjects.[31]
In the course of further correspondence he had, it seems, written
in his wonted disputatious and superior style, and this tone,
as well as the contents of his letters, had greatly exasperated
Calvin. This only too grimly appears from a letter which he
wrote to Farel on the same date as that to Frellon and which is
a terrible blot on his memory. " Servetus lately wrote to me
and conjoined with his letters a long volume of his delirious
fancies, with the Thrasonic boast that I should see stupendous
and hitherto unheard of things. If I am agreeable he promises
to come here. But I am unwilling to pledge my faith for him.
For if he should come and my authority avails aught, I shall
never suffer him to depart alive." [32]

In his letters [33] he adopts the tone not of an inquirer, but
of an equal and even of a superior, and he occasionally indulges
in the crass objurgations characteristic of sixteenth-century
theological controversy. It was the manner as well as the
matter of them that provoked Calvin into the above deplorable
utterance, and, as he tells Frellon, to write, in one of his replies
at least, " more sharply than is my custom, being minded to
take him down a little in his presumption." Despite his bad
impression of the writer, he must have been impressed with
the originality and reasoning power which these letters reveal.
They are by no means those of the pretentious smatterer.
They are far more philosophical than the early works on the
Trinity, are, in fact, the mature product of the resourceful

[30] " Opera Calvini," viii. 832 f. [31] *Ibid.*, viii. 482 f.
[32] " Opera," xii. 283.
[33] Thirty of them are given in " Opera," viii. 649 f.

thinker who, not unnaturally, deemed himself entitled to adopt the magisterial tone. Their argumentative power, backed by an astonishing erudition, as well as their provocative style, must have made him feel rather uncomfortable at times.

In them he maintains his characteristic conception of the Son and the Trinity against the orthodox one, and treats Calvin as he had treated the German Reformers and the scholastic and patristic theologians as "a metaphysical sophist." He tells him that these Trinitarian Gods are as false as the gods of the Babylonians. This metaphysical doctrine is, in fact, the greatest blasphemy and imposture of the papal Antichrist.[34] To aggravate the enormity of his offence in Calvin's eyes, he develops a conception of God as the all-pervading power or essence of which all things are the manifestation, and thus gives a pantheistic colouring to his teaching. God, he contends, is everywhere and in all things, which are the modes of His manifestation. Calvin was prepared to admit this, if taken in the conventional theological sense. But he appears to have divined the pantheism lurking in such expressions, and such pantheistic reasonings were for him deadly poison. He further attacks the doctrine of justification by faith alone and not by works. Belief in his conception of the Son of God is the essential thing for salvation, not faith, as the principle of deliverance from the guilt and penalty of sin, of which he has no vivid sense. Faith is assent to this conception. But mere assent is not enough. It must be a living and efficacious faith and must, therefore, be joined with charity and good works with fasting and prayer. "That," he says, "is a living faith by which, in believing in Christ, we feel Him to live in us." [35] He strenuously rebuts the evangelical assumption that man is totally corrupt, that works have no intrinsic value or merit, are in fact damnable in God's sight, and deserve only eternal death. He will hear nothing of justification merely by imputed righteousness. Man's actions are good or bad in themselves. Theft, murder, adultery are evil and carry with them the penalty of wrongdoing. *Per contra*, the good a man does has an inherent moral validity. From this point of view alone, to talk of good works as evil and damnable, as essentially corrupt

---

[34] See the first nine epistles, " Opera," viii. 649 f.
[35] " Opera," viii. 690.

because of the false assumption of the utter badness of human nature, is rubbish. If evildoing in itself merits punishment, is there no reward, no merit to be attached to the doing of good ? Is there no distinction in the nature of things and in God's sight between the adulterer and him that eschews such a crime ? If we can increase in wickedness, can we not increase in righteousness, and is this increase compatible with justification merely on the ground of an imputed righteousness ? " Thou art a wicked blasphemer " (" tu improbus et blasphemus "), he angrily exclaims, " in thus calumniating the work of the Spirit." [36] Besides, this doctrine is utterly at variance with the teaching of Jesus and the apostles and makes Christ and Paul liars. Did not Christ bless the pure in heart ? Did not Paul exhort to be faithful in welldoing. Your doctrine, he concludes, for these and additional reasons, is a mere fabrication, a magical fascination.[37]

He challenges Calvin's doctrine of regeneration and urges his own doctrine of baptismal regeneration against his view of baptism as merely a sign of our adoption. He confutes his arguments in favour of infant baptism and maintains that baptism cannot be effective without understanding and faith on the part of the recipient, which infants cannot have. It can, therefore, he holds with the Anabaptists, only be rightly performed in the case of adults. He calls him a thief and a robber (" tu fur es et latro ") in thus seeking to introduce them into the kingdom of heaven otherwise than by the door, i.e., faith. If, he reasons, you would introduce them into the kingdom, pray for them that Christ, who was only baptized as an adult, may receive them, as He showed Himself eager to do.[38]

On the subject of the Church his view is more in keeping with that of the sects of the Reformation than with that of Calvin. The Church consists of those who have been regenerated by baptism. It is the spiritual kingdom founded by Christ, governed by the Holy Spirit, and subject in matters of faith to the authority of Scripture. But Scripture is not the only authority. Nay, there was a Church before the New Testament Scriptures were penned, and the living voice of the spiritually illuminated who compose it is to be preferred to the

[36] " Opera," viii. 672.
[37] See Epistles, 10-14 and 21, " Opera," viii. 669 f., 688 f.
[38] Epistles 15 and 16, " Opera," viii. 676 f.

dead word. This Church judges what is true and what is false. To Calvin this subjectivism must have appeared pure Libertinism, Anabaptism, and he must all the more, on this account, have resented the claim of the unconscionable writer to be the agent of a further regeneration of the Church in this sense. Servetus tells him that its degeneration began with the development of an unscriptural theology under the influence of Greek philosophy and the papal Antichrist, and this long period is coextensive with the 1260 years of the Apocalypse, and was also foretold by Daniel. But its duration is about to end. The signs of this are manifold, and to Michael Servetus is assigned the rôle of the angel Michael, who will lead the battle of the angels against the Antichrist and revive the reign of the true Church on earth. Thus will be realised the real restitution of the Church to its pristine purity.[39]

Finally he attacks his doctrine of the unfree will,[40] his legalist conception of Christianity,[41] and his view of the Lord's Supper, which he interprets in a realistic sense. The correspondence was, in fact, a searching criticism of his whole theological system in the most uncompromising tone. From beginning to end he treats Calvin as a false teacher and perverter of true Christianity, and the weight of some of his arguments only made the offence the more galling. Even the most patient, the meekest of men would have been stung into anger by such a series of proddings, and to a man of Calvin's sensitive and dogmatic temperament these proddings were deadly wounds. It hardly required, in addition, the equally mordant criticism of the " Institutes," which Calvin had sent him, and which he returned with outrageous marginal notes, to complete his alienation from the writer.[42] Calvin, who could neither understand nor brook free theological discussion of this kind, henceforth, as his letter to Farel proves, thirsted for the blood of the heretic.

" THE RESTITUTION OF CHRISTIANITY "

Servetus incorporated these letters to Calvin in " The Restitution of Christianity." Part of this work he had sent in

[39] Epistle 20, " Opera," viii. 686 f.
[40] Epistle 22, " Opera," viii. 691 f.
[41] Epistles 23-26, " Opera," viii. 694 f.   [42] " Opera," viii. 481.

manuscript to him in the beginning of 1546, since it is apparently to it that Calvin refers as "the bulky volume of delirious fancies" in his letter to Farel in February of this year.[43] This manuscript he enlarged and, in a fateful moment, determined to print anonymously for the propagation of his views on a wider scale. The difficulty was to find a publisher bold enough to undertake the hazardous enterprise. In the spring of 1552 he appealed to his friend, the Basle publisher, Marrinus, who declined to run the risk and returned the manuscript.[44] Ultimately he succeeded in persuading the publisher Arnoullet of Vienne to undertake the work. It was printed in a press outside the town with the utmost secrecy, and some of the bales seem to have been dispatched to Frankfort and Basle in the beginning of 1553. There was nothing to indicate the author except the initials M. S. V. (Michael Servetus Villanovanus) on the last page, and Servetus, who was known at Vienne and in France only by the name of Villeneuve might reasonably hope that no one would think of identifying the cryptic letters with the bearer of this name. He forgot, however, that he had sent part of the work in MS. to Calvin who, if the printed work came into his hands, would have no difficulty in concluding who the author was.[45] This is what happened, and it was through Calvin, indirectly, if not directly, that he was discovered to the Inquisition as the author of the obnoxious volume. It is a miscellany rather than an organic work. It consists of five books on the Trinity, two dialogues on the same subject, a number of disquisitions on Faith, Righteousness, the Law and the Gospel, Love, Regeneration, thirty letters to Calvin, the Signs of the Kingdom of Antichrist, and an Apology addressed to Melanchthon and his colleagues. The collection reflects his anti-Trinitarian teaching in its more mature form under the influence of the Platonic and Neo-Platonic philosophy, which he had studied more intensively in the interval since he wrote his two early works on the Trinity.

[43] Bolsec in his "Life of Calvin" states categorically that he sent the "Restitutio" in MS. to Calvin, and there seems no adequate ground for doubting his testimony. Willis, "Servetus and Calvin," 169 f.

[44] See his letter to Servetus in "Opera," viii. 835.

[45] Willis thinks that Servetus sent Calvin a copy of the printed book (196, 231-233). See also N. Weiss, "Calvin, Servet, G. De Trie et le Tribunal de Vienne," *Bulletin de la Soc. de l'Histoire du Protestantisme Français*, lvii. 399 (1908).

It reflects, further, his distinctive apprehension of the other doctrines of the Christian religion in opposition to the doctrinal teaching of both Roman Catholics and the evangelical Reformers. It contains his discovery of the pulmonary circulation of the blood—a partial anticipation of that of Harvey. In respect of this discovery, Willis, himself a physician, called him " the physiological genius of the age." [46]

[46] Only three copies of the first printed edition have survived—one in the Library of Edinburgh University, one in the Imperial Library at Vienna, and one in the National Library at Paris. An exposition of its contents is given by Willis, 191 f.; Trechsel, " Die Protestantischen Antitrinitarier," i. 120 f. The copy in Edinburgh University Library lacks the first sixteen pages, which have been abstracted, and eighteen written pages substituted for them. This seems to be the copy at Geneva from which Trie abstracted these pages and sent them to Vienne to be used against Servetus by the Inquisition. The written pages are conjectured to have been derived from the MS. copy which Servetus had sent to Calvin. See Cuthbertson, " A Tragedy of the Reformation," 37 f. (1912). There is a German translation of the " Restitution " by Speiss (1895). Moeller (" History of Christian Church," iii. 447) erroneously says that, in addition to the M. S. V. at the conclusion of the " Restitution," he revealed his name on p. 199 of the work. The " Michael " of the dialogue on this page is fictitious. On his discovery of the pulmonary circulation of the blood in detail see Tollin, " Die Entdeckung des Blutkreislaufs Durch Michael Servet " (*Physiologische Abhandlungen*, ed. by Preyer, Erste Reihe, 1876).

CHAPTER IX

THE PROSECUTION OF SERVETUS

THE INQUISITION AND SERVETUS

THE process of discovery started with a letter written on the 26th February 1553 by W. De Trie, Lord of Varennes, a French refugee at Geneva, to his cousin Antoine Arneys of Lyons, who had reproached him with his apostasy from the true Church and accused the Protestants of licence in life and doctrine. Trie retorted not only by denying the accusation, but by turning it against his opponent. The Roman Church, he told him, was harbouring a heretic of the worst type in the person of a Spaniard residing at Vienne, who called himself Villeneuve, but whose real name was Michael Servetus, and who had formerly been condemned by the Reformed Churches. He gave some particulars of his heretical teaching, adding that he had recently printed a book, through the publisher Arnoullet at Vienne, a copy of which had evidently been sent to Geneva. In proof of his assertion he sent him the first leaves of it.[1] Trie mentions the fact only for the purpose of retaliating his cousin's charge of licence on the Roman Church itself, not, professedly at least, in order to institute proceedings against Servetus for heresy, though he enlarges on the enormity of his heresy and says that such a heretic ought to be burned wherever he may be found. He does not mention Calvin's name, and there is nothing in the letter to suggest that it was inspired by him, though he may, as Gordon suggests in a recent article in the " Encyclopedia Britannica," have derived the enclosed leaves from him.

Arneys promptly handed the letter and the accompanying leaves to the Inquisitor Orry, whom Cardinal Tournon, Archbishop of Lyons, had summoned from Rome to aid in the suppression of heresy in his diocese. The Inquisitor at once

[1] " Opera," viii. 835 f.

requested the Vicar-General of Lyons to inform the cardinal, who was then residing at the castle of Rousillon, near Vienne, and who directed the Lieutenant-General of Dauphiné, M. Maugiron, to investigate the case.[2] The result was that Villeneuve was summoned before the Procurator of the King and the Fiscal of Vienne as suspect of heresy. He denied the charge and a search of his house as well as of the printer's establishment failed to yield any confirmation of the suspicion, since both had taken the precaution to print the book at a secret press outside the city. The civil authorities, in consultation with the Archbishop of Vienne, accordingly decided that there was not sufficient evidence to warrant his imprisonment. The Inquisitor Orry thereupon suggested the advisability of obtaining further information from Geneva. He himself dictated a letter on the subject which Arneys wrote to his cousin. In reply, on the 26th of March, Trie protested that his intention had not been to involve Servetus in a charge of heresy, and that what he had written was meant solely for his cousin's edification. He is nevertheless glad that this private communication may be instrumental in purging Christianity of such filth and pestilential doctrine, and proceeds with evident zest to amplify the evidence. Though unable " for the present " to send the printed book, he forwards " a couple of dozen of pieces," which Servetus had written to Calvin—evidently part of his correspondence. As these are in his own handwriting, it will, he adds, be impossible for him to disown their authorship, as he might do in the case of the printed book. He had, he tells him, the utmost difficulty in persuading Calvin to hand over these documents, inasmuch as he did not consider it to be part of his duty to punish heresy with the sword, but to refute it by argument. Calvin had, however, yielded to his importunities in view of the awkward predicament in which his refusal would place himself, since it would expose him to the accusation of having made a charge which he could not substantiate. He hoped, in fact, to be able to extract more from him. For the present this consignment will suffice to run the heretic to earth.[3] Five days later (31st March), in a third letter, in response apparently to another request for further proofs, he is still unable to send the printed book, but promises, if necessary, to send it

    [2] " Opera," viii. 838 f.   [3] Ibid., viii. 840-843.

and the MS. of the " Restitution," which Servetus had formerly
sent to Calvin, but which was then, and had been for two years,
in the possession of Viret at Lausanne. He specially directs
the attention of his cousin to one of Servetus' letters to Calvin
(already forwarded) in which the heretic had explicitly identified
himself with Villeneuve, and added some information about
his early condemnation by the German theologians.[4]

In these letters Trie has evidently no scruples about setting
the Inquisition to work against Servetus. Calvin has, and
De Trie represents these scruples as due to his conviction that
it is not his business to punish heresy by the sword. Calvin
evidently felt the invidiousness of acting as informer to the
Inquisition, which was persecuting his own brethren in France,[5]
even in the case of one who, like Servetus, was obnoxious to
both parties. He emphatically denied, subsequently, that he
had exposed Servetus to " these savage beasts, the professed
enemies of Christ," as he calls the Inquisition. Was it likely,
he asks, that he should suddenly enter into familiar communication with " the satellites " of the Pope, with whom he had as
little in common as Christ with Belial ? The thing is a pure
slander, not worth wasting his time in refuting.[6] We may, I
think, accept this emphatic disavowal of the odious charge of
deliberately betraying the arch-heretic to the Inquisition. He
had evidence enough in his possession years before to have
done so, and yet had refrained from playing the part of informer.
Moreover, there is no reason for doubting De Trie's assertion
that he only yielded to his importunities in order to shield
him from the reproach, to which his refusal to do so would
expose him, of having led his cousin to bring a charge against
an apparently innocent man, which he could not make good.
In so doing, he was, indeed, giving up private documents,
without obtaining their author's permission. But Servetus
had himself published them in the " Restitution " without
asking his permission, though naturally enough suppressing

[4] " Opera," viii. 843 f.
[5] Five French students, who had studied under Viret and Beza at
Lausanne, had been arrested at Lyons in the previous year and had been
sentenced to death for heresy. They were still in prison, awaiting the issue
of an appeal to the Parliament of Paris. See Choisy, " Almanach Jean
Calvin," 1935.
[6] " Opera," viii. 479. " Defensio Orthodoxæ Fidei De Sacra Trinitate "
(1554).

his signature, and Calvin might argue that they were no longer to be regarded as confidential. Further, he might justifiably see in the publication of them a set attempt not only to controvert, but to subvert his teaching and destroy his influence through the circulation of the book at Geneva, to which Servetus had sent a consignment, and elsewhere. This consideration would doubtless weigh with him in yielding to De Trie's repeated solicitations.

On the other hand, while this may explain, it hardly justifies his ultimate, if reluctant complicity in the exposure of the heretic to the Inquisition. This complicity certainly does not look well on the part of one who, though very reluctantly complying with Trie's reiterated request, professes, in condemnation of the practice of the Inquisition, the enlightened principle of dealing with heretics by persuasion, and not by force. Some historians [7] have gone farther and have seen in Trie's letters all through a crafty expedient, engineered by Calvin, for compassing the destruction of the arch-heretic under the screen of a hypocritical profession of enlightened principle. In other words, Trie was only the ostensible performer in a plot hatched by Calvin himself against the heretic. This seems to me very unlikely in itself. It is not borne out by the Trie correspondence, and Calvin, as we have seen, emphatically denied such an insinuation. At the same time, his attitude was by no means blameless. Even if he felt that it was no concern of his to shield the heretic from the punishment which, as his letter to Farel shows, he believed to be his due, his profession of enlightened principle, as against the Inquisition, left him no alternative as a man of honour but to refuse to have anything to do with it. He should either not have made this profession, or, having made it, should have acted on it, and refrained from abetting Trie's tactics even for the sake of saving his friend's reputation.

[7] Roget, " Histoire du Peuple de Genève," iv. 21 f. ; Willis, " Servetus and Calvin," 235 f. (1877). Kampschulte is inclined to agree, ii. 180. Trie wrote " in vollem Einverständniss mit Calvin." On the other side, Choisy, " La Théocratie à Genève au temps de Calvin," 131 (1897), " Calvin, Sa Vie et son Œuvre," 30 (1909), and " Calvin," 150 f. (1925) ; Doumergue, " Jean Calvin," vi. 276 f. (1926) ; N. Weiss, " Calvin, Servet, G. de Trie, et le Tribunal de Vienne " (1908), and " Servet et Calvin," " Foi et Vie " (October 1909) ; Hunt, 207 f. (1933). Rilliet refrains from stating his opinion, but seems to accept Calvin's disclaimer, " Relation du Procès," 70, Eng. trans. by Tweedie (1846) under the title " Calvin and Servetus."

In consequence of these two communications, Servetus and his publisher were arrested and imprisoned on 4th April. During his examination on the following two days he admitted the authorship of the letters to Calvin submitted to him ; denied that he was the Servetus who had written the books on the Trinity, though he confessed that during his sojourn in Germany he had read these books and had thought well of them ; asserted that when Calvin had taxed him during their correspondence with being Servetus, he had rebutted the inference, whilst retorting that, for the purpose of this disputation, he was ready to personate Servetus ; disclaimed holding the opinions expressed in these letters, which he had written only for the purpose of eliciting Calvin's opinions on these subjects ; and professed his readiness to revoke them. He had merely put them forward as matters of debate and had no intention of sustaining them. He was ready to submit to the determination of the Church.

All this was, of course, sheer prevarication and reveals a lack of moral courage and straightforwardness. The only palliation is that he knew that he was a doomed man if he owned the heresies charged against him and his identity with Servetus, and that the temptation to outwit his persecutors was a strong one. In this respect, he makes, indeed, a sorry figure compared with the martyrs of the evangelical faith. His offer of submission was not likely to save him from a heretic's doom. He could only make sure of safety by flight, and in the early morning of the 7th April succeeded, probably with the help of some of his friends, in making his escape. Some weeks later followed the discovery of the secret printing press at Vienne, the seizure of five bales of the " Restitution " at Lyons, and his condemnation as a heretic of the first magnitude.[8] He was accordingly burned in effigy along with the bales of his book [9] (17th June).

TRIAL AND MARTYRDOM AT GENEVA

Meanwhile the fugitive seems to have decided to make his way to Italy, and it was with this intention that he reached

[8] *Maximum fuisse hereticum.*
[9] See the " Procès de Servet à Vienne," " Opera," viii. 833 f.

Geneva on the 12th of August. Geneva, of all places!
exclaims the astonished reader. Surely he must have known
that, in resorting to the city of Calvin, he was exposing himself
to the danger of a renewed inquisition. He seems to have
concluded that there was less risk of persecution for heresy
among the enemies of the Roman Church, who made profession
of liberty of thought, at least against that Church. He seems,
too, to have concluded that, by remaining quiet, he could keep
his identity with the obnoxious heretic concealed, since he
only intended to make a short halt in his journey over the Alps.
Despite his experience at Vienne of the risk of discovery, he
was still very ingenuous. Next day, Sunday, 13th August, he
even ventured to hear Calvin preach. He was recognised.
Calvin was informed of the discovery, and at his instigation he
was straightway arrested.[10]

To secure his trial, it was necessary that some one should
come forward with a definite charge within twenty-four hours.
The rôle of accuser, who was under obligation to constitute
himself a prisoner and was liable to the penalty attached to
the crime if he failed to prove it, was undertaken for Calvin
by his secretary, the refugee Nicolas de la Fontaine. Next
morning, 14th August, the secretary accordingly presented to
the Lieutenant of Criminal Justice, Tissot, forty articles which
had been drawn up overnight by Calvin, and arraigned his
teaching as set forth in his writings, including the " Restitution " ; accused him of defaming Calvin and his teaching;
and asserted that he had been condemned about twenty-four
years before in Germany, and was an escaped prisoner from
Vienne. In his replies to Tissot, who examined him on these
articles, he acknowledged that he had written the books on the
Trinity published in Germany, but denied that he had been
condemned by the German Churches. He acknowledged, too,
the authorship of the " Restitution " and other works and the
opinions set forth in them, whilst stating them as far as possible
in orthodox language and professing his readiness to receive

[10] " Opera," viii. 725. The historians disagree over the question whether
he spent some time, and how long, at Geneva before his arrest. For discussion of various views see Doumergue, vi. 306 f. It seems to me most
probable that he was arrested the day after his arrival. Gordon gives the
date of arrival 7th August (Art., " Ency. Brit."), Hunt, the 12th, " Calvin," 210.
Holl suspects that he went to Geneva in order to stir up opposition to
Calvin, " Aufsätze," iii. 271 (1928).

correction on the subject of infant baptism. He accused Calvin and Trie of instigating his imprisonment at Vienne, said quite frankly that he had broken prison because the priests wished to burn him, and that he had been given a chance of escape by the authorities. As to the charge of defaming Calvin, he had only paid him back in his own coin, and boldly stated that his works contained many errors. He denied the charge that he disbelieved in the immortality of the soul.[11]

Both parties were thereupon remitted to prison by the Lieutenant of Criminal Justice, who on the following day, 15th August, communicated the result of his examination to the Small Council, along with a request for the trial of the accused. In deference to this request and a petition presented by La Fontaine, the Council resolved in the affirmative and proceeded with his examination on the articles of indictment. He reiterated the answers already given, whilst contesting the accuracy of some of the charges, and declaring that his intention was not to calumniate Calvin, but only to show him his errors. Next day (the 16th) La Fontaine was represented by the advocate Colladon, like himself a refugee and a staunch adherent of Calvin, whilst Berthelier, his sworn enemy, actuated apparently by his antagonism to the Reformer, intervened on the side of the accused. Colladon, who seems to have been well schooled by Calvin in the controversy, attempted to show from his writings that he did not hold the doctrine of the Trinity in the orthodox sense of three hypostases, as he now professed to do, and Berthelier seems to have contradicted his contention. The result was an angry scene and the suspension of the sitting for the day.

His intervention brought Calvin himself into the debate on the following day (the 17th), in consequence of the decision of the court to permit him to act with Colladon in the case. The trial threatened to become a trial of strength between him and his Genevan enemies, and besides his zeal for the purity of doctrine, it was essential for the vindication of his authority against the anti-Calvinist party to secure the condemnation of the heretic at all hazards. Unfortunately for Servetus, his heresies were so unspeakable, from the current orthodox point of view, that even the anti-Calvinist opposition could not make

[11] " Opera," viii. 726 f.

much capital out of his cause. Calvin had undoubtedly a strong case as defender of the faith against such a blasphemer (as the age undoubtedly reckoned him). In the course of his examination at this sitting, Colladon adduced his notes on Ptolemy and Pagnini's Bible, and accused him of calumniating Moses and of interpreting the fifty-third chapter of Isaiah of Cyrus and not of Christ. The first of these notes to which exception was taken questioned the truth of the statement that Palestine was a land flowing with milk and honey. The note, he said, quite truthfully, was not his, but incorporated from another writer, adding that, in his opinion, it contained nothing reprehensible and referred to the condition of Palestine at the present time. This expression of opinion roused the ire of Calvin, who exclaimed that this was to accuse Moses of lying. Servetus refused to admit the inference and stuck to his opinion. He was equally tenacious in maintaining against Calvin his interpretation of the fifty-third chapter of Isaiah as the true historical one, whilst admitting that it prospectively referred to Christ, and appealed to Nicolas of Lyra in support of his contention. He further angered Calvin by maintaining his pantheistic conception of God. "All creatures," he insisted, " are of the proper substance of God ; everything is full of God." "What," cried Calvin, " if anyone in stamping on this floor should say that he had stamped on God, would you not be ashamed of such an absurd assertion ? " " I do not doubt," was the cool reply, " that this bench and all that you see here is of the substance of God." " Then," retorted Calvin, " the devil must be of the substance of God." " Do you doubt it ? " queried Servetus, relaxing into a smile. " To me all things are part and parcel of God. Nature is substantially God." [12] Angry and horrified though he was by such imprudent outbursts, Calvin had reason to be satisfied with the encounter, which tended to compromise the accused in the eyes of his judges. This unfavourable impression was heightened by certain discrepancies in the answers regarding his escape and the printing of his book, which did not harmonise with what he had previously said. The citing of his criticisms of " The Institutes " which Calvin had sent him, and the reading of his

[12] For these details, which are not given in the official " Procès," see Calvin's " Defensio," " Opera," viii. 496.

letter to Abel Poupin, one of the ministers of Geneva, in which he bitterly aspersed their teaching, were likewise fitted to create an unfavourable impression. At all events the court agreed with Colladon that sufficient had been proved against the accused to warrant the discharge of his accuser, La Fontaine.[13]

At the next sitting on the 21st there was another encounter between Calvin and the accused on the question whether the Ante-Nicene Fathers had used the term Trinity, and on that of the sense in which the three persons were to be understood. Calvin referred him to the works of Justin Martyr, Irenæus, Tertullian, Clemens, and Origen in order to prove that the early Fathers did not hold the Trinitarian doctrine in his sense.[14] He instanced in particular passages from a work of Justin— the " De Expositione Fidei "—in which the term Trinity occurred. Servetus asked for a Latin translation of the work. As no such translation existed, Calvin held him up to ridicule as a tyro in Greek,[15] whilst pretending to quote the Greek Fathers in support of his blasphemous heresies. He must have known from the perusal of his works that the charge was baseless, and the attempt to represent him as an ignorant smatterer, and thus score against him by the tactics of the clever advocate, certainly does not say much for his sense of fairness. Servetus was fain to admit that as far as the work of Justin was concerned his contention was erroneous.[16] While the admission was rather damaging to his reputation, as a matter of fact Justin did not use the term Trinity nor did he hold the doctrine in the later Trinitarian sense, in spite of Calvin's dogmatic assertion to the contrary. The " De Expositione " was in reality not written by him. It was a later forgery meant to buttress the Nicene doctrine of the Trinity. Servetus' contention was right and that of Calvin wrong as far as Justin, who had not used the term Trinity in his authentic works, was concerned. Had he only known the spurious character of the work in question he could have tellingly turned the tables on his opponent by exposing his lack of critical judgment.

[13] For these proceedings before the Council see " Opera," viii. 735 f., and Calvin's " Defensio," " Opera," 496 f.

[14] " Opera," viii. 759 f.

[15] " Defensio," " Opera," viii. 498.

[16] " Opera," viii. 759.

Warned by such an exhibition of the rancour of his opponent, Servetus on the following day appealed by letter to the Council against the injustice of trying a man in a civil court for his religious opinions. He denounced the practice as an innovation unknown to the apostles and the ancient Church. He quoted the Scriptures, and referred to the attitude of the Emperor Constantine in support of his contention that it was for the Church, not the State, to deal with matters of doctrine, and that the only punishment applicable to the delinquent was excommunication. To make heresy a criminal charge in a civil court was contrary to Scripture and ancient practice. Moreover, he had been guilty of no offence within Genevan territory, and was no seditious propagandist. The questions at issue were difficult and fitted to be discussed only by learned men. He had not spoken of them to anyone in Germany besides the theologians Oecolampadius, Bucer, and Capito. Nor had he mentioned the subject to anyone in France, and had never countenanced the seditious views of the Anabaptists against the civil power, of which he disapproved. He added a request for an advocate to plead for him in view of his ignorance of the Genevan forms of law.[17] The letter is a moving protest against the injustice of making a man's theological opinions the subject of a criminal accusation in a civil court. Its moderate spirit contrasts most favourably with the narrow and fierce zeal of Calvin, who, in his thirst for the condemnation of his antagonist as a criminal in the sight of God and man, was merely the mediæval inquisitor in the guise of the evangelical Reformer.

His request was refused, and the Attorney-General Rigot, to whom the conduct of the case was now entrusted, subjected him on the 23rd to a series of searching interrogations relative to his past life and his moral character. The object of this examination was evidently to prove him a dangerous agitator as well as a heretic.[18] In reply to his questions he gave what seems a straightforward account of his career, though chronologically it is not quite correct. He asserted in all sincerity that he was impelled by his conscience and by the precepts of the Gospel to spread the light that God had given him, and that he had done so with no intention to incite anyone to

[17] " Opera," viii. 762 f.   [18] Ibid., viii. 763 f.

sedition. His sole aim was to restore primitive Christianity
from the corruptions of the later Church. He had written for
theologians and educated men, after the manner of such disputations, in the interest of what he considered to be the truth,
and without malicious intent towards individuals or Churches.
He had never been imprisoned before his arrest at Vienne
except for a few days, on one occasion, as the result of wounding
a man in self-defence. He had never married because he did
not feel capable of entering on the married state. He had
never led a dissolute life and had ever sought to regulate his
conduct by the Scriptures. He had never written a single
word for the purpose of corrupting the young or inciting them
to licence. He had never thought that his teaching would do
harm to Christianity or favour the religion of Turks or Jews
at its expense, though he had read the Koran. His intention
in coming to Geneva was merely to pass through it on his way
to Italy, not to propagate his doctrine or sow dispeace in
the Genevan Church.[19] All this makes the impression of
honesty and sincerity. The Attorney-General had completely
failed to prove his case. Had the court been less under the
influence of theological animus, it ought to have had little
difficulty in waiving further proceedings.

The Attorney-General professed to see in his answers a
tissue of falsehoods and attempted, evidently with the aid of
Calvin, to state anew the case against him, adding a new series
of articles relative to his life, character, and opinions. He
was especially concerned to refute his letter to the Council,
particularly his contention that it is not permissible by the
Gospel and the ancient practice to arraign a heretic before the
civil court and punish him with death. At the sitting of the
28th August he replied to this new inquisition with equal force
and sincerity.[20] This reiterated defence had evidently made
a favourable impression on the court, which refused the request
of the authorities of Vienne for his extradition as a fugitive
from justice in reply to the letter addressed by the Council to
them, requesting them to forward the documents relative to
his case. At the sitting of the 31st August the court adopted
the more honourable course of allowing the fugitive to decide
whether he should be handed over to the officer whom they

[19] " Opera," viii. 767 f.   [20] *Ibid.*, viii. 771 f.

had sent to take him into custody, or remain in its hands. Throwing himself on his knees, he implored his judges with tears not to send him back to Vienne, but to do with him what seemed to them good. The officer was accordingly dismissed without his victim and the Viennese authorities firmly, if politely, informed that their request could not be granted.[21]

The favourable impression produced by the accused in his duels with the Attorney-General seems to have revived the activity of the anti-Calvinist party on his behalf. Hence the renewed effort of Calvin to counteract it in another encounter which took place between them at the sitting of the 1st September. The debate was cut short by the court which directed Calvin to draw up a new series of articles from the writings of the heretic, to which Servetus should reply in writing. The trial thus once more took a more theological turn. This change proved to be a fateful one for the accused, though it appears to have been suggested by his friends among the Calvinist opposition in the belief that his reply would strengthen his case, in view of the appeal to the Swiss Churches which the Council had resolved on, but had not yet made. Had they been better versed in the subtleties of the theological questions at issue, they would have known that such an appeal would only call forth the condemnation of these Churches, and ultimately render it difficult, if not impossible, to secure his vindication. With the skill of the expert theologian Calvin had no difficulty in composing a formidable series of propositions out of his writings utterly at variance with the orthodox faith. To these Servetus penned a reply in which he imprudently treated Calvin in his old contemptuous manner. For him Calvin is a second Simon Magus. To this Calvin and the ministers retorted with a lengthy refutation couched in their harshest manner.[22] This document Servetus subjected to a searching criticism in which he aggravated his former imprudence by indulging in downright vituperation. He liberally spices his comments with such epithets as " Liar," " Thief," " Impostor," " Bestial Fellow," " Perfidious Blasphemer," " Cacodemon." In palliation it has to be remembered that he saw in Calvin the agent of the persecution from which he had suffered at

[21] " Opera," viii. 783 f.
[22] For these Documents, see " Opera," viii. 501 f.

Vienne and was now suffering at Geneva. He was justly angered by his barbarous confinement in a noisome cell where, as he told the Council, he was " devoured by vermin," and had had no change of linen for five weeks, and by the refusal to allow him counsel, as had been done in the case of his adversary.[23] The Council granted him a change of garments at his own expense, though it appears that the order to this effect was not carried out.

Instead of proceeding further with the trial, it at length determined to carry out its resolution to appeal to the Swiss Churches, and on the 21st September sent these documents, along with a copy of " The Restitution," to the ministers of Bern, Basle, Zürich, and Schaffhausen for their opinion. On the following day Servetus, who was emboldened by the outbreak of bitter strife between the Calvinist and anti-Calvinist parties over the Berthelier affair, denounced Calvin as a false accuser and demanded his arrest and trial " until the case should be decided by his death or mine or other penalty." " I demand from you justice, gentlemen—justice, justice, justice." Along with the letter he submitted certain articles ascribing to Calvin the action of the Inquisition against him and giving reasons why he ought to be condemned.[24] The Council took no notice of his demand and a pathetic appeal for a hearing on the 10th October was equally fruitless.[25]

At length on the 19th the replies of the Swiss Churches had all come to hand. As might have been expected, they were unfavourable to the accused. His theology was plainly too much at variance with their confessions of faith to allow any alternative but that of its condemnation. Moreover, Calvin, with the Bolsec case fresh in his memory, had no liking for the course pursued by the Council, though he agreed to it, and had taken the precaution to write to his friends among the Swiss ministers representing Servetus in the worst light and emphasising the extreme danger of his opinions to the Reformed cause.[26] There could be no doubt of his heterodoxy. His exculpation would certainly be damaging to the orthodox view of the Trinity and would afford the Romanists a dangerous pretext for discrediting the Reformation. Calvin undoubtedly

---

[23] See his letter to the Council, 15th September, " Opera," viii. 797.
[24] " Opera," viii. 804 f.   [25] *Ibid.*, viii. 806 f.   [26] *Ibid.*, xiv. 610 f.

felt it his duty, as the guardian of the faith, the watchman of the evangelical cause, to warn his brethren against the enemy. But in his zeal for the faith he seems not to have realised how invidious and unfair it was for him as prosecutor to attempt to influence those whom the Council had virtually appointed arbiters in the case. Such intervention is one more proof of the lack of fairness and justice with which the religious zealot pursued his victim. This tactic would alone have sufficed to put him and his case out of court in the eyes of enlightened judges. Whether his judges knew of this tactic does not appear, and it is certain that his correspondents did not resent his interference with the exercise of their judicial function. The ministers unanimously condemned the heresies of Servetus in the strongest terms and exhorted the Council to deal with him in exemplary fashion.[27] These letters were as much partisan effusions on behalf of Calvin as deliverances in support of the orthodox faith. They were, too, words of doom. In view of the spirit and practice of the age, his judges could not do otherwise than condemn, and they had been sufficiently, if not in so many words, notified what the penalty should be.

At the sitting of the 26th October Perrin, the leader of the opposition, strove in vain to secure a verdict of not guilty. In vain, too, his proposal to remit the case to the Council of Two Hundred. Equally futile the appeal for a lesser penalty than death.[28] The majority voted for the extreme penalty and directed that he should be burned alive on the following day, along with his books, in punishment of " his great errors and blasphemies."[29]

Sure of his prey Calvin had been quiescent during the previous days, and he now intervened with the request to substitute death by the sword for death by burning.[30] Though the request was refused, it does credit to his sensibility in recoiling from the ghastly mode of punishment meted out to heretics in accordance with the practice of the age. The sentence was only intimated to the unhappy man, who hoped to the last for acquittal, or at most a light penalty, on the

---

[27] " Opera," viii. 555, 558, 808 f.   [28] *Ibid.*, xiv. 657.
[29] " Opera," xxi. 557. For the trial in detail see Rilliet, " Relation du Procès Criminel Intenté à Genève Contre Michel Servet," 1844 (Eng. trans. by Tweedie, 1846).
[30] " Opera," xiv. 657.

following morning. Recovering calmness after a paroxysm of despair, he asked, apparently through Farel, who visited him in his cell, for an interview with Calvin. Accompanied by two members of the Council, Calvin accordingly repaired thither and asked him what he wanted. " To ask your pardon," was the reply. Disclaiming all personal enmity, he told him to ask pardon of God and reproached him with his heresies. The assumption that, in differing from him, he had offended God, exasperated Servetus and stung him into a passionate defence of his convictions. Calvin thereupon left him to his fate, " self-condemned," as he says.[31] A few minutes later he was conducted to the porch of the Hôtel de Ville to hear the sentence of the Lord Syndics, as judges in criminal causes, and the grounds of it read out in the presence of the crowd. He begged for a milder form of death lest his sufferings should drive him to belie his convictions. If he had erred, it had been in ignorance, and in the conviction that what he wrote was in accordance with Scripture.[32] His appeal was refused, and he was led away under guard to the stake at Champel, accompanied by Farel, some " of the brethren," and the crowd. Pressed by Farel to confess his errors, he staunchly refused, said that his sentence was unjust, and prayed God to forgive his enemies. At Farel's threat to go no further with him if he persisted in thus justifying his past conduct, he ceased to dispute on the subject and continued to invoke the name of God till he reached the spot where the faggots were piled.[33] After prostrating himself in prayer he was bound to the stake, a chaplet of twigs covered with sulphur placed on his head, and the fire lighted. A piercing cry of anguish as the fire shot up into his face sent a thrill of horror through the crowd. Perhaps, as Doumergue argues, the sulphur fumes speedily suffocated the martyr.[34] According to Bolsec and Castellion, the wood was wet and he suffered terrible torture from the slow-burning faggots before he expired. His last words were, " Jesus, Son of the eternal God, have mercy upon me." His fidelity to his convictions is seen in the fact that, in invoking Jesus, he refrained from the orthodox formula, " eternal Son of God."

[31] " Defensio," " Opera," viii. 460; cf. Farel's account, "Opera," xiv. 693.
[32] " Opera," xiv. 693-694.
[33] See Farel's letter to Blarer, " Opera Calvini," xiv. 693 f.
[34] " Calvin," vi. 360 f.

CHAPTER X

SEQUEL OF THE TRAGEDY

CRITICISM OF PROSECUTION

THE trial and its tragic finale form one of the worst scandals of Reformation history. Admitting that the death of Servetus was in accordance with what was, and had for centuries been, law and practice, it was utterly at variance with the protests of the Reformers against their application to themselves and their adherents. Calvin himself was unwearied in thus protesting on behalf of his persecuted brethren in France and elsewhere. Granted that it might well appear in his eyes and those of his fellow-Reformers an audacious and intolerable evil to deny the orthodox doctrine of the Trinity, was it not equally an audacious and intolerable evil, in the eyes of the Roman Church, to deny, say, the doctrine of transubstantiation? Consistency alone ought to have taught them to refrain from thus justifying the brutal tactics of their opponents and stultifying their own principle of the right of the heretic to maintain his religious convictions in deference to conscience and the Word of God. Moreover the bitter and vindictive spirit with which Calvin pursued his adversary even unto death was totally at variance with the teaching of the Gospel which he professed to vindicate. Even making allowance for the unenlightened spirit of the age, it is difficult to understand how a man who, like Calvin, claimed to be following in the footsteps of his Master, could not see that he was dishonouring Him and belying the spirit of the Gospel in the interest of his own dogmatic beliefs. Equally reprehensible is the conduct of the Council in condemning a man to death who was no subject of theirs, whose trial was instigated not by a citizen of the republic, but by an alien refugee, and on whom expulsion from their territory was the only penalty that could equitably have been inflicted. True, according to canon law it was the duty of the State to abet the Church in the prosecution and punishment of a heretic, wherever he might be found. But the Reformers and the Reformed State had, in 1536, thrown off allegiance to the papal authority and were no longer bound to take their cue from the law and practice of the Roman Church. Still more objectionable was the conduct of Calvin and the Council in view of the high character and deep religious spirit of their victim. Servetus was undoubtedly a sincere and even passionate believer in Christ, though not in the metaphysical Christ of later Greek theological speculation. His striving to substitute what he conceived to be the Christ of Scripture for the Christ of this speculation was only the application of the Reformed and also the humanist principle of resorting to the sources for the true knowledge of early Christianity. In so doing, he anticipated, in his own fashion, a tendency in modern Christological discussion to diverge, in some respects, from the Christology of the Councils of the fourth and fifth centuries to the historic Christ as the authentic record of His own teaching reveals Him.[1] He was absolutely sincere in maintaining his convictions, profoundly religious, erudite and extraordinarily able in developing these convictions, and in spite of certain weaknesses of temperament and conduct, deserved on these grounds the respect of his opponents. To pursue such a man to death for opinions which differed from those alike of Reformers and anti-Reformers was a melancholy exhibition of theological intolerance and human perversity. The only excuse that may be adduced on behalf of his fellow-Reformers is that, in spite of their professions and principles, they were but men of their age and did not truly understand the cause they espoused. As human nature and human intelligence are constituted, men as a rule can only see with the eyes of their time, and the progressive, independent thinkers must battle and suffer for the truth that is in them. In the sixteenth century the penalty for such independence was still persecution and even death, with nothing but a good conscience and the conviction of dying for posterity as their reward. Happily the time was to come when even the disciples

---

[1] He appears to have divined this tendency. Future generations, he says, will be stupefied by the metaphysical verbiage of these Councils, " De Erroribus," 42.

of Calvin, if not the descendants of the men of the Vienne
Inquisition, would recognise his services to the cause of liberty
of thought and erect a monument to his memory in expiation
of the blunder and the crime perpetrated in his trial and
barbarous death.

Happily, too, even in that age of religious dogmatism, there
were not lacking voices raised in his vindication and in condemnation of his persecutors. Beza himself informs us that
hardly were the ashes of Servetus cold when the question of the
punishment of heretics began to be agitated, some contending
that, while heretics should be repressed, they should not be
put to death ; others that they should be left to the judgment
of God.[2] Perrin and a number of his followers had even tried
to bring in a verdict of not guilty and, failing this, had voted
for a milder penalty. Sulzer, one of the Basle ministers, wrote
shortly before his condemnation that there were many who
vehemently censured the persecuting tactics of Calvin and the
Council.[3] The minister Vergerius testifies to the same effect
and the refugee Italian jurist Gribaldi did not hesitate to
assert that it is inadmissible to penalise errors in doctrine,
because the faith of the individual is free.[4]

CALVIN'S DEFENCE

Doubt or dissatisfaction was so widespread that Calvin felt
it necessary to write a defence of the punishment of heresy,
and, in particular, of the justice of the execution of the heretic.
It appeared in Latin and French in the beginning of 1554.[5]
His thesis is that true doctrine is made known in the Word of
God and is thus founded not on the authority of man, because
God Himself speaks to us in the Word. He claims to be in
possession of this doctrine in contrast to papists and heretics
alike, who have no true knowledge of the Divine teaching.
To allow such false doctrine, which is apostasy from God,

----

[2] " Vita Calvini," " Opera," xxi. 149.
[3] Letter to Bullinger, " Opera," xiv. 627, 28th September 1553.
[4] " Opera," xvi. 463-464 ; Trechsel, ii. 282.
[5] " Defensio orthodoxæ fidei," etc. ; " Declaration pour maintenir la
vraye foi," etc. The Latin edition is in " Opera," viii. 457 f. It consists
of a number of documents relative to the trial of Servetus with a disquisition
on the question, Whether it is permissible to Christian judges to punish
heretics.

is to subvert religion and render certainty impossible. It is, therefore, absolutely necessary for the preservation of true religion and the honour of God to punish such apostasy with the sword. This power has been invested in kings and magistrates. It does not invalidate this contention to adduce the barbarities perpetrated by the papists against the Protestants. The papists persecute the truth, and where no true knowledge of the truth prevails such persecution is to be condemned. In accordance with this dogmatic assumption of a monopoly of truth, he replies to the objections based on the example and teaching of Christ Himself. To understand the command to allow the tares to grow up with the wheat in a literal sense would deprive the magistrates of the right to exercise justice and frustrate all laws and government. In commanding Peter to sheathe the sword, Christ wished to avoid tumult. In so doing He only forbids the use of the sword to His ministers, not to the magistrate in defence of the Church. It is absurd to punish a thief for depriving us of our property and yet refrain from punishing the impious wretch who seeks to deprive God of His glory. Whilst the kingdom of Christ is to be advanced by the preaching of His ministers, who are to suffer and make use only of spiritual weapons, the Lord has directed *where?* kings to maintain true doctrine against apostates, who seek to overthrow His worship and corrupt the true faith. Witness the command of the Lord to the children of Israel in Deuteronomy xiii. to kill the prophet who seeks to reduce them to false gods, even if he were a son or a brother. To quote this terrible injunction as a warrant for burning a theological opponent is grim enough in a preacher of the Gospel. To wrest the words of Christ Himself for the same purpose shows a strange lack of insight into the Gospel. Calvin does not hesitate to do both in defence of his action in persecuting Servetus to the death. His argumentation, of which this is a sample, is more remarkable for its ingenuity than for its force from the Christian point of view. While it failed to remove the doubts of many even of his friends, it roused the strenuous opposition of those who, like Castellion, dissented from his dogmatism. In a letter of 10th February 1554 his friend Zerchintes (Zurkinden), Chancellor of Bern, told him plainly that his experience of the persecution of Anabaptists had convinced him of the futility of using force against heretics, reminded him that clemency can do more than violence in winning back the erring, and expressed his regret that he had undertaken the defence of such an odious practice.[6]

CASTELLION'S PLEA FOR TOLERATION

A public refutation was soon forthcoming from the hand of Castellion under the pseudonym Martinus Bellius and purporting to be published at Magdeburg. It bore the title "De Haereticis an sint Persequendi," etc., and was really published at Basle in March 1554.[7] It took its rise in the circle of Italian refugees at Basle (Curione, Laelius Socinus, etc.), to which Castellion belonged and whose members, in their antagonism to the doctrines of the Trinity, predestination, etc., were the forerunners of the modern Unitarians. Though the main portion is attributable to Castellion, he seems to have incorporated some pieces written by his associates and edited by him.[8] Besides the long preface addressed to the tolerant Duke of Würtemberg, it contained a number of citations from the writings of the Fathers and the Reformers, including Calvin himself, against persecution, and an epilogue by Basil Montfort, perhaps another pseudonym for Castellion. In the preface he denounces the spirit of theological contention, dogmatism, and intolerance so detrimental to true religion, which consists in faith and charity. All this zeal for abstruse doctrines is totally unnecessary for salvation. Every party condemns the other in order by the help of persecution and punishments to reign alone. Hence the calumnies hurled against the heretic in order to make him odious to the people and incite their ferocity against him. And all this in the name of Christ and in obedience to His will ! Satan himself could not excogitate anything more repugnant to the mind and will of Christ. Think you that He will approve and praise all this when He shall appear ? Will He condemn a man for believing as his conscience dictates in regard to all these inter-

---

[6] " Opera," xv. 19 f.
[7] A French edition appeared some weeks later under the title, " Traicté des Hérétiques," etc.
[8] Buisson, " Castellion," ii. 12 f. (1892).

minable points in dispute. Even if Servetus has erred, did
He not say that we are to forgive the erring seventy times seven ?
Who is there that, knowing the infinite number of his own sins
and shortcomings, dare think that he is entitled to pluck the
beam out of his brother's eye and not rather concern himself
with the correction of his own life than with the condemnation
of others ? What is a heretic ? " After having long tried to
find out what a heretic is, I can discover no other answer than
that we esteem all those heretics who do not agree with us in
our opinions." The real heretic is he who lives a life unworthy
of Christ—the persecutor, for example—and it is just to such
that we do not apply the term. Each sect regards the other
as heretical and the sects are so numerous that if you are
accounted a believer in one city, you become a heretic in another.
If you wish to preserve your life, you must have as many
faiths, as many religions as there are cities or sects. There is,
of course, manifest exaggeration in this rhetoric presentation of
the divergence of evangelical teaching. Apart from the radical
wing of the evangelical party and individual dissenters who
belonged to no party, there was, in reality, except in regard to
particular doctrines like that of the Lord's Supper, a remarkable
unanimity of teaching in the evangelical Churches, as their
Confessions amply show. With a caveat against the prevalent
practice of throwing about the odious term heretic, he concludes that the only punishment permissible by Scripture is
excommunication or separation from the faithful, and proceeds
to show the disgrace and detriment done to Christ and
Christianity by the violent methods in vogue, more especially
in view of the obscurity of many of the questions at issue. To
persecute is to teach those who are not Christians—Turks
and Jews—to hate Christ and the Gospel, which persecution
only dishonours and deforms. He closes the preface with an
eloquent and moving plea for toleration in the name and for
the honour of Christ.

There follows a series of quotations in favour of toleration
from the works of Luther, Brenz, Erasmus, Franck, Hedion,
Regius, Calvin, and other Reformers, and from the Fathers—
Lactantius, Chrysostom, Jerome, and Augustine. The name
of Melanchthon is absent from the list, probably on account
of the approbation with which he had hailed the burning of

Servetus. Luther, too, had sadly lapsed from his early defence of toleration. But his vindication of liberty of conscience against a persecuting Church or State, in his earlier days of struggle against both, was so splendid that Castellion places him at the top of his list, whilst pointing out that too many of the Reformers, who began, under the influence of affliction, with such noble professions, proved untrue to them after success had given them the power to repress their opponents. Happily this reproach did not apply to Brenz, the Reformer of Suabia, who continued strenuously to maintain that the magistrate had no coercive jurisdiction in the spiritual sphere, and that the heretic is to be judged by the Word of God and punished only by excommunication. It was somewhat hazardous to cite the judicious Erasmus, who was not the man to endanger his life in defence of heretics, and after denouncing persecution against the Sorbonne in 1526, thought it prudent in 1529, after the second Diet of Spires, to maintain its validity against the Protestants. Nevertheless, it was not difficult to show him in his less apprehensive moments as a friend of toleration, though his testimony was not likely to have much weight in the eyes of Calvin. It is rather pungent to find Calvin himself among the advocates of clemency, if the choice of extracts from his writings was certainly limited. In the epilogue, he adds an energetic refutation of the attempt to wrest New Testament texts in support of the right to persecute and denies the applicability of Old Testament examples under the Gospel.

It is a remarkable production considering the age in which it appeared, and its author amply deserves the credit, which M. Buisson claims for him, of enunciating and demonstrating at length the true principle of religious liberty which the Reformers, with the rarest exceptions, only partially understood and so unworthily represented.[9]

Beza's Reply

This indictment of persecution greatly angered the zealots and Beza rushed into print with a refutation entitled

[9] Buisson gives a detailed exposition of the work, to which I confess my indebtedness, i. 360 f.

" De Haereticis a civili Magistratu puniendis Libellus." He maintains the threefold thesis that it is necessary to punish heretics, that this duty belongs to the magistrate, and that the death penalty may be inflicted on them. Like Calvin, he attacks the assumption that dogmatism is not essential to religion, which he denounces as blasphemy and sacrilege. False doctrine means the ruin of the Church, and the heretics are the agents whom the devil uses to overthrow it. Hence the necessity of repressing them, as the Old Testament and even the New as well as the universal practice of the Church amply prove. This being so, it is the duty of the civil magistrate to take this function on himself. His office is to secure the end for which society exists, viz., that God be duly honoured. But God cannot be duly honoured unless those who despise true religion are repressed by the sword. This the ministers cannot do, since the power of the sword is outside their province, and for them to use it would be to usurp a power that is not theirs, as the Roman Antichrist has done. They can only excommunicate the offender. But mere excommunication cannot prevent the heretics from propagating their views, and thus the Church would become the victim of endless dissension, division, and confusion. The only remedy is to have recourse to the magistrate, and he appeals to the Word and to the opinions of the Reformers to prove his right and his obligation to vindicate the true religion against its contemners. But may he inflict the death penalty for heresy ? Most certainly, in accordance with the principle that the greater the crime, the greater the penalty. Heresy being the worst of crimes, it deserves the extremest of penalties, in the interest both of the preservation of society and the vindication of God's glory.[10]

Beza wrote this misguided effusion at Lausanne, where he was Professor of Greek. He was a refugee from persecution in France. If he had crossed the French border, this specious plea would have been used to send him to the stake. He was evidently unconscious of the fact that in seeking thus to refute Castellion, he was doing his best to justify the persecution of himself and his French brethren. Castellion seems to have

---

[10] Buisson, ii. 19 f. ; Baird, " Beza," 52 f.

paid no attention to his fulmination. But he had another shot at Calvin in the " Contra Libellum Calvini," in which in the form of a dialogue between Calvin and Vaticanus (Castellion) he scathingly continues his criticism of the dogmatic, persecuting spirit and contentions of his book in defence of the trial and burning of Servetus.[11]

[11] For detailed account of it, see 'Buisson, ii. 33 f. Stickelberger proffers a weak defence of Calvin in relation to Servetus in his recent " Calvin," 192 f. French trans., 1936.

CHAPTER XI

THE TRIUMPH OF THE THEOCRACY

CALVIN SUPREME

WITH the burning of Servetus and the repression of the Perrinists, Calvin's doctrinal and ecclesiastical system had won a decisive victory. His personal influence was henceforth supreme in the Councils. Organised opposition to his will was now hopeless, and individual opposition appears as rare as it was hazardous. There is a marked change in the entries in the Registers in this respect from 1556 onwards. The oft-recurring criticism of previous years largely disappears. There are few charges of this kind and when they occur the delinquents are summarily dealt with.[1] In the Councils his word is received as an oracle not only in matters ecclesiastical, but in all matters affecting the State. His proposals and requests, whatever the subject of them, are as a rule granted as a matter of course, and he is constantly consulted on questions of policy or administration. The closest and most cordial co-operation exists between him and the Government, and it is not too much to say that his will is the dominating force of the republic. Appreciation and deference take the place of the recrimination and ill-will of the years of conflict with the Perrinists. The Council gives expression to its sense of " the great and inestimable services " he has rendered to the State,[2] and in December 1559 it invites him to accept the right of citizenship, which he had hitherto abstained from asking for fear of incurring the suspicion of self-seeking.[3] It takes every opportunity of showing him personal attention. It resolves, for instance, on the 7th October 1557, " in recognition of his many services to give him a good robe for the winter." [4] The

[1] See, for instance, " Opera," xxi. 673 f.
[2] " Opera," xxi. 723.
[3] *Ibid.*, xxi. 725.
[4] *Ibid.*, 676.

frequent illnesses from which he suffers in these last strenuous years arouse the greatest solicitude and it directs the physicians and apothecaries to spare no expense in treating him.[5] It shows him a reverence, a deference, a submission which even the Pope might have envied.

GOVERNMENT ACCORDING TO THE WORD

From 1555 onwards the Government of the Republic became practically a full-fledged theocracy, or better expressed, perhaps, a clerocracy, inspired and directed by Calvin and the ministers. The ideal of government in accordance with the Word of God now becomes a reality. Its recognised principle is that the magistrates act in the place of the sovereign God and that the supreme law is the Word, as interpreted by Calvin. In this sense we might also, with M. Goyau (*Revue des Deux Mondes*, July 1914), call it a Bibliocracy. The sole motive in the conduct of affairs of State is professedly the maintenance of God's sovereignty, the advancement of His honour and will, of which the ministers, the Church, are the guardians and the interpreters. To them the Government must have recourse for direction in the exercise of its functions, which embrace the whole life of the citizens, private as well as public, individual as well as corporate. The people of Geneva are regarded as the people of God and shall be ruled as the people of Israel were ruled in accordance with His declared will. Calvin adopts the part of the Old Testament legislator and prophet, speaking in the name of God, as well as the New Testament apostle and evangelist, who preaches the Christian Gospel, and in this latter sense the régime might also be called a Christocracy. Both Government and people are bound to accept his interpretation of the law and the Gospel, and act in accordance with it. He therefore frequently appears in the Council to remind the members of their responsibility to God, on whom the Government of the city depends, and exhort them to humble themselves before Him, to confess their sins, and to have regard to His honour in the repression of all vice.[6] At his instigation the Council resolves that on the occasion of the annual election of the magistrates, in particular, one of the

[5] " Opera," xxi. 707.   [6] *Ibid.*, xxi. 671.

ministers shall instruct the electors and the magistrates in their duty to God in the discharge of their functions.[7] The appeal, of which the following is a characteristic sample, was usually made by Calvin himself. " After prayer," we read in a notice of the meeting of the General Assembly on the 4th February 1560, " Mr John Calvin, minister of the Word of God and burgess of this city, made the Christian admonition and exhortation for the election of the syndics and the treasurer by this Assembly. He set forth the imminent dangers, menaces, and troubles which presented themselves from all sides and the necessity of electing capable and suitable men for this weighty office. It was to-day especially requisite to consider the gravity of the occasion and, having God as the President and Governor of our elections, to choose with a pure conscience, without regard to anything but the honour and glory of God, for the safety and defence of the republic. He also adduced the example of the good King Josaphat in that, having constituted judges in the provinces of Judea, he warned them that they took the place of God. This he did in order to show that those who are chosen may not pollute a seat so sacred, and insisted at large that the electors should have regard to this." [8]

So amenable was the Council to the influence of its spiritual mentor that it even decided, at his request, in December 1557, to institute a quarterly sitting, on the model of the meetings of the Venerable Company, for the mutual criticism of the public and private conduct of its members (the Grabeau). There is to be a frank interchange of opinion on one another's failings, in a spirit of charity and brotherly love, in order that the grace of God may prevail among them and all enmities and bitterness may be eliminated. To ensure due edification the conference is to be held with closed doors and each is bound on his oath not to reveal what is said in these secret sessions, or indulge in reproaches, or vaunt himself at another's expense. It was a severe test for a body of men associated in the task of administration to submit to these brotherly censures, and its institution shows the extraordinary influence which Calvin was now able to bring to bear on the government of the republic. The institution is unique as an attempt to apply the Christian spirit

[7] Choisy, " La Théocratie à Genève," 199 f.
[8] " Opera," xxi. 728 ; cf. 685, 743.

to the art of politics, to ensure the observance of rectitude in the conduct of government, and from this standpoint, as I have pointed out in a previous chapter, there is something to be said for Calvin's theocratic view, despite the criticism to which it has been subjected and to which it, indeed, lends itself. That in a Christian nation men should rule in the spirit of the religion they profess, in strict conformity to the moral law and the Christian law of love, is for him the only rule that is permissible in both national and international affairs. He deserves the credit of insisting on this in his own characteristic fashion, and striving according to his light to make the Government of the State a reflex of the kingdom of God. The theocracy and the Grabeau are his method of ensuring that government shall be the real and not merely the professed exemplification of the sovereignty of God, of honesty, righteousness, justice in the conduct of public affairs. Magistrates and rulers are to submit their actions to the test of criticism, based on the Christian standard, and govern in the Christian spirit. There is to be no playing with words, no sophistry about the end justifying the means, no deception of self or others for political purposes, no make-believes, no mere profession of principles to hide a diabolic practice. God, he says in effect, is to rule through you on earth, the God of the moral law and the Christian Gospel. Examine yourselves and submit yourselves to examination, therefore, individually and corporately, in order to ensure this Divine government. The ideal is of the highest, the motive of the best, and the intention absolutely sincere—to establish righteousness, justice, the fear of God among men. It produced men of high and strong character and undoubtedly tended to make the Reformation and the republic a great moral force far beyond its narrow confines.

Unfortunately the ideal is not always according to knowledge, nor truly enlightened, and the methods of its realisation are at times mistaken and reprehensible. Calvin's conception of the sovereignty of God is that of the Jewish theocracy rather than of the Gospel and of the moral law in the strict sense. His sovereign God reflects the crude as well as the more developed notions of the Old Testament, and is, besides, shaped in the mould of a rigid, intolerant dogmatic spirit. The theocracy thus tends to become a politico-ecclesiastical tyranny and in this respect repels the enlightened Christian spirit.

GENEVA A CITY OF REFUGE

Calvin's power was greatly strengthened by the ever-swelling number of fugitives from persecution. Geneva became more and more a city of refuge for the persecuted of Italy, Spain, France, England, Scotland, Poland. Under the new régime the dislike and suspicion of these immigrants disappeared. The restrictive legislation against them was modified and the rights of citizenship were bestowed with a liberal hand. The Registers contain numerous entries relative to their admission by the hundred. On 14th October 1557, for instance, 50 English, 25 Italians, 200 French, and 4 Spaniards take the oath as inhabitants.[9] In the following year the number was as high as 360, among them John Knox and Christopher Goodman, who were received gratis in recognition of their services as ministers of the Word of God.[10] In 1557 the enfranchised immigrants were already considerably more numerous than the citizens by birthright.[11] Separate Italian and English congregations were assigned the church of Notre Dame La Neuve for their worship, and it was in this church that Knox ministered.[12] Even the Spaniards were numerous enough to form a separate congregation, which was assigned the church of St Germain for its worship.[13] By their numbers and their zeal for the cause for which they had been driven into exile, these refugees contributed powerfully to leaven public opinion in favour of the new régime. They included many men of rank and culture, and among them Calvin

[9] " Opera," xxi. 671.

[10] *Ibid.*, xxi. 697 ; Kampschulte, ii. 285.

[11] Kampschulte, ii. 285.

[12] " Opera," xxi. 608, 615, 619 f. The order of worship, discipline, and administration of the Sacraments, as used in the English Church at Geneva, was drawn up by Whittingham and other refugees and approved by Calvin. See Colligan, " Whittingham," 74 f. (1934). It was adopted by the Church of Scotland in 1565. First printed at Geneva, 1556. It is given in Knox's " Works," iv. 157 f., and in " Phenix," ii. 204 f. (1708). On the English Church and English refugees at Geneva, see Martin, " Les Protestants Anglais refugiés à Genève au Temps de Calvin " (1915). See also Heyer, " La Colonie Anglaise à Genève," *Mem. de la Soc. d'Hist. et d'Archéologie de Gen.*, ix., and A. F. Mitchell, " Le Livre des Anglais," containing their names.

[13] " Opera," xxi. 706.

found his staunchest abettors in the task of establishing his theocratic system. Knox, Goodman, Beza, Laurent de Normandie,[14] for instance. There was among them, however, an element of questionable character and antecedents, and Calvin is found, in November 1556, complaining to the Council of " the scandals " which their conduct is causing, and which were tending to compromise the good name of the republic. These scandals may, in part, have been due to an unwillingness to submit to his puritanic régime, which was evidently not quite to the taste of some of his French fellow-countrymen of high rank who, in espousing the evangelical cause, had not renounced the luxury and the free code of morals obtaining among the French nobility. The complaint contains, however, substantial evidence of immoral practices such as bigamous marriages, and the Council hastened to take measures for the stricter super-vision of these " *mauvaises gens*." [15] Certain it is that there were some arrant hypocrites even among those who professed the greatest zeal for the Puritan Gospel and won the confidence of Calvin, but who, like M. de Passy, the fugitive Bishop of Nevers, ultimately belied this profession by their vicious conduct.

Others gave trouble by their inability to accept his teaching without demur. The centre of this dissent was the Italian congregation, some of whose members, including the dis-tinguished jurist Gribaldi, the physician Blandrata, or Biandrata, Alciati, and Gentile, criticised the condemnation of Servetus and questioned the received doctrine of the Trinity. Gribaldi, who lived on his estate at Farges, was ordered to quit the city. As the dispute in the congregation became acute, Calvin and the Italian pastor Ragnoni appealed to the Council against these " fantastic spirits," as they termed Blandrata and the others, whom they accused of holding the opinion of Servetus, and demanded that the members of the congregation should accept a short Confession of Faith which they had drawn up.[16] To this end Calvin, accompanied by the syndic, repaired to the church with the Confession, and after discussion and further negotiation, all, with two exceptions, professed their

---

[14] For de Normandie, see " Opera," xxi. 695.
[15] " Opera," xxi. 654 f. ; Kampschulte, ii. 370 f.
[16] " Opera," xxi. 691.

agreement [17] (May 1558). Blandrata and Alciati retired from
the city, but Gentile remained to continue the agitation and
was arrested and thrown into prison (9th June 1558). According to the accusation against him, he not only charged Calvin
with " oppressing the truth by his cavillations," but boldly
attacked the official doctrine of the Trinity.[18] At first he
showed a disposition to maintain his opinion in defiance of
Calvin, who ascribed his " horrible blasphemies " to the
instigation of the devil. But he had no wish to incur the fate
of Servetus and erelong offered to accept the Confession and
apologise to Calvin for his rash utterances against him. The
Council was not satisfied with these professions of repentance
and referred the case to a commission of five jurists, who were
of opinion that his retraction was not sincere and that he merited
death by decapitation (6th August). The Council accordingly
sentenced him to be beheaded and he only saved himself from
this fate by the most explicit confession of his errors and
declaration of penitence. This confession and declaration the
Council was ultimately prevailed on to accept and contented
itself with sentencing him to appear before the Hôtel de Ville
in his shirt and torch in hand, to make the tour of the city,
and to burn the document containing his heterodox views [19]
(1st September 1558). His penitence, it appears, was, after
all, only a makeshift, and in spite of the prohibition to leave
the city without the licence of the magistrates, he escaped
shortly after and continued in the course of his wanderings in
France and Poland to champion his anti-Trinitarian heresies
until he at last, in 1566, suffered at Bern the fate which he had
with difficulty evaded at Geneva.

DOMINANCE OF CONSISTORY

The grand adjunct and instrument of the theocracy is the
Consistory, which now becomes all-powerful and with which
the Council energetically and deferentially co-operates in the
policy of establishing the rule of God in the republic. The
clerical membership increases with the increase in the number

---

[17] " Opera," xxi. 693-695.   [18] *Ibid.*, xxi. 698.
[19] " Opera," xxi. 698 f. ; Colladon, " Vie de Calvin," 85 f. ; Choisy,
" La Théocratie," 193 f. ; Schaff, " The Swiss Reformation," 652 f.

of the ministers, and in 1557 it equals that of the elders.[20]
At Calvin's request the Council resolves in this year to choose
as members God-fearing men of exemplary life.[21] Its influence
is augmented by the accession of Beza, who quitted Lausanne
and settled in Geneva in 1558, of Viret, who followed him some
months later.[22] For the more effective detection and punishment of delinquents, the Council empowers it to examine
witnesses on oath,[23] and takes steps to give effect to its demand
for the stricter supervision of the people and the stringent
enforcement of the edicts relative to vice, abstention from
Communion, and excommunication. To this end it directs
that the ministers shall be housed throughout the city " for the
better invigilation of vice," [24] commissions two of the syndics
to take part in the house-to-house visitation, and promulgates
an edict punishing with a year's banishment all who abstain
from the Communion for a year, and even excommunicated
persons who neglect to apply for readmission within the same
period.[25] It further submits to the Council of Two Hundred
a series of edicts for the punishment of fornication, adultery,
swearing, blasphemy, and contempt of religion. The Two
Hundred give their sanction, but in the General Assembly
several speakers object to them as "too drastic" ("*trop rudes*").
" We are not now under the law, but under grace," insisted
one of these objectors, " and to punish adultery with death is
to return to Judaism. Moreover, to pass these edicts would be
to banish half the population of the city." Despite the efforts
of their supporters to silence such objections, they were sent
back to the Councils for revision and modification, and the
Consistory was fain in the meantime to be content with less
heroic measures. It took what revenge it could by summoning
several of the critics to its bar and sending them to the Council
for punishment.[26] It was more successful in the attempt to
check by puritanic legislation the luxury which it deemed
unworthy of the city of God. In September 1558 the minister
Des Gallars appeared as its spokesman before the Council
to represent " the great scandal " arising from the rampant
superfluities and excesses in the matter of dress and meat.

[20] Kampschulte, ii. 358.
[21] " Opera," xxi. 660 f.
[22] *Ibid.*, xxi. 706, 711.
[23] *Ibid.*, xxi. 639.
[24] *Ibid.*, xxi. 670 f.
[25] *Ibid.*, xxi. 667.
[26] *Ibid.*, xxi. 654 f.

Remonstrance has hitherto been unavailing to restrain the extravagance of both sexes, especially among the refugees, in dress, ornament, and feastings. The state of things, it seems, was worse than in pagan times, and if the Romans by sumptuary laws thought fit to repress such luxury, it was all the more incumbent on the legislators of a Christian State to free the republic from this reproach. On both religious and economic grounds the Council resolved to set about the work of reform in a number of edicts which minutely prescribed the dress and diet of the various classes in the spirit of puritan simplicity, with special penalties for the tailors and cooks, as well as their clients, who should contravene these regulations [27] (October 1558).

REVISION OF THE ORDINANCES OF 1541

Fifteen months later Calvin and Viret ventured to represent to the Council the desirability of recognising more definitely than in the Ordinances of 1541 the distinction between the ecclesiastical and the temporal spheres and the independence of the ecclesiastical jurisdiction as wielded by the Consistory. The object of the representation was, they avowed, to bring this jurisdiction into conformity with the Word of God and the practice of the ancient Church and thus realise Calvin's ideal of the autonomy of the Church in spiritual things, which the State in 1541 had refused to recognise. On this occasion both Councils were far more amenable to his ideal of spiritual independence, and substantially legislated his behests in the new set of edicts, which were incorporated in a revised edition of the Ordinances promulgated in 1561. The first of these edicts accordingly enacts that the syndic or magistrate who may be chosen a member of the Consistory shall act only in his capacity as an elder and shall not, as hitherto, bear his baton of office " in order the better to mark the distinction which Holy Scripture emphasises between the sword and authority of the magistrate, and the jurisdiction with which the Church is invested for maintaining all Christians in the obedience and true sense of God, and preventing and correcting all scandals." The temporal sovereignty and the spiritual

[27] " Opera," xxi. 706 f. ; Kampschulte, ii. 349 f.

régime are, indeed, conjoined and inseparable in the maintenance
of the Divine rule. But they are not to be confused, and in
thus discerning between them both Councils desire to acknowledge their subjection to Him who, in His Word, teaches this
distinction. Here at last we have the explicit recognition of
the Calvinist conception of the two powers, secular and
ecclesiastical, and their co-ordination in the maintenance
of the Divine rule in the community. The second edict
acknowledges the right of the ministers, which has hitherto by
a " vicious usurpation " been ignored, to a voice in the choice
of elders by the Council, and directs that henceforth none
shall be chosen without their knowledge and advice. The
third declares that all members of the Councils—native citizens
and affranchised burgesses alike—shall be capable of election
as members of the Consistory. The fourth, which deals with
the subject of excommunication, and enjoins that those whom
the Consistory has excommunicated on account of scandals
and who persist in their evil course, shall be publicly proclaimed
in the churches as " rejected from the flock," until they confess
their faults and seek reconciliation. In particular, those guilty
of denying the Gospel in order to save their lives, or relapsing
into popery, must present themselves in the congregation as
penitents and demand pardon of God and His Church [28] (February
1560). Finally the right of the people to a voice in the
election of ministers, hitherto ignored by the Council, receives
recognition in the enactment that the names of those presented
for the office of pastor shall be publicly proclaimed beforehand
in the church, in order that the people, if necessary, may state
their objections, and, in case these are sustained, a new election
may be made by the Council and the ministers. The right of
popular objection is likewise to apply to the election of elders.[29]

" THE MOST PERFECT SCHOOL OF CHRIST "

Under such favourable auspices the Consistory during these
latter years of Calvin's life laboured effectively at the task of
disciplining the people into conformity with the theocratic
ideal. The Registers bear ample testimony to its zeal and
rigour in the prosecution of delinquents. We are sufficiently

[28] " Opera," xxi. 726 f. ; x^a. 120 f.   [29] *Ibid.*, x^a. 94.

familiar with the characteristic features of this prosecution as
delineated in a former chapter and need not adduce further
particulars here. The only difference compared with previous
years consists in the fact that its activity is now energetically
abetted by the Council, and that there is no chance, as formerly,
of successful appeal from it to the magistrates. Opposition to
or criticism of its proceedings is effectively suppressed. The
conduct of the citizens is subjected to a searching inquisition
carried out not only by the ministers, but by the magistrates
and their officials. Something like an ecclesiastical reign of
terror, based on a system of espionage, prevails. Liberty of
thought is strangled by the exercise of a strict censorship of the
press, which is entrusted to the ministers, and any modification
of the text of a book, which has received their sanction, renders
the culprit liable to the death penalty.[30] Liberty of conscience
does not exist for those who dissent from the Calvinist creed
and worship, and a determined crusade is initiated against
papists and Anabaptists, who are imprisoned or banished.[31]
The relics of popery in the shape of the crosses on the spires
and the images, which apparently still remained in the churches,
were removed, and it is characteristic to find John Knox taking
a leading part in this iconoclastic activity.[32] Very significant of
this intensified disciplinary régime is the number of excommunications, which shows a marked increase on that of previous
years. Whereas the total number for the four years 1551-54
was only 80, it rises to nearly 100 in 1555 and 140 in the
following year. In 1559 it rises to over 300.[33]

In virtue of this rigorous régime, Geneva became to all
appearance the most religious and moral city of Europe. To
John Knox it seemed " the maist perfyt schoole of Chryst
that ever was in the erth since the dayis of the apostellis." [34]
" In the streets of Geneva dare no notable malefactor more
shew his face than dare the owle in the bright sunne." [35] The
people resorted to the churches in crowds, especially to hear
Calvin and Viret, and it became necessary to appoint additional
ministers and to reopen the church of St Germain.[36] Equally

---

[30] " Opera," xxi. 710.   [31] Ibid., xxi. 664-666, 722 f.
[32] Ibid., xxi. 652, 656, 717.
[33] Kampschulte, ii. 286-287, 361.
[34] " Works," iv. 240 (Laing's ed., 1895).
[35] Ibid., v. 212.   [36] " Opera," xxi. 688, 713, 718, 720.

gratifying was the concourse at Calvin's lectures, which were attended by the notables of the city from the magistrates downwards.[37]   Lectures and sermons were the absorbing topic of discussion. All this zeal for the things of the spirit was undoubtedly an index of the deep religious zeal, the earnest conception of life which Calvin and the more devoted of his fellow-preachers succeeded in nurturing in their adherents. It is, indeed, a striking testimony of the power of his personality and preaching. At the same time, the number of excommunications in a city of about 13,000 inhabitants would seem to show that there was a strong undercurrent of laxity, judged at least from the standpoint of the puritan ideal. If it is a testimony to the thoroughness with which the Consistory sought to enforce this ideal, it is also an indication of the unwisdom and the partial failure of this system of minute artificial regulation of the moral and spiritual life. Even if, as John Knox says, vice disappeared from the public view, it was, it is to be feared, only driven behind the scenes. This excessive regulation indubitably nurtured the hypocrite as well as the strong and sincere character of puritan mould.

EDUCATIONAL REFORM

A highly creditable feature of the later Calvinist régime is its active interest in educational reform. In the Ordinances of 1541 Calvin, as we have seen, had laid stress on the importance for Church and State alike of an adequate educational system. Hence the prominence of " the doctor " in these Ordinances. The scheme of educational reform therein adumbrated had unfortunately proved but a pious wish. It had not got beyond the embryo stage in spite of Calvin's interest in the subject. His old teacher at Paris, Maturin Cordier, whom he had brought to Geneva in the early period of his reforming activity, had followed him into exile and could not be persuaded to return after his recall in 1541. Castellion, who took his place in this year, was well fitted to realise his educational ideal. But, as we have seen, he was too independent to run in harness with the masterful reformer, and with his withdrawal and the outbreak of the struggle with the Perrinists, educational reform was

[37] Colladon, " Vita," " Opera," xxi. 87.

practically at a standstill. Higher education seems to have been confined to the exegetical lectures which Calvin regularly delivered and which attracted a large number of hearers.[38] Parents who wished to give their children the benefit of a good education were obliged to send them elsewhere. The reputation of Geneva as a centre of culture as well as the stronghold of the Reformation had still to be made, and Calvin was even accused by his opponents of striving to keep the people in ignorance in the interest of his doctrinal system. He had a profound sense of the value of knowledge for both the religious and civic life and his conversion to the evangelical faith had not stifled his ardour in the pursuit of it, though it gave it a definite theological bent. Throughout these years of effort to establish the Calvinist discipline he never lost sight of his original plan of organising and developing a sound educational system as the indispensable completion of his work as a reformer. The Registers of the Council and his correspondence attest alike the continued solicitude for the instruction of the young and the failure of his efforts to improve it. It was only in 1559 that he at last succeeded in realising his original plan by the reorganisation of the school and the foundation of an academy for higher studies. In March of the previous year he persuaded the Council to sanction the erection of a new college on a more salubrious and commodious site than that of the school in the convent of Rive,[39] and set about raising a building fund, which the Council was unable to provide out of the revenue of the city. With its active patronage, he collected a considerable sum in legacies and donations and supervised the construction of the new edifice, which was not completed till 1562, and which remains as a monument of his enlightened educational policy. He appears to have taken as the model of the new institution that founded and developed by Johann Sturm at Strassburg, which he had visited during a journey to Frankfurt in 1556, and where he had lectured in theology during the years of his exile from Geneva. This institution consisted of a school or college in which a graduated course of instruction was imparted as a preparation for more advanced studies in arts and theology under separate professors. As thus developed

---

[38] Colladon, " Vita," " Opera," xxi. 70.
[39] " Opera," xxi. 687; cf. 631.

under Sturm's auspices, the institution at Strassburg was a combination, in two distinct departments, of the secondary school and the university. The advanced department ultimately, in 1566, received from the Emperor Maximilian II., under the official title of Academy, the status of a university with the right to confer degrees.[40] With this model before him, Calvin drafted the constitution and plan of courses for his combined college (*schola privata*) and academy (*schola publica*) at Geneva. The pupils of the college are graded in seven classes. In the lowest class, the seventh, they are taught writing and the elements of the Latin and French languages. This instruction is progressively continued in the sixth and fifth. In the fourth they begin Greek and read Cicero and Ovid. In the third they study the Greek grammar more intensively and read the orations of Isocrates, continue the study of Cicero, and add that of the Æneid and Cæsar's " Commentaries." In the second, attention is given particularly to the Latin and Greek historians, Livy, Xenophon, or Polybius, with the addition of Homer, the elements of logic, and the Gospel of St Luke in Greek on Saturdays. In the first class they continue the study of logic and add that of rhetoric in connection with the orations of Cicero and Demosthenes and the works of Homer and Virgil, with special exercises in style, declamations twice a month, and the reading of a New Testament epistle in Greek on Saturdays. Each class is divided into groups of ten, with a head boy, who acts as monitor of each group, and is taught by a regent. The regent is elected by the ministers and the professors of the academy and presented to the Council for acceptance and confirmation, according as it shall see fit, and takes the oath binding him to the faithful performance of his function. The general supervision is entrusted to a Principal Regent, and the methods of instruction and discipline are minutely defined. The advancement of the pupils from a lower to a higher class is decided by an annual test on a prescribed theme, and the results are declared in a public assembly in the church of St Peter's, at which prizes given by the Council are presented to the best two pupils of each class.

The training is thus specifically humanist. Calvin ranged himself on the side of the more enlightened pædagogues as

[40] Borgeaud, " Histoire de l'Université de Genève," 27 f. (1900).

against the votaries of use and wont in education—of his old
master Cordier, of his friends Gouvea, Sturm, Budin, Baduel,
who were among the more celebrated of these practical educational reformers.   Characteristic is the important part assigned
to religious instruction.   Each class is opened with prayer
and the morning instruction closes with the repetition of the
Lord's Prayer.   On resuming they spend an hour singing the
Psalms, and at the close of the afternoon lessons the Lord's
Prayer is again repeated, with the addition of the Creed
and the Ten Commandments.   The pupils must attend the
Wednesday sermon under the charge of a regent, and both
sermons on Sunday, in addition to the Catechism, those who
absent themselves or listen carelessly being publicly punished
on the following day.   On the Saturday afternoon they spend
an hour on the Catechism in preparation for the lesson on the
Sunday, and each quarter before the celebration of the Communion one of the ministers attends and addresses the whole
school on the subject.   Calvin evidently believed in dosing
them with religion.   He certainly succeeded in making it a
burden grievous to be borne by these long-suffering innocents.
The regents are particularly enjoined to teach them to love
God and hate vice—an admirable precept which might have
been adequately observed without so much church-going and
such frequent repetition of prayers in the course of instruction.

The head of the higher department, or *schola publica*, is the
Rector, who also exercises the chief supervision over the college.
He is chosen by vote from the ministers and the professors and
holds office for two years, but is eligible for re-election.   His
duty is to superintend the whole educational establishment, to
admonish the principal, regents, and professors in case of
dereliction of duty, to deal with cases of friction arising among
the teachers or the students, to see that the students receive
the right of residence in the city from the Council, to inscribe
their names in the matriculation list, and receive their subscription to the Confession of Faith.   Before entering office
he is sworn to perform his functions faithfully.

There are three professors of Greek, Hebrew, the arts, and
two of theology, who, as in the case of the Rector, are bound
on oath faithfully to discharge the duties of their office, which
are prescribed in detail.   The number of lectures given each

week totals twenty-seven. There are, besides, a weekly discussion, presided over by one of the ministers, for those who
desire to exercise themselves in the exposition of the Scriptures,
and a monthly disputation on some theological theme under
the presidency of one of the theological professors. Freedom
of discussion is allowed, subject to the reservation that " all
sophistry and impudent and audacious curiosity tending to
corrupt the Word of God and all ill-disposed contention and
stubbornness be avoided." [41] Otherwise the students are
allowed complete freedom from the discipline to which the
pupils of the college are subjected. The obligatory subscription
of the Confession, however, bars anything like liberty of thought
or research in theology. This document requires, at the outset
of their career as students, the absolute acceptance of all the
subtleties of Greek theology as legislated by the General
Councils, in addition to the specific Calvinist theology. The
student must begin his studies by solemnly professing the
current orthodox doctrines before he has had the opportunity
of submitting a single one of them to independent investigation.
In this respect the higher instruction sketched by Calvin
cannot be described as educationally sound. The ecclesiastical
influence is supreme, and this influence, in its rigid Calvinist
form, was certainly not fitted to nurture the scientific spirit
in spite of the noble motto above the entrance of the academy,
" Post Tenebras Lux." It may, indeed, claim the merit of
recognising the value of a thorough intellectual training by means
of the classic languages, and of contemplating the systematic
formation of character on a serious religious basis. But from
the educational point of view in the larger sense the scheme is
far too one-sided. The intense and almost exclusive study of
the classics leaves too little room for the study of science [42]
and history. This was, indeed, the weakness of the humanist
educational reform, and Calvin could not be expected to be
wiser than the educational reformers, to whom the knowledge

---

[41] " Leges Academiæ Genevensis," " Opera," xᵃ. 65 f.

[42] For the attitude of Calvin to science see Lecerf, " De l'Impulsion
Donnée par le Calvinisme a l'Étude des Sciences Physiques et Naturelles,"
Bull. Soc. Hist. du Prot. Français, 1935, 192 f. If he did not assign a place to
science in the curriculum, he professed against the obscurantists a sense of
the utility of the " Arts libéraux et honnêtes sciences " for the knowledge
of God and the conduct of life. His own special interest was, however,
theological, not scientific, and he shared the crude scientific views of his time.

of classic literature and antiquity was a sort of fetish and the wider knowledge of nature and history was a sealed book. Despite this narrowness of vision and lack of a larger educational outlook, the new foundation was a great achievement. Its formal inauguration in St Peter's on the 5th June 1559, when Calvin preached and Beza as Rector orated in impressive fashion, was the beginning of a long period of enhanced prestige for the little republic, whose intellectual and spiritual influence it contributed materially to spread from the Alps to the Highlands of Scotland.

Calvin strove betimes to secure for it a staff of competent teachers and professors. He attempted unsuccessfully to lure Mercier (Mercerus), Vatable's successor at the Collège de France, from Paris, and Tremellius, rector of the college of Hombach in the Duchy of Zweibrücken, for the chair of Hebrew.[43] His task was fortunately facilitated by the secession of the professors and regents of the college at Lausanne in consequence of a dispute with the Bernese Government over the introduction of the Genevan system of discipline. Chevallier became professor of Hebrew, Berauld of Greek, in place of Beza, who was originally nominated, and who was elected Rector, Tagaut professor of arts or philosophy, whilst Calvin himself and Beza professed theology. Among the regents [44] was Calvin's old teacher Cordier, who had for many years taught at Neuchâtel and Lausanne, and who, owing to his advanced years, was attached to the college in an honorary capacity and pensioned by the Council. With such a staff the number of pupils and students swelled rapidly, and in the year of Calvin's death, 1564, it reached the total of 1200 and 300 respectively. The list of matriculated students during the first three years is largely an international one and contains the names of not a few who afterwards attained celebrity as pillars of the reformed cause in their respective countries.[45] The concourse of students from Italy, France, the Netherlands, Germany, England, and Scotland was a striking testimony to the international influence of its founder and of his far-reaching activity as the leader and organiser of the Reformation in Western Europe.

[43] Borgeaud, 36 f.

[44] Their names are given in the Latin preface to the " Leges," x^a. 68.

[45] A facsimile for the years 1559-61 is given in Borgeaud, 56-63. A list from 1559 to 1859 in the " Livre du Recteur " (1860).

CHAPTER XII

CALVIN AS CHAMPION OF THE REFORMATION

DURING the twenty-eight intervening years between Calvin's
first arrival at Geneva in 1536 and his death in 1564 he rendered
incalculable service as the champion of the reformed cause,
in controversy with its Roman Catholic opponents ; as mediator
in the internal quarrels among its adherents in Germany and
Switzerland, as inspirer and director of its missionary activity
in his native France and other western lands, and as its
diplomatic protagonist in the sphere of international politics.
Long before his death in 1564 Geneva had become not only
a city of refuge for the persecuted of many lands, but the
headquarters of militant Protestantism in these lands—the
Rome of the Reformed Churches.

NECESSITY OF THE REFORMATION

We are already acquainted with his masterly defence of
the Reformation in reply to Sadolet. His next encounter
was with Albert Pighius, a notable Dutch theologian and
Archdeacon of Utrecht, who in 1542 attacked the doctrine of
the slavery of the will with the usual arguments [1] and against
whom he wrote a " Defence." [2] Pighius' teaching was too
Pelagian even for the Romanists, and his book was ultimately
placed on the Index by the Inquisition. The controversy, it
seems, had some influence in leading the Council of Trent
to disown the Pelagian and semi-Pelagian heresies, and Calvin
might claim that, in controverting the Dutchman, he had done
a good turn in support of Romanist as well as Protestant orthodoxy. His performance was, however, little to the taste of
Melanchthon, to whom he dedicated it and whom he claimed

---

[1] " De Libero Arbitrio."
[2] " Defensio Sanæ et Orthodoxæ Doctrinæ de Servitute et Liberatione
Humani Arbitrii " (1543), " Opera," vi. 233 f.

as a supporter of his views. Melanchthon had already swerved from the extreme Lutheran conception of the unfree will. Whilst appreciating the compliment and expressing admiration of Calvin's talents as a controversialist, he suggested that he should exercise them on subjects of more fruitful utility to the Protestant cause.[3]

Far more effective, from this point of view, were his refutation [4] of the Articles issued by the Sorbonne in 1542 in defence of the Roman faith, and the treatise " On the Necessity of Reforming the Church " in the form of an " Exhortation," [5] in 1543, to the Emperor Charles V. and the Diet of Spires. The refutation of the Sorbonne doctors takes the form of a proof of each Article proffered in a vein of racy sarcasm and followed by the relative antidote in the form of a statement of the reformed teaching. In the " Exhortation " to the Emperor and the Diet he dwells on the abuses in the Church which the Reformers have sought to remedy, on the salutary remedies they have adopted, and on the necessity of the adoption of these remedies. The worship of God, the doctrines of the Gospel, the sacraments, and the government of the Church were, he maintains, miserably corrupted before Luther and others arose to bear aloft the torch of reformation. True worship consists in worshipping God in spirit and in truth. It is that prescribed by God Himself. By disregarding this prescription, the Church has been led astray into a multitude of superstitious and human devices, " teaching for doctrines the commandments of men." Only what is expressly sanctioned by the Word of God is permissible. From this standpoint he reviews and condemns the extraneous observances invented by men—prayer to the saints, which deprives God of His sovereign function as the hearer of prayer and is incompatible with the office of Christ as sole intercessor ; adoration of images, which has led to gross idolatry ; the multiplication of religious rites borrowed in part from paganism and more adapted to a theatrical show than to the spiritual worship of God. Similarly the true doctrine of salvation, which teaches us to realise our depravity,

---

[3] See his letter to Calvin in " Opera," xi. 539 f. (May 1543).
[4] The title of the Refutation is " Articuli a Facultate, etc., cum Antidoto " (1544), " Opera," vii. 1 f. Translated by Beveridge in " Calvin's Tracts," i. 71 f.
[5] " Exhortatio," etc., vi. 453 f. ; Beveridge, " Calvin's Tracts," i. 123 f.

to trust only in the sacrifice of Christ, and seek in Him alone righteousness and life, has been perverted by the schoolmen in their doctrine of work righteousness and merits, satisfactions and the consequent suspense and uncertainty which annihilates all real confidence in God's promises. Moreover, the sacraments instituted by Christ have been utterly obscured by extraneous beliefs and ceremonies and others added by perverse human invention. Equally fictitious and unscriptural is the government of the Church, which is simply a travesty of that instituted by Christ. Its place has been taken by "a new and mongrel species of government," under which the bishops have ceased to be pastors and are become secular princes. Neither they nor the lower orders of the clergy discharge the primitive pastoral function of feeding the flock with the Word. The whole clerical order is a disgrace to their profession ; no other is more addicted to all kinds of wickedness. The manifold vices of the ecclesiastical establishment need no detailed demonstration. The government of the Church has become a lawless, licentious, unlimited domination over souls, and he challenges his readers to say whether Luther and his fellowreformers were not amply justified in their demand for the radical remedy of all these glaring and intolerable abuses.

These remedies, he next contends, have the merit of restoring the worship, doctrine, sacraments, and government of the Church to the ancient form in accordance with the Word of God. This thesis he elaborates by an examination of the positive reforms effected and exemplified in these respects in the Reformed Churches, and by answering the objections, reproaches, and calumnies of their opponents. But granting the existence of these abuses, is this a sufficient cause for disrupting the Church and convulsing the world ? Have the Reformers not been guilty of desolating the Church with strife and schism ? It is not the Reformers, he retorts, but their opponents that have made themselves guilty of these evils by their refusal to amend abuses and the cruel persecution of those who have sought to do so. To have kept silence would have been to betray the truth, and in battling for the truth the Reformers have been fighting for God, not in order to excite tumult and sedition. It has been the fate of the Gospel from the beginning to excite the rage and resistance of the wicked and to be preached amid great contention. But may not abuses be corrected by gentle as well as harsh remedies? The Church, he admits, neither is nor ever has been perfect, and strife is not to be nurtured for small and trivial errors. But what the Reformers have contended for are neither small nor trivial matters. They are questions of the utmost moment. They involve the whole substance of the Christian religion. Is it, for instance, a trivial thing to countenance idolatry in the Church of God? What say Moses and the prophets of this heinous sin? Is it a trivial thing to corrupt the doctrine of salvation, to ascribe to the priest the power to offer that sacrifice which Christ alone performed for us, to subject men to the tyranny of a corrupt hierarchy? For such enormities there can be no toleration and no moderation. To be indifferent or tolerant in their presence would be to suffer the name of God to be impiously blasphemed. But has not the cure been worse than the disease? Has not the Reformation movement given rise to universal licentiousness, moral degeneration, and spoliation? He admits that the movement has not accomplished all that is to be desired. But the Reformers have done their duty. They have planted and watered as God has commanded. If there have been unfortunate results, the fault is not theirs. Let his opponents, if they will, expostulate with God, who giveth the increase. But he rebuts as absolutely false the assertion that no benefit has resulted from the movement, and he appeals, in proof of his contention, to its spiritual and moral effects in the lives of multitudes of those who have been quickened by the preaching of the Word of God. If some pervert the Gospel, it is not because the Reformers have taught them to do so. And it is not for the enemies of the Reformers to charge them with lack of discipline, which he admits is not without some foundation, since they have done their utmost to thwart and bring to naught all their efforts. Let them also bear in mind how difficult the task of reconstructing the Church out of the ruin to which they have reduced it by their perversions and corruptions. And with no little force he bids them clear away their own perversions and corruptions, of which he gives a scathing delineation, before attempting to throw dirt at the Reformers. " I mean not to palliate or flatter our defects when I thus speak. I know how much we require to be improved. Undoubtedly, were God to call us to account, excuse would be difficult. But when called to answer our enemies, we have a better cause and an easier victory than we could wish." He frankly admits, too, the spoliation, the secularisation of Church property. He confesses the sin of it and will on no account excuse such wrong. It ought to be rectified, and too many of the Lutheran members of the Diet must have felt uneasy under this frank confession. But what right, he asks with great force, have simoniacal bishops and priests to make such a charge, who misuse the revenues of the Church so scandalously. The paragraphs in which he labours this point are very damning to these hypocritical censors. Whilst he will not excuse the secular princes who have been guilty of unworthy conduct in this matter, he thinks that the clergy have justly forfeited their right to the ecclesiastical property by the gross and widespread perversion of these revenues to unworthy ends. He concludes with a refutation of the charge of schism, in which he seeks to show that it is not the Reformers but their opponents who have departed from the true Church, which consists in the preaching of sound doctrine and the pure administration of the sacraments, in allegiance to Christ its head and not to the Roman pontiff.

The passionate conviction, the heroic endurance for a great cause, which lends a tremendous force to this plea for the Reformation, are finely expressed in its closing sentence. "We will die, but in death even be conquerors, not only because through it we shall have a sure passage to a better life, but because we know that our blood will be a seed to propagate the Divine truth which men now despise." Calvin is, indeed, seen at his best in such an indictment and defence. The moral and spiritual intensity of the man finds powerful expression with far less of the doctrinaire vehemence, the dogmatic acerbity that mars too much of what he wrote. The intolerant spirit is there and with " the papists," as well as the heretics who withstand what he regards as the truth, there can be no compromise. But here he is fighting against a system which is not merely for him a travesty of Christian truth, as tested by the primitive standard, but is freely admitted by its more impartial and earnest votaries to be corrupt in head and members and the nurse of scandalous corruption in both the Church and the world. Whatever Christianity might be, it could not possibly be this travesty of it. That this justified the Reformers in attempting to mend, and, if this was denied, to end it, he shows with a logic and a moral and religious power that rises far above the level of mere theological controversy. Even from the specifically theological point of view, it would take no small amount of special pleading to make plausible against such arguments the claim of the papal mediæval Church to be the Church of Christ and the apostles. The contrast between this Church and the secularised and corrupt Church is very glaring, and in the face of the scandalous evils which he arraigns, the necessity of the Reformation is, on practical grounds, an exceedingly cogent one.

CALVIN AND POPE PAUL III.

The concessions to the Lutherans made by the Emperor at the Diet of Spires in 1544 were resented by Pope Paul III., who wrote him a paternal admonition reproaching him with his presumption in deciding matters pertaining to religion without consulting him. To undertake to call a Council and grant other concessions in virtue of the imperial will was to encroach on the papal jurisdiction, to truckle to wicked rebels against the Holy See, to court the fate of Korah, Dathan, and Abiram, and other contemners of God like the Emperors Anastasius and Frederick II.,[6] etc. The letter gave Calvin the opportunity of penning some scathing criticisms of the Pope and the papal claims in a series of comments on the papal effusion.[7] His pitiless exposure of the Pope's morals are not in the best of taste. But the scandalous private life of Paul Farnese certainly invited plain speaking. The Pope reminds the Emperor of the punishment incurred by Eli in not chastising his sons. What about the Pope's sons? "Paul Farnese has a son and by him grandsons, besides bastards who still spring from the old dotard and his half-rotten carcase. What kind of person is Pier Luigi? I will say the severest of all things that can be said, and yet most true—Italy never produced

---

[6] "Admonitio Paterna Pauli III." (August 1544), "Opera," vii. 249 f. Translated by Beveridge, "Calvin's Tracts," i. 237 f.
[7] "Admonitio, etc., cum Scholis," "Opera," vii. 249 f. Translated by Beveridge, "Calvin's Tracts," i.

such a monster before ! Paul, why do you not bestir yourself ?
. . . Then what has the world long been indignantly saying
of your grandsons and of your whole family ? If Eli was
punished for indulgence, will you pass with impunity when
you not only in silence connive at the horrid crimes of your
sons, but lend them a helping hand ? . . . But now more
than enough of actual sons. You give out that you are the
father of all Christians. In the deplorable corruption of the
world, is there any room for taciturnity ? You are silent,
though you know and with your own eyes see that the world
is rushing to destruction. If God did not spare Eli, what
punishment, think you, is impending over yourself ? I come
nearer home. In what state is your See ? What Sodom will
you find for me where there ever was greater impunity for
all kinds of evil ? . . . And now, just as if you had nothing
to do at home, you fear lest the wrath of God may be impending
over your head for this one fault—if you silently allow peace
and equality of rights to be conceded to the Protestants, until
the question of religion shall be discussed, if you tolerate
Cæsar in promising, without your order, a Council as well as
a legitimate determination of the cause." [8] From this introduction he proceeds to traverse the papal contentions and
claims and the papal reading of history and Scripture in support
of them, and in conclusion bids him awake to the fact that
men are now living in another age than that of papal absolutism,
and that the Emperor will not allow himself to violate his
word like another Sigismund at the behest of a perfidious
Farnese.

Exposure of Relic Mania

In a more popular and sarcastic vein he rallies the Roman
Church on its ridiculous relic mania in the form of an "Address
showing the Advantages which Christendom might derive
from an Inventory of Relics." [9] The practice, he shows, has
resulted in gross superstition and cheatery, downright idolatry,
the perversion of the religious instinct. It is against these
abuses, not the sentiment of reverence in itself for the memorials

---

[8] " Latin Tracts," i. 257 f.
[9] " Advertisement très utile, etc." Also known as " Traité des Reliques,"
vi. 405 f. (1543). Eng. trans., " Calvin's Tracts," i.

of the dead, that he directs the shafts of a biting ridicule. In order to expose completely the crass ignorance, the stupidity, the lying and deception on which this superstition thrives, it would be necessary to make an inventory of all the relics of Christendom, which is impossible. But even the most partial inventory may suffice to discredit the wretched business. It would, for instance, reveal the fact that the same relic is possessed by several churches. The foreskin of Christ is, for example, to be found at Charrons in the diocese of Poitiers, and is nevertheless shown at the Lateran Church in Rome. The blood of Christ is shown in at least a hundred churches—in some in drops, in others in phials, in others in goblets. So in regard to many other articles supposed to be relics of Christ—His cradle, the vessels containing the water made into wine, His shoes, His garments, the table at which He ate the last Supper, the cup, the towel with which He dried the apostles' feet, etc. These are more or less ubiquitous, although for hundreds of years after He lived no one ever heard of them, until they were invented and passed off on a credulous and ignorant people. In this querulous and ironic strain he passes in review the fabrications purporting to be relics of the virgin, of the angel Michael, of Joseph, of John the Baptist, of the apostles, some of the notable saints. Those who think of Calvin only as the austere reformer and the terribly logical theologian should read this biting philippic, if they would realise what a master of sarcasm and even of humour of the blistering sort lurked beneath the puritan moralist and the abstruse exponent of the theory of original sin and predestination. One cannot help wondering how, after this exposure, the Roman Catholics could still have the courage to palm off the contents of this vast ecclesiastical museum as genuine articles, and not rather consign them to the rubbish heap. Calvin thinks it was because God had blinded them in order to punish them for their incredible stupidity and rascality. Of the stupidity at any rate there can be no doubt.

CALVIN ON THE COUNCIL OF TRENT

The decrees of the Council which at last met at Trent in December 1545, and sat till March 1547, gave him an opportunity of once more entering the lists in defence of the Reformed cause. These decrees related to the rule of faith, the equal validity of Scripture and tradition, as sources of doctrine, and the infallibility of the Vulgate, original sin, free will, justification, the sacraments, and ecclesiastical reform. These Calvin subjected to a lengthy criticism in an attack entitled, " The Decrees of the Council of Trent, with the Antidote." [10] The address with which the papal legates, who presided in place of the Pope, opened the Council and in which they not only confess the gravity of the abuses rampant in the Church, but place the responsibility for them on the Church itself, seems to give the case away in favour of the Reformers. At last, cries Calvin, the culprit candidly confesses his sins. But he refuses to believe in the honesty of the confession and he was not far wrong. The Pope and the curial party at least were strongly opposed to any adequate practical reform and were resolved to make no concession to the Reformers in the matter of doctrinal reform. The Council, in fact, whilst enacting a few reform measures, reaffirmed the Roman doctrines on the subjects discussed, which Calvin refutes from the orthodox Protestant point of view. He denies at the outset the claim of the Council to represent the Church and to pass decrees in its name, and in view of the meagre attendance his denial was well founded. Neither in numbers, nor in ability, nor in influence were its members, consisting chiefly of obscure and dependent Italian bishops, entitled to legislate the mind even of the Roman Catholic Church, let alone the Church of the Reformers. For the latter their acts could not possibly have the validity which the Pope vainly sought to impart to them by according his ratification, and Calvin's powerful attack materially contributed to deprive them of any chance they had of settling the controversy in favour of Rome. He has, for instance, no difficulty in showing that the Vulgate version, which is declared to be the only authentic and authoritative one, teems with errors, and disposing of these would-be monopolists of the Holy Spirit as obscurantists, who wilfully shut their eyes to the light, claim for the Church the sole right of interpretation, and set its imprimatur on ignorance and absurdity.

[10] " Acta Synodi Tridentinæ cum Antidoto " (1547), vii. 371 f. ; " Calvin's Tracts," ii. 18 f.

DENOUNCES THE AUGSBURG INTERIM

He was equally hostile to the Augsburg Interim (May 1548), by which Charles attempted, in spite of the Pope and his skeleton Council, now assembled at Bologna, to settle, temporarily at least, the Reform conflict as far as Germany was concerned. This compromise appeared to Calvin and to all staunch Protestants who would not follow the pliant Melanchthon, merely political patchwork. He therefore lost no time in upholding the evangelical faith in a work in which he first gave the text of the obnoxious Interim and then set forth " The True Method of Reforming the Church and Healing its Dissensions." [11] He treats the Interim as an adulteration of the pure doctrine of Christ, shows why this is so by refuting the arguments adduced in support of this compromise in doctrine and usage, and denounces the attempt to secure peace by the sacrifice of what he holds to be the truth. The Interim is a specious pacification which leaves us only a half Christ and, by falsifying every part of His teaching, can only lead to the ultimate undoing of the Reformation. That he refuses to yield a jot or tittle in the matter of such doctrines as free will and justification, etc., is, of course, a foregone conclusion. He is here, as in his other doctrinal writings, the confirmed dogmatist, to whom it is impossible to agree to differ. To the moderate mind he may seem unreasonably tenacious. But a compromise that retained the Roman Catholic rites, including the worship of the virgin and the saints and the Roman sacraments, reaffirmed the dogma of transubstantiation and the papal jurisdiction, was a real menace to the Reformation as an emancipation movement. He was amply justified in refusing unity and peace at such a price. After this onslaught the Interim had no chance of acceptance in the Reformed Churches outside Germany, and even in Germany it proved an ultimate failure.

[11] " Interim Adultero-Germanicum," etc. (1549), " Opera," v. 549 f. ; " Calvin's Tracts," iii. 190 f.

CHAPTER XIII

MEDIATOR BETWEEN THE REFORMED CHURCHES

CONCILIATORY ATTITUDE TOWARDS LUTHERANS

HIS contribution as the champion of the Reformation against its Romanist opponents is only one side of Calvin's international activity. Scarcely less prominent is the part which he played as mediator in the controversies of the Reformed Churches for the purpose of assuring their unity in the essentials of the faith. The best defence of the Reformed cause was to weld the ranks of its adherents into a united force against the enemy, and this union he strove, as far as his own dogmatic convictions would allow, to further. On the occasion of his visit to the Conferences at Frankfurt, Hagenau, Worms, and Ratisbon in 1539-41 he endeavoured to mediate a better understanding between the Lutheran and the Swiss and South German Reformers on the crucial question of the Lord's Supper, and on ceremonies and discipline. He and Melanchthon became friends at once when they met at Frankfurt in 1539, and the friendship increased with each subsequent conference. Melanchthon had no hesitation in assenting to a number of articles on the Supper, which he had previously sent him, whilst confessing that some of his fellow-theologians were obstinately addicted to the grosser conception of the real presence. Though doubtful of the possibility of a closer concord, he was desirous that this partial concord should be nurtured until it might please God to lead both sides to complete unity. In regard to discipline Calvin found the Lutheran Churches greatly lacking from his more puritan standpoint, and in its worship too many elements savouring of Judaism. Melanchthon admitted that the Lutherans had retained too many of the old rites and hoped that they would gradually be diminished, though he was reluctant to enter on the discussion

188

of the question.[1] On the other hand, Calvin endeavoured to disarm the suspicion which Farel, Zebedee, and others of his Swiss colleagues entertained of Melanchthon and also of Bucer, whom they accused of too great latitude on the matter of the Lutheran ceremonies. Difference on such points, he told Farel, was no sufficient cause for fanning dissension.[2] The Lutheran League of Schmalkald, he added, has resisted the attempt of the papal legate to fan discord between it and the Swiss Reformers. Its leaders have told the legate plainly that they are in fraternal communion with those whom he calls Sacramentarians.[3] He rebukes the sectarian spirit of Zebedee, a zealous Zwinglian, who was agitating against Bucer and the Lutheran theologians. These recriminations in an extreme spirit only injure the Reformed cause and are unjust to men who are rendering such effective service to it. Difference of opinion on such points should not be allowed to break the bond of brotherly union with those who are working with us in a common cause.[4] In the same tone he writes to another Swiss minister, Du Bois, who was disturbing the peace of the Swiss Churches by his exaggerated defence of the Lutheran doctrine against the Zwinglians.[5] Bullinger, Zwingli's successor, was also, it appears, not too keen to hold out the hand of fellowship to Luther, and protested against the assumption that when Luther has spoken, no one may open his mouth to contradict him. He would have nothing to do with a concord of which this was a condition. Luther is only a man, liable to err and ought to be told so.[6] He was, too, accused of harbouring ill-feeling towards Bucer and the Strassburg theologians on account of their pliancy to Luther.[7] To him also Calvin addressed an epistle in reference to these reports in favour of conciliation and mutual understanding.[8]

To those who are acquainted with his own polemics against opponents the rôle of conciliator must appear rather surprising. From this point of view, the friendship with Melanchthon, who was no longer so sound as he had been on the question of

---

[1] See letters to Farel, " Opera," x[b]. 330 f.; Herminjard, " Correspondance des Réformateurs," v. and vi.

[2] " Opera," x[b]. 341.

[3] *Ibid.*, x[b]. 341 f.

[4] *Ibid.*, x[b]. 344 f.

[5] *Ibid.*, x[b]. 444 f.

[6] *Ibid.*, x[b]. 322.

[7] Doumergue, " Calvin," ii. 543.

[8] " Opera," xi. 27 f.

predestination, is also somewhat of a mystery. His prestige as a scholar and a Reformer and his affectionate appreciation of his younger colleague doubtless influenced his judgment. Still more decisive was the consciousness of the necessity of unity, compatible with the maintenance of what he deemed essentials, if the Reformed cause was to prevail. In this he certainly showed a grasp of the right policy, and his conciliatory attitude, as far as it goes, is altogether to his credit. In the interest of this conciliatory policy he even signed the Augsburg Confession at Ratisbon after Melanchthon had modified the article on the Supper.[9] He published a French translation of Melanchthon's "Loci Communes" with a commendatory preface [10] in 1546, though it contained a view of free will and predestination different from his own. To agree to tolerate dissent from his pet doctrine was, indeed, in view of his rabid intolerance on this point within his own sphere at Geneva, a signal testimony of his self-sacrifice for the sake of unity. To bless where it was usual for him to curse was a rare tribute alike to the depth of his friendship and his sense of the imperative necessity of agreeing to differ for the sake of conciliation.

Unfortunately on Luther himself, who in his later years renewed the controversy with the Zwinglians over the sacramental question in his fiercest vein, he was able to exercise little influence in favour of conciliation. He never met him and he only wrote him one letter about a year before his death, which he never received. Luther was even more intolerant on the question of the real presence than Calvin on the question of free will and predestination. In 1544 he wrote a "Short Confession on the Supper" in which he abusively denounced the Sacramentarians. The effusion caused the keenest pain to both Melanchthon and Calvin, and Calvin seems to have given him up as hopeless.[11] "With what fury is your Pericles carried away in thus giving vein to his tendency to fulminate, especially since his cause is not the better one. And what does he effect by storming in this fashion except that the whole world judges him to be mad ? I am thoroughly ashamed of

[9] See Schaff, " Swiss Reformation," ii. 665 f.
[10] " Opera," ix. 847 f.
[11] See Letter to Melanchthon, " Opera," xii. 98 f.

one whom I venerate with all my heart.   And the worst of it
is that no one dares to stand up against such violence, or even
to mutter a word against it.   We all, I confess, owe much to
him. . . . But we ought to see to it in the Church that we
do not defer too much to men." Of Calvin's own doctrine
he seems to have expressed his appreciation, and of Calvin
himself he spoke highly on various occasions.[12]   He even seems
to have repented shortly before his death of his rabid treatment
of the question and to have recognised in Calvin the man
fitted to bring about an accommodation.   " He is certainly a
learned and pious man," he remarked to the Wittenberg
bookseller Goltsch, on perusing in his shop in April 1545 the
Latin translation of his tract on the Supper.   " If Oecolampadius
and Zwingli had expressed themselves thus at the outset, we
should never have been in so long a controversy." [13]

Luther's irreconcilable polemics were continued after his
death, from 1552 onwards, by his fanatic followers Westphal,
pastor at Hamburg, and Hesshusius, the General Superintendent
of the Lutheran Church in the Rhine palatinate.   With them
Calvin maintained a long and heated controversy in favour of
his own mediating conception of the Supper.[14]   Unfortunately
it only resulted in a permanent schism between the Lutheran
and the Reformed Churches.   But if he failed to convert the
zealots who attacked the Philippists, as the more moderate
Lutherans who followed Melanchthon, were called, he at
least succeeded in winning over the palatinate, Hesse, Bremen,
Anhalt to the Reformed doctrine.

OTHER CONCILIATORY ENDEAVOURS

Equally unfortunate was the attempt to negotiate an understanding between the ultra-Lutherans and the French congregation at Frankfurt during a second visit to the city, which he
undertook for this purpose in 1556.   He had a special interest
in this congregation, which largely consisted of the French

---

[12] See, for instance, his appreciation of his " Epistle to Sadolet," " Opera,"
x[b]. 402.
[13] See Doumergue, ii. 573.   On his later polemic against the Sacramentarians, see my " Luther and the Reformation," iv. 179 f.
[14] See his various writings against them in " Opera," ix.   A good account
of this controversy is given by Schaff, ii. 659 f.

refugees to whom he had ministered at Strassburg and whose refusal to accept the Interim had driven to seek an asylum in England. The accession of Queen Mary forced them to leave England in search of a new refuge on the Continent. This they ultimately found at Frankfurt, where the Council assigned them and their pastor Pullain a church for worship in April 1554. Internal dissension and quarrels with the Lutheran pastors threatened to end in its dissolution, and Calvin obtained from the Genevan Council permission to repair thither on a mission of conciliation in the late summer of 1556.[15] He found it impossible to abate the implacable violence of the Lutheran preachers towards his French brethren. They denounced them, he wrote, in language more hostile and furious than if they were Jews or papists.[16] They refused to meet him in conference, and at their instigation the Council would not allow him to preach even to the French congregation. They refused his request to be allowed to bid them good-bye. By a lucky chance he encountered them the day before his departure on the 24th September at the door of the Town Hall (the Römer), and took his revenge by saluting them in the most friendly manner and giving them his blessing [17] ! As far as accommodation with the Lutherans was concerned, his mission was a failure, and in spite of repeated appeals on behalf of concord, which he wrote from Geneva in the following years, the Council ultimately, in 1563, decreed that the refugees should accept both the Wittenberg Formula of Concord and the Augsburg Confession and adopt the Lutheran rite in the celebration of the Supper.

Not much more successful was his effort to allay the dissension which had broken out in the congregation of English refugees at Frankfurt over the question of the unmodified use of the English Prayer Book. On this question the party, led by John Knox, whom the refugees had called from Geneva as one of their ministers in October 1554,[18] had quarrelled with

---

[15] " Opera," xxi. 645 f.
[16] Letter to Wolmar, " Opera," xvi. 284.
[17] " Opera," xvi. 319 f.
[18] Knox's " Works," iv. 12 f., which gives the story of the dissension at Frankfurt under the title " A Brief Discourse of the Troubles begoune at Franckford, A.D. 1554 " (1575), doubtfully attributed to Whittingham. It is also given in enlarged form in " Phenix," ii. 44 f. See also Colligan, " Whittingham," 35 f.

that led by Richard Cox, and the quarrel had resulted in Knox's exile by the Frankfurt magistrates at the instigation of the latter party and his return to Geneva in the spring of 1555. Both parties appealed to Calvin, and in a letter written from Geneva in February of this year he urged them to come to an understanding on the basis of mutual concessions. In his opinion there were many things in the English liturgy that were not advisable from the standpoint of purity of worship. But they were not of such fundamental importance that they could not be tolerated meanwhile, and he counselled, on practical grounds, a gradual amelioration. He condemned both the obstinacy of those who were, on principle or by prejudice, opposed to change and the extreme zeal of those who were eager to enforce forthwith their puritan views. His sympathies were, however, more with the contentions of the latter than with those of the former party, and he keenly resented the treatment of Knox, albeit Knox was not a very judicious controversialist and was not an easy man to negotiate an amicable arrangement with on the basis of take and give. He had, moreover, himself partly to blame for his dismissal from Frankfurt by his rash aspersion of the Emperor in his " Faithful Admonition to the Professors of God's Truth in England," which made it very risky for the Frankfurt authorities to harbour him in their midst. In reply to Calvin, Cox reminded him that he and his party had made considerable concessions in the matter of ceremonies, such as kneeling at Communion, the surplice, crosses, and other things " in their own nature indifferent." [19] Calvin retorted that crosses, candles, and such trifles savoured of superstition, and failed to see why Cox and his friends should persist in burdening their fellow-Christians with such trifling and unprofitable dregs of popery. He charged them, too, with their underhand and unbrotherly treatment of Knox and again counselled moderation. [20] In response the Coxian party explained and defended their action against Knox, whose extremist effusion against Queen Mary and the Emperor had gravely endangered his brethren as well as himself, and finished by telling Calvin to mind his own business. [21]

[19] Knox's " Works," iv. 55 f.
[20] " Opera," xv. 628 f.   [21] Knox's " Works," iv. 62 f.

Archbishop Cranmer's project of a synod of the representatives of the Reformed Churches to negotiate a common doctrinal agreement, as an offset to the Council of Trent, evoked his whole-hearted approval. In response to Cranmer's letter on the subject,[22] he deplored the doctrinal division within the Reformed ranks and declared his readiness " to cross ten seas " if necessary in order to serve the cause of union and heal the bleeding body of Christ, which this division has lacerated.[23] He was even prepared to accept the episcopate in the modified form of a superintendence, whilst ruling out the hierarchical conception of apostolic succession.[24] Unfortunately the project did not get beyond the stage of a pious wish. On the other hand, he had the satisfaction, in 1549, of negotiating with Bullinger an agreement which harmonised the Churches of Geneva and Zürich, and erelong of the whole of Protestant Switzerland, except Bern, on the question of the Lord's Supper (*Consensus Tigurinus*). The way for this harmony had already been prepared in the First Helvetic Confession of Faith which Bullinger and Myconius, along with Bucer and Capito of Strassburg, had drawn up in 1536 for the Swiss Churches, and in which the Zwinglian doctrine was already modified in the direction of the more developed Calvinist view.

[22] " Opera," xiv. 306.
[23] *Ibid.*, xiv. 312 (April 1552).
[24] Choisy, " Calvin et l'Union des Églises," *Bulletin de la Soc. de l'Hist. du Prot. Français*, 1935, 87. See also Pannier, " Calvin et l'Episcopat," " Revue d'Histoire et de Philosophie Religieuse de l'Univ. de Strasbourg," 1926.

CHAPTER XIV

DIRECTOR OF THE EVANGELICAL MISSION

GENEVA CENTRE OF MILITANT EVANGELISM

THE services thus rendered by Calvin as controversialist and conciliator to the Reformed cause were enhanced by his activity as the inspirer and director of its missionary activity. Under his auspices Geneva not only became the city of refuge *par excellence* for the persecuted of many lands. He transformed it into the headquarters of a powerful missionary activity. Geneva, in fact, ultimately superseded Wittenberg as the centre of militant evangelism. " Calvin," says Holl, " did much more than the German Reformers for the general interest of Protestantism. His intervention signified everywhere two things—decision and organisation. Thereby he rescued the Reformation from running to sand. Protestantism owes to him, outside Germany and the northern lands, its maintenance and extension." [1] In his correspondence he appears as a sort of universal mission bishop inspiring and directing the evangelical mission throughout a large part of Europe. In furtherance of the Gospel he addresses missives or deliverances which read like encyclicas. Witness that on " Offences," inscribed to his friend, Laurent de Normandie, in which he strove to confirm the faith of the adherents of the Reformation and increase their number against the scepticism of radical humanists like Dolet and Rabelais, as well as the slanders of the Romanists.[2] A critic of the Calvinist régime is accused by the Consistory, in 1561, of saying that Geneva had become a second Rome and Calvin the idol of the Protestants.[3] The remark, though made in an ill-natured spirit, was not far from

[1] " Aufsätze," iii. 273.
[2] " De Scandalis," " Opera," viii. 6 f. ; latest edition of the French version by Schmidt, " Trois Traités," 149 f. (1934).
[3] " Opera," xxi. 752.

the truth. The Register of the Venerable Company contains many notices of the sending forth of pastors and evangelists for the nascent Reformed Churches of France and other lands, and of the active interest of Calvin and his fellow-ministers in this work.[4] The founding of the academy was in part actuated by the desire to provide a supply of trained evangelical missionaries. Even some years before its foundation the requests for ministers from the French churches are considerable. After it they begin to multiply in a remarkable degree and their increase must have been a gratifying evidence of the substantial spread of the movement over a large part of France. These requests come from Paris, Blois, Tours, Rouen, La Rochelle, Aix-en-Provence, Bordeaux, Bergerac, Aube, Havre, Dieppe, Caen, Nerac, Chateauroux, Villefranche, Tarascon, Valence, Nantes, Chatellerault, Montpellier, Angoulême, Libourne, Angers, Orange, Nismes, and many other places. On one day, 6th September 1557, as many as five such requests are dealt with. On another—13th July 1559—as many as six, and six more on the 28th August of the same year.[5] Cities like Paris, Tours, Poitiers, Cognac, Libourne, Nismes, even find it necessary to ask for additional ministers,[6] and letters arrive with encouraging accounts of the progress of the mission.[7] So great is the demand that Calvin is at times at his wits' end to comply with it.[8] In addition to these mission pastors, members of the Venerable Company are occasionally commissioned to proceed to Paris and other places to encourage and strengthen the Reformed congregations. Des Gallars, Morel, Machard, for instance, are dispatched on such a commission to Paris.[9] Requests come from lands beyond France—from Piedmont and from England. In April 1560 Des Gallars is accordingly deputed to reform and sustain the churches in England which have united in this petition.[10] Charles IX. was amply justified in ascribing, in a missive to the Genevan Council in January 1561, the religious upheaval in France to the activity of the

---

[4] See, for instance, " Opera," xxi. 681 f.
[5] " Opera," xxi. 674, 718, 720. In addition to the increasing notices in the Registers from 1556 onwards see " Histoire Ecclesiastique," i. 134, 160, 235, 244 f.
[6] " Opera," xxi. 662, 666, 745, 771.
[7] Ibid., xxi. 742 f., 747, 751.
[8] Ibid., xxi. 772.
[9] Ibid., xxi. 672-673, 709.
[10] Ibid., xxi. 730 f.

preachers sent from Geneva to propagate the Reformed faith. These preachers, he complained, not only steal from house to house sowing diversity of opinion in religion. They dare to preach to large assemblies of his subjects and scatter broadcast a mass of seditious literature to the great peril of the State. He therefore demands that the Council shall recall these seditious emissaries and forbid such missions for the future, under threat of hostilities in case of refusal.[11] Calvin and his fellow-ministers could not deny the fact of these missions in France,[12] and the Council, whilst professing ignorance of them, admitted that, in reply to questions, the ministers have confessed that they have commissioned some preachers to spread the Gospel in France in the interest of true religion. But, it adds, they emphatically deny that they have attempted to seduce his subjects from their allegiance, and they have striven to discourage all seditious enterprises. It certainly was the case that Calvin had opposed the Amboise conspiracy, and the assurance of the innocence of both the Council and the ministers of any political motive in connection with the propaganda was honestly meant. Whilst also disclaiming any such intention for the future, the Council does not explicitly undertake to prevent the continuance of this activity.[13] As a matter of fact, as the Registers show, the mission continued as before, though Calvin expressly undertook to conduct the business of supply without the cognisance of the Council " in order to exonerate it in future from the charge of sending ministers to France." [14] In August 1563 a deputation of the French ministers visited Geneva for the purpose of formally thanking the Council for all the benefits which, by its protection of the persecuted and its active interest in the cause of the Gospel, it has conferred on the French Church.[15]

INTERNATIONAL PROPAGANDA

Calvin showed his active interest in the spread of the Reformed faith not only by training and sending forth an ever-increasing band of missionaries. He laboured successfully to

[11] " Opera," xviii. 337 f.
[12] Ibid., xxi. 742.
[13] Ibid., xviii. 343 f.

[14] Ibid., xxi. 753.
[15] Ibid., xxi. 807.

further it by means of a vast correspondence with its leaders in Central and Western Europe—in France, England, Scotland, the Netherlands, Germany, Denmark, Sweden, Poland. During the progress of the movement in England in the reign of Edward VI. he appears in close co-operation, through his letters, with Somerset and Cranmer, and seeks to fan the zeal of the young King himself. In October 1548 he exhorts Somerset to proceed with the work of establishing the true religion, in spite of the difficulties and afflictions that beset him, and enlarges on the means to this end—the instruction of the people in pure doctrine, the extirpation of abuses, and the repression of all manner of vice. He tells him in characteristic fashion that the opponents of the Reformation, whether adherents of Antichrist or Protestant Radicals (*gens fantastiques*), ought to be repressed by the sword as rebels against God ! This grim exhortation contrasts strangely with the pleas for toleration which he put forth for his persecuted brethren in France and other lands, and is a very ugly feature of his missionary zeal in the cause of the pure Gospel.[16] In another epistle, written two years later, he urges him to secure an effective ministry by checking the misappropriation of university and ecclesiastical funds. Unfortunately Somerset was himself deeply involved in the policy of spoliation and was besides no longer in power.[17] To Edward himself he dedicates his Commentaries on Isaiah and on the Catholic Epistles, and sends his exposition of Psalm 87.[18] In the dedication of his Isaiah he holds up as models for his imitation the pious kings of Israel, exposes the corruption of Christianity by the Roman Antichrist, and summons him to take a lead in the work of restoring its purity.[19] In that of the Catholic Epistles he fulminates against the Council of Trent, warns him against too great indulgence in the matter of ecclesiastical usages, such as the intercession of the saints, which obscure the clarity of the Gospel, and emphasises the necessity of taking measures to prevent the funds of the universities from being spent on those who make no secret of their hostility to the pure Gospel.[20] In sending his exposition of Psalm 87 in the following year

[16] " Opera," xiii. 65 f.   [17] *Ibid.*, xiv. 155 f. (July 1551).
[18] He sent Des Gallars to present these Commentaries.
[19] " Opera," xiii. 669 f. (January 1551).
[20] *Ibid.*, xiv. 30 f.

(July 1552) he impresses on him anew the duty and privilege
of using his office for the advancement of the kingdom of
Christ, and reminds him of the danger which kings and princes
run of forgetting this kingdom in the pursuit of earthly power
and pleasure. "The recognition of the many special benefits
which you have received from God's infinite goodness ought
to incite you to employ all your powers in His honour and
service, giving an example to your subjects in doing homage
to the great King, to whom your majesty is not ashamed
to subject yourself in all humility and reverence under the
spiritual sceptre of His Gospel." [21]

He was not satisfied with the gradual progress of Cranmer
in the work of reformation, and in 1550 urged him to greater
zeal and more radical measures. He recognises, indeed, that
much has been accomplished in the previous three years. But
the residuum of superstition is all too great, and he tells him
that religion will never flourish until the English Church is
better provided with suitable pastors for the preaching of the
pure Gospel, and until a stop is put to the scandalous spoliation
of its revenues. He greatly fears that, with his advancing
years, the cold of a perpetual winter will set in after the
autumns have been allowed to pass in procrastination.[22] He
was evidently insufficiently acquainted with the difficulties of
Cranmer's position. England was not Geneva, and if it took
Calvin nearly fifteen years of conflict to establish his theocratic
rule over a small republic, he might well have adopted a
less impatient tone in criticising the progress of the English
Reformation. Cranmer was moving as fast as the difficult
situation in which he was placed would allow. His pace,
under Northumberland's auspices and with the aid of Peter
Martyr and other refugee theologians, had, in fact, become too
fast for the bulk of the nation to follow, as the insurrections of
Edward's reign and the reaction that followed it amply prove.
The Second Prayer Book and the Forty-two Articles reveal
this imprudent acceleration, and Calvin is found in 1552
congratulating him on his "auspicious" and splendid zeal
and, as we have seen, cordially supporting his plan of an
International Council of the Reformed Churches in opposition

[21] "Opera," xiv. 341 f.
[22] Ibid., xiii. 682 f.

to the Council of Trent.[23] In the Vestiarian controversy
which the puritan Bishop Hooper raised in 1551 he even advised
moderation, and urged him not to stickle over such trifles as
cap and vestments.[24] After the tragic reaction of the reign of
Queen Mary, he renewed his efforts to stimulate the English
Reformation. He dedicated the second edition of his " Commentary on Isaiah " to Queen Elizabeth, and in congratulating
her on her escape from the tyranny of the late reign and on her
accession, exhorted her to follow the footsteps of her deceased
brother in restoring true religion.[25] His dedication met with
no gracious reception. Elizabeth, who resented Knox's
" Blast " against her sex, assumed that the obnoxious effusion
had been published with Calvin's approbation and expressed
her dissatisfaction to his messenger in no kindly terms. He
wrote to Cecil disclaiming any knowledge of or responsibility
for the publication of the work and dissenting from its thesis.[26]
He did not, however, succeed in overcoming the dislike of the
Queen to the Genevan system of ecclesiastical government and
discipline, and though he continued to exercise an influence
on the development of the English Reformation through the
returned English refugees, and entered into correspondence
with Grindal and other English Churchmen,[27] he lost the
chance of modelling the government and usages, if not the
doctrine, of the English Reformation after the pattern of
Geneva.

On the other hand, he exercised through Knox a decisive
influence on the establishment of the Scottish Reformation.
It was to Calvin that the Lords of the Congregation appealed in
1558 to use his authority to move Knox to return and co-operate
with them in the aggressive movement, which eventuated two
years later in the overthrow of the Roman Church in Scotland.[28]
It was on the Calvinist model in government and worship as
well as doctrine that the Scottish Church was organised. He

[23] " Opera," xiv. 312 f.
[24] Letter to Bullinger, " Opera," xiv. 74 f. (March 1551).
[25] " Opera," xvii. 413 f.
[26] Ibid., xvii. 490 f. ; cf. Knox's " Works," iv. 356 f.
[27] See, for instance, " Opera," xviii. 87 f. His influence on the doctrine
of the Anglican Church appears in the relatively mild Calvinist character
of the doctrines of election and predestination as set forth in the " Forty-
two Articles," subsequently reduced to Thirty-nine. See Curtis, " History
of Creeds and Confessions," 176, 182 (1911).
[28] Knox's " Works," i. 274.

rejoiced in the extraordinary success of Knox's leadership, but found it necessary in 1561 to caution him against an excessive rigour in the matter of ceremonies. Care is to be taken to purge the Church from all defilements which have flowed from error and superstition, and especially that the mysteries of God be not polluted with ridiculous and insipid mixtures. But, with this exception, certain things are to be tolerated even if they may not be approved.[29] He also sought to direct the movement through his correspondence with Moray and Hamilton, Duke of Chatellerault.

To King Christian of Denmark he dedicated the first part of his " Commentary on the Acts of the Apostles " in 1552, and to his son Frederick the second part in 1554, with the object of stimulating their zeal against Romanism.[30] The friction with the Lutherans over the sacramental question frustrated further overtures in this direction, as also in Sweden, to whose king, Gustavus Vasa, he dedicated his "Minor Prophets." [31] In August 1560 he rededicated the revised edition of the " Commentary on the Acts " to Prince Radzivil in the hope of strengthening the Reformed movement in Poland.   Through him [32] he strove to influence the Polish king, Sigismund II., to whom he had already in 1549 inscribed his " Commentary on the Epistle to the Hebrews." [33] The way for the spread of the movement in Poland had been paved by the tolerant spirit which recognised the rights of the Greek Church in the Lithuanian half of the kingdom and welcomed Hussite and Jewish refugees from Bohemia and Germany. It had already made substantial progress in the reign of Sigismund's father, Sigismund I. The influence of Luther's teaching and the activity of the Bohemian Brethren swelled the number of its adherents, and many Polish students who repaired to Wittenberg, Strassburg, Zürich, and later Geneva returned as its zealous emissaries. The national antagonism of the Poles to the Germans favoured the growth of Calvin's influence at the expense of that of Luther. Both the political and the religious situation thus contributed to secure for his overtures to Sigismund a sym-

---

[29] " Opera," xviii. 433 f.   On Calvin in relation to Knox see the monograph of Mezger, " John Knox et ses Rapports avec Calvin " (1905).
[30] " Opera," xiv. 292 f. ; xv. 14 f.
[31] *Ibid.*, xvii. 445 f.
[32] *Ibid.*, xv. 428 f. (Feb. 1555).   [33] *Ibid.*, xiii. 281 f.

pathetic reception. The king was disposed to favour the movement to the extent at least of a reformation of practical abuses, whilst Prince Radzivil and many of the leading nobles were eager to establish the evangelical faith. Calvin took advantage of this promising situation to advocate the cause of the Reformation in a second appeal to the king himself in December 1554. The letter is a remarkable evidence of the liberality in the matter of Church government which he could display on occasion in order thereby to advance this cause. Whilst combating the claim of the Pope and the hierarchy to divine jurisdiction over the Church, he was ready to recognise, as in the case of the English Church, the patriarchal and episcopal system of government as suitable for a large kingdom like Poland and as conforming to the development of the ancient Church. "The ancient Church established patriarchates and set primates over separate provinces in order, by this means, the better to bind the bishops in concord. In the same manner it is right that to-day one archbishop should preside over the illustrious kingdom of Poland, not indeed that he should dominate others or arrogate to himself an authority filched from them, but that for the sake of order he should hold the first place in synods and nurture a holy unity among his colleagues. Similarly there might be bishops of cities and provinces for the purpose of preserving order, as circumstances require, and one elected by his colleagues should be charged with this duty on the occasion of episcopal assemblies. But it is a very different thing to confer on a man a moderate dignity of this kind, in accordance with the powers which it involves, from investing in one man an immense dominion over the whole earth. Entirely worthless, therefore, is the chatter of the Romanists about one supreme head. It is in accordance neither with the sacred ordinance of God nor with the sacred usage of the ancient Church." [34] He energetically kept up the crusade in a series of letters in the following year to a number of the nobles as well as the king.[35] His influence is seen in the union effected between the Calvinists and the Bohemian Brethren in Poland at a meeting held at Kozminck in 1555, which greatly strengthened the Reformed cause, and in the resolution of the Diet, convened at Petrikau in the same

[34] "Opera," xv. 332 f.   [35] See "Opera," xv. 892 f.

year, to summon a national synod for the Reformation of the Church on scriptural lines and to invite him, along with Beza, Melanchthon, Vergerio, and other leading Reformers to take part in it. The plan was frustrated by the opposition of the bishops. But the Diet in the following year, 1556, secured at least that each noble should be at liberty to decide the religious question for himself.

The movement received a great impulse from the arrival in 1556 of John à Lasco from his chequered exile in Germany, England, Friesland, and Geneva,[36] and in him and his helper, the Italian Lismannini, Calvin found a zealous champion both of the Reformed cause and of the Genevan system of doctrine and discipline. As his correspondence with them and the nobles shows,[37] he strove to widen the Protestant union so as to include the Lutherans. He was unable to accept the invitation of a number of the Polish ministers and nobles to visit their native land in the interest of the evangelical cause. But he continued to abet à Lasco, Radzivil, and their fellow-workers in this cause and encouraged à Lasco, Tricesius, and others in the work of translating the Bible into Polish. The movement suffered a great loss by the death in 1560 of à Lasco, who had been appointed superintendent of the Reformed Churches in Lesser Poland. It was hampered, too, by dissensions over the Trinitarian question, which was aggressively agitated by Blandrata, Faustus Socinus, Gentile, and Alciati, who sought a field in Poland for the propagation of their anti-Trinitarian views, and on which Calvin wrote his " Admonition to the Poles." [38] The reform movement was largely confined to the aristocracy and the middle class of the towns. It had taken no hold on the peasantry, and many of the nobles, including even Radzivil, sympathised with the anti-Trinitarians. The Jesuits were exerting themselves to fan a Romanist reaction, and before his death in 1564 Calvin had good reason to be apprehensive for the future of Polish Protestantism which the activity of the Jesuits was ultimately to blast. On the other hand,

---

[36] For à Lasco's early career in Poland and during his exile, see Dalton, " Johannes à Lasco," Eng. trans. by Evans (1886).

[37] With à Lasco, " Opera," xvi. 170 f., 263 ; with Lismannini, " Opera," xv. 913 f. ; xvi. 180 f ; with the nobles, " Opera," xvi. 674 f.

[38] " Opera," ix. 633 f. See the same volume for other writings addressed to them on this subject.

Calvinism took a firm and permanent grip on Hungary,[39] and through the activity of Olevianus, a former student of the Genevan Academy, and joint author with Ursinus of the Heidelberg Catechism (1563), gained the supremacy over Lutheranism in the palatinate. To its elector, Frederick III., an ardent Calvinist, Calvin dedicated his "Commentary on Jeremiah." [40]

MISSION TO THE NEW WORLD

Calvin even contemplated a mission to the New World on the other side of the Atlantic in connection with Coligny's scheme of settling a colony of French Protestant refugees in Brazil. This scheme, which Villegaignon attempted to realise in 1555, "gave," in the words of a contemporary historian, "a marvellous hope of advancing the kingdom of God even unto the ends of the earth." [41] Unfortunately, Villegaignon, a knight of Malta, who had risen to be Vice-Admiral of Brittany and had suggested the enterprise to Coligny, was by no means the man to carry it to a successful issue. He settled on an island in the Bay of Rio de Janeiro, to which he gave the name of Coligny, and wrote to his patron to send him ministers and more settlers. Coligny applied to Calvin, who in September 1556 entrusted the ministers Richer and Chartier with the mission.[42] Two months later (19th November) they left Honfleur with a second expedition consisting of three vessels, carrying about 300 refugees, including six young children " in order to learn the language of the country." After their arrival in March 1557 they wrote encouragingly of their reception by Villegaignon and of his zeal for the true faith. They were, however, anything but enthusiastic over the country

[39] Though Calvinism ultimately succeeded in gaining the ascendancy over Lutheranism in Hungary proper (see my " Luther and the Reformation," iv. 344), Calvin himself appears to have taken little part in the spread of the evangelical movement in this region. " Calvin s'intéressa vivement au sort de la Hongrie dès la chute de Budé aux mains des Turcs en 1541. Cependant, parmi les documents retrouvés jusqu'à present, il n'y a pas, à cette époque, trace d'intervention personelle, immediate en faveur de la Réforme hongroise. Dans la correspondance de Calvin ne figure aucune lettre écrite par lui aux Hongroises." Revesz, " L'Influence du Calvinisme sur la Réforme Hongroise," Bull. Soc. Hist. du Prot. Français, 1935, 93.

[40] " Opera," xx. 72. For Calvin's activity in greater detail as director of the Reformed cause in Europe, see Doumergue, vii. 479 f. (1927).

[41] " Hist. Ecclésiastique," i. 184.

[42] " Opera," xvi. 279.

and the natives, whose barbarism could not be worse. They differ little from the brutes, they reported, and they have no hope of winning them for Christ. Ignorance of their barbarian language is another insuperable difficulty, and the only hope of their evangelisation lies in the youths whom Villegaignon has placed under training, and by whose means they trust ultimately to be able to pursue the work of evangelisation more effectively.[43] At the same time, Villegaignon wrote to Calvin thanking him effusively for sending him the ministers and professing an ardent zeal for the spread of the true religion.[44] Richer and Chartier also wrote a glowing account of his piety and his soundness in the Reformed faith.[45]

Unfortunately, it erelong appeared that both they and Calvin had been miserably deceived by these professions. Villegaignon proved a treacherous patron of the faith which he professed. Dissension broke out between the ministers and one of the settlers, who had been a student at the Sorbonne and who objected to the celebration of the Lord's Supper after the simple reformed rite. Villegaignon took the part of the opposition, ceased attending sermon, and declared that he would have nothing to do with the Calvinist sect. At length, on the resumption of persecution in France, he prohibited the preaching of the Gospel and proclaimed his adherence to the faith as held by the Sorbonne. Chartier had already sailed for home in order to lay the contested points before the Churches of France and Germany. Richer and a number of his adherents set sail shortly after. The vessel sprung a leak a short distance from the land and three out of the five of its passengers, who returned in a small boat to beg assistance, were thrown by the merciless governor over a precipice. The others managed after terrible hardships to make the coast of Brittany. The first evangelical mission to the heathen, organised by Calvin and Coligny, thus ended in disastrous failure.[46]

[43] " Opera," xvi. 433 f.
[44] Ibid., xvi. 437 f.
[45] Ibid., xvi. 440 f.
[46] " Hist. Ecclésiastique," i. 184 f. ; Parkman, " Pioneers of France in the New World," 16 f. ; Heulhard, " Villegaignon " (1897) ; Smith, " Villegaignon " (1898).

CHAPTER XV

CALVIN AND INTERNATIONAL POLITICS

His Diplomatic Activity

In the interest of the Reformation Calvin sought to make his influence felt in international politics. To this end he laboured incessantly to cultivate the favour and goodwill or disarm the hostility of the rulers and statesmen of his age from the Emperor downwards. He was a diplomatist as well as a theologian and made ample use of the diplomatic art in the service of God, subject to the maintenance of what he deemed the truth, which permitted no compromise for the sake of mere political ends. He was careful to address those in high authority with due respect, and opposed the extremists whose zeal led them to hurl defiance at the potentates of this world. In this respect he was more judicious, one might almost say opportunist, than his bellicose friend, John Knox. Like him he never feared the face of man. But he knew better how to adopt on occasion the felicitous and politic tone needful to win support or modify opposition in the international sphere.

On Behalf of the German Reformation

As we have seen, he first appears in the rôle of ecclesiastical diplomatist on a large scale in the conferences of 1539-41 relative to the religious question in Germany. In these conferences, following in the footsteps of Zwingli and the Landgrave Philip of Hesse, he laboured to bring about a Franco-German Protestant alliance against Charles V. in the interest both of the Reformation and of France, of which he was a loyal son.[1] For this service he received the thanks of

Kampschulte, i. 331 f.; De Crue, " L'Action Politique de Calvin," 19 f. (1907); Doumergue, ii. 594 f.

Francis I., which were conveyed to him through his sister, Margaret of Angoulême, better known, through her marriage with the King of Navarre, as Margaret of Navarre. The projected alliance failed to mature, and in view of the insincerity of the profession of goodwill to the German Reformation on the part of the French king, who resumed the policy of persecution in France during the last years of his reign, its failure is not surprising. None the less, Calvin deplored the short-sightedness of the German Protestant princes in supporting the Emperor in the war with France, which broke out in 1542, and the successful conclusion of which at last brought him the opportunity of crushing the Protestant League of Schmalkald in Germany.

He had foreseen this danger to the Reformed cause in Germany, and the defeat of the Elector of Saxony and his Protestant confederates through the treachery of Duke Maurice of Saxony, which ensued in 1547, threatened to undo it even in Switzerland. The Registers of the Council record his efforts to ward off the danger by negotiations with the ministers and Governments of the Swiss Protestant Cantons for the defence of the common cause.[2] The defeat of the German Protestant princes was a sore trial to his faith and his courage. This disastrous check to the work of Luther might well have unnerved even a man of his iron will and indomitable faith. He realised the magnitude of the disaster which he had foreseen and feared. But he also read in it the divine admonition of the futility of relying on mere political expedients, mere human help in the Lord's cause, and in this conviction he penned some of his most heroic epistles to his brethren in Switzerland, France, and Germany. God, he writes to Bullinger, will not permit his elect to perish.[3] " The Lord," he writes to M. de Falais, " wills to take from us this triumphant Gospel in order to compel us to fight under the cross of Jesus Christ. Let us console ourselves that His purpose is to uphold His Church by His miraculous power, without the aid of human arm." [4] It is by spiritual arms, he tells his French brethren, that God will vindicate His cause. " True it is that to all human appearance (in view of the debacle in Germany) there seems no assurance that this will be the case. But in commending to

[2] " Opera," xxi. 398 f.   [3] Ibid., xii. 591.   [4] Ibid., xii. 552.

Him His pure Church and the kingdom of His Son, let us hope that He will lend His hand to the work beyond our expectation. . . . Remember how He has preserved His Church in time past, and doubt not that He will glorify Himself in such a fashion that we shall be astounded." [5] *Esperons et nous verrons* is the keynote of these incessant exhortations.

He did not, however, neglect human means in striving to rally the discomfited and discouraged adherents of the Reformation in Germany and elsewhere. He strove, in the interest of this cause, to renew the alliance of France and the Swiss Cantons.[6] He wrote against the Interim and severely reproached the pusillanimous Melanchthon, to whose example he ascribed the success of what he called " this deceitful deformation." The hoped-for Divine deliverance came, indeed, in the very human form of the second treachery of Maurice, who had been rewarded with the Saxon electorate, in 1552, and his alliance with Henry of France against the Emperor, whose triumph was thus frustrated in the most unexpected fashion. Henry II., who succeeded Francis in 1547, broke with the Pope over the Council of Trent, whilst he had come to terms with Calvin's patron, Edward VI. In this strange international revolution Calvin saw, as far as Germany was concerned, the star of the Reformation emerge from the cloud that had enveloped it for three dark years.

On Behalf of the Reformation in France

Unfortunately, his hope that Henry would finally abandon the policy of persecution at home was blighted by the edict of Chateaubriand in June 1551,[7] which he launched against the French Protestants at the instigation of the all-powerful Guise and Montmorency. Calvin's efforts at intercession were in vain. Henry curtly told the envoy of Zürich, through whom he attempted this intercession, to leave him to govern his kingdom as he thought fit.[8] The next half-dozen years up to the death of Henry were full of anxiety. England was lost to the

[5] " Opera," xii. 561.
[6] *Ibid.*, xiii. 266 f. ; Crue, 29 f.
[7] MacKinnon, " Growth and Decline of the French Monarchy," 163 f. (1902).
[8] Crue, 35.

Reformation for the time being. The breach with the extreme Lutherans closed a large part of Germany and the northern lands to his influence. The renewal of the struggle between France and Spain resulted in the peace of Câteau Cambrésis in April 1559, and the victories won by Duke Philibert Emmanuel of Savoy for Philip II. against Henry greatly increased the prestige and influence of the duke and seemed to portend danger to Geneva itself. The treaty of peace contained, in fact, a clause binding Philip and Henry to unite their forces for the rehabilitation of the Church at the expense of the Protestants.[9] Montmorency even proposed to the Duke of Alva to destroy Geneva, " that nest of heresy." Persecution had meanwhile continued in France, and Calvin, besides writing to the King of Navarre,[10] dispatched Farel, Beza, and Budin in September 1557 on a mission to Germany to beg the intervention of the German Protestant princes in support of a direct appeal made by an embassy of the Cantons on behalf of their French brethren.[11] Henry practically told the embassy to mind their own business. " He desired to be spared such representations, since he had never taken upon himself to lay down the law to their subjects." [12]

In view of the threatening international situation, Calvin also strove to revive the alliance between Bern and Geneva, which had been strained to the breaking point by the conflict with the Perrinists, whose cause Bern had espoused. Throughout the long and acrimonious negotiations [13] from 1556-58 he wrote many of the diplomatic documents, and it was largely due to his persistence and political ability, backed by the apprehension of the designs of the Duke of Savoy, that the negotiation was brought to a successful issue in the beginning of 1558. A few weeks after the conclusion of the Treaty of Câteau Cambrésis, the Genevese were working day and night to put the citadel of Protestantism in a state of defence against the expected attack. " All set their hands to the work," we read in a letter of Haller to Bullinger in June 1559, " magis-

[9] " Growth and Decline of the French Monarchy," 175.
[10] " Opera," xvi. 730 f.
[11] " Opera," xvi. 635 f. ; xxi. 675 f. ; xvii. 100 f. ; " Growth and Decline of the French Monarchy," 170 f.
[12] Schmidt, " La Vie et les Travaux de Jacques Sturm," 102 f. (1855).
[13] See " Opera," xxi. 630 f. ; Dunant, " Relations Politiques de Genève avec Berne et les Suisses," 151 f. (1894).

trates, ministers, nobles, people." [14]   Calvin himself is believed
to have lent a hand in the urgent enterprise,[15] whilst writing
letters of encouragement and comfort to the French churches.[16]

Despite this long-continued repression the Reformed
Church of France had steadily grown.   It was in this menacing
year that it organised itself as a national Church after the
Calvinist model of doctrine, discipline, and government,
though Calvin, who seems to have drafted its Confession of
Faith, disapproved of its proposed publication as impolitic.[17]
It already counted among its adherents or sympathisers many
of the French nobility, such as Coligny and his brother, and
even members of the French royal house itself, such as Navarre
and his brother Condé.   Through these and other influential
supporters he laboured to mitigate the intensified persecution
instigated by the Duke of Guise and his brother, the Cardinal of
Lorraine, during the short reign of Henry's son, Francis II.
(1559-60), and sent Beza once more to Germany to negotiate
the intervention of the Count Palatine.[18]   The inevitable
result of this intensified persecution was the abortive revolt
engineered by La Renaudie against the tyranny of the Guises.
The malcontents consulted Calvin, Hotman, Beza, among other
theologians and jurists, on the right of resistance to such tyranny.
Hotman and others seem to have answered in the affirmative,
on the assumption that, in case of misgovernment, the princes
of the blood were entitled to rescue the kingdom from such
tyranny.[19]   Calvin might have acquiesced if the king had
been a minor and if Navarre had expressed his willingness to
act.   But Francis was not a minor, and Navarre, unlike his
brother Condé, was not disposed to take the lead in such an
enterprise.[20]   He therefore opposed it as both illegitimate and
imprudent, and would have nothing to do with the particular
plot of La Renaudie, who attempted during a visit to Geneva
to inveigle him into compliance.   The attempt proved a
fiasco (March 1560) and brought in its train a terrible retri-

[14] " Opera," xvii. 564 f.   [15] Borgeaud, 82 f.
[16] " Opera," xvii. 570 f.
[17] *Ibid.*, xvii. 525 f. As a matter of fact the Confession was not then
published. See Doumergue, vii. 202 (1927). It is given in " Opera," ix.
731 f. Along with it the Church adopted a system of ecclesiastical polity or
" discipline." See " Hist. Ecclésiastique," i. 198 f.
[18] " Opera," xvii. 687 f. ; *cf.* xviii. 97 f.
[19] " Hist. Ecclésiastique," i. 285.   [20] Crue, 50-51.

bution on its perpetrators. It tended, too, to compromise Calvin, who was accused, without the slightest foundation, of complicity,[21] and categorically declared that he had opposed it from the outset.[22] On the other hand, he was not averse to raising a force in the southern and western provinces for the protection of Navarre and Condé against the hostile designs of the Guises. In July 1560 he sent Beza to Nérac to stir up Navarre to take action against them [23] in the interest of the welfare of the State as well as religion. The arrest and condemnation of Condé at Orleans and the virtual imprisonment of his brother confirmed his foresight in urging these precautions for their safety, which they had unwisely disregarded.

Deliverance from this new danger unexpectedly came in the death of the young king in the beginning of December 1560. In this sudden stroke Calvin saw the hand of the Lord. "There seemed," he wrote to Sturm, "no remedy for the extreme calamities in France when, suddenly, God appeared from on high, and He who had transfixed the eye of the father (Henry II.) pierced the ear of the Son." [24] His persecuted French brethren, he adds, take no pains to conceal their exultation, and even accuse him of slackness in not sharing their too sanguine hopes. Their rejoicing as well as Calvin's reference to the causes of the death of father and son was not in the best of taste, though it was natural enough. The death of the king put an end to the tyranny of the Guises and transferred the chief influence in the Government for the time being to Navarre and Condé, and the chancellor L'Hopital, as members of the Council of Regency, under Catherine de Medici, who ruled in the name of her son, Charles IX.

Calvin hastened to give them the benefit of his advice in "a memoir on the measures to be adopted by the agency of the King of Navarre in order to achieve a peaceful and equitable solution of the political and ecclesiastical difficulties" in France [25] (December 1560). In this document he demands immunity from persecution and liberty of worship for his co-religionists. To judge from the spirit that found expression

---

[21] "Opera," xviii. 70.

[22] *Ibid.*, xviii. 38 f.; *cf.* 83 f., 427.

[23] *Ibid.*, xviii. 97 f., 177 f., 204; Bohatec, "Calvin und das Recht," 174 f. (1934).

[24] "Opera," xviii. 270.

[25] *Ibid.*, xviii. 281 f.

in the States General which assembled at Orleans in the same
month, the public feeling was all in favour of religious toleration
and political reform. In the reaction from the Guise régime,
France appeared ready to take the lead in a movement in favour
of both, and under the impulsion of this reaction the Government went the length of attempting a conference between the
two religious parties in the Colloquy of Poissy (September
1561). Calvin was not expressly invited to take part in it and
had no great liking for such a compromising conference with
his Romanist antagonists. Moreover, the Genevan Council
refused to permit him to attend without the most explicit
guarantee of his safety.[26] At the request of the King of Navarre,
Beza and Peter Martyr took his place and he could rely on his
alter ego Beza to stand firmly by the Reformed doctrines. As
he expected, Beza's firmness, especially on the subject of the
Eucharist, rendered the attempt at an accommodation hopeless.
It at least gave the French Protestants the opportunity of
discussing the religious question on equal terms with their
opponents and showing their strength as an organised body.
The lesson was not without its effect on the Government
which in the Edict of St Germain accorded them a comparatively large measure of toleration (January 1562). The
reply of the Guises, who had won over the vacillating King of
Navarre, was the massacre of Vassy two months later, and the
outbreak of the first civil war between Catholic and Huguenot
in France. Calvin had no hesitation this time in supporting
the party of active resistance, whilst deploring and condemning
the excesses to which it led on the Huguenot as well as the
Catholic side. It was no longer a question of the right of
revolt against constituted authority. The massacre of Vassy
was a brutal infringement of the Edict of St Germain, and the
Huguenots, in seeking to avenge it, were, he might well argue,
vindicating the royal power as well as the true religion. He
therefore permitted Beza to remain in France in order to
further the Huguenot cause,[27] and sought to raise men and
money in Protestant Switzerland.[28] He exerted himself to
secure the help of England and Germany for Condé and Coligny,
only to discover that Condé, who consented to an unsatisfactory

26 " Opera," xxi. 754 f.
27 *Ibid.*, xxi. 773 f.   28 *Ibid.*, xxi. 785 f.

peace (Peace of Amboise, March 1563), was almost as un-reliable as his brother. To Condé he did not conceal his disappointment. " If," he wrote, " you do not make your authority felt, the peace will be but a body without a soul." [29] His hope for the future lay in Coligny, who was made of sterner stuff, in the Queen of Navarre, Jeanne D'Albret, and her son, the young Prince of Navarre, to whom he dedicated his " Commentary on Deuteronomy " in August 1563.[30]

[29] " Opera," xx. 13.   [30] *Ibid.*, 116 f.

CHAPTER XVI

CALVIN AS THEOLOGIAN

" THE INSTITUTES OF THE CHRISTIAN RELIGION "

In Calvin the scholar and thinker were combined in a rare degree with the man of action. In the early period of his activity at Geneva as preacher and organiser he had given proof of his powers as a controversialist in his defence of the Reformation against Sadolet and in his encounter with Caroli. Before he set foot in Geneva he had established his reputation as a theologian by the publication of the first edition of his " Institutes of the Christian Religion " at Basle in 1536. From 1541 onwards he was engaged in defending his distinctive teaching, particularly the doctrine of predestination, against a series of theological antagonists. In addition, he waged war with the ultra-radical reforming sects of the Spirituals and the Anabaptists and with the anti-Trinitarian Servetus. At the same time he was occupied in elaborating the *opus magnum* which won him the first place among the Reformed theologians of the century, and in which he distinctively systematised the Reformed theology. The work passed through four stages represented by the editions of 1536, 1539, 1543, and 1559, when it assumed its final form.[1] Compared with the last, the first is merely a sketch in six chapters, and the elaboration which the work underwent in the interval between 1536 and 1559 appears in the increase of the number of chapters in the final edition to eighty. Despite this elaboration, the work of 1536 contains expressly or implicitly his characteristic teaching. At the age of twenty-six Calvin had already grasped the theological system, of which the edition of 1559 is only the mature expression. Only four years earlier he had made his debut in the world of letters as an erudite scholar of the humanist type. In the

[1] There were several other editions, but these show little change.

short interval between 1532, when he published his edition of the " De Clementia," and 1536, when he sent forth the first edition of his " Institutes," he had mastered the new theology and fashioned it in the mould of his acute and powerful mind. From this point of view the " Institutes " is an extraordinary *tour de force*. In little more than three years Calvin develops from the budding humanist into the master theologian of the Reformed movement with a set of conceptions that nearly thirty years of further study will not essentially modify. The fact betokens superlative intellectual power as well as strength of conviction. M. Doumergue rightly expresses his astonishment at his " incredible precocity." [2] It reveals, too, what we may call his dogmatic faculty—the faculty of swift and intense conviction, which is impervious to change or compromise in the light of further experience or increasing knowledge. His mind is not of the progressive order that is susceptible to such influences. For him truth is not a growth—the growing result of an enlarging experience and knowledge. It is an intuition that abides and changes not. There is only elaboration, not essential development. His conceptions are for him, from the outset, imperative dogmas, in virtue of the dogmatic type as well as the strength of his mind. " In the doctrine which he taught at the beginning," says Beza, " he remained firm to the end and changed nothing, and this has happened to few theologians." [3] The question, however, remains whether this distinction had not its disadvantages, and whether even in theology it is not better to grow with increasing experience and knowledge. The question never seems to have suggested itself to Calvin, though he was long dissatisfied with the performance of his task and devoted years of intense labour to the extension and perfecting of his work. In all essentials the theology of 1559 is the theology of 1536—Calvin the infallible.

At the same time, the work, in its original and in its later form, shows the influence of other leading reformers on his thought—of Luther, Melanchthon, Bucer, Zwingli. To Luther he owes the evangelical background of his teaching. The Lutheran conception of God as omnipotent will, of His glory [4]

---

[2] " Calvin," iv. 9.　　　　[3] " Opera," xxi. 170.
[4] Seeberg, " Dogmengeschichte," iv. 152. So spielt der Gedanke der Ehre Gottes bei Luther eine kaum minder erhebliche Rolle als bei Calvin. For the subject in detail, see Storch, " Die Ehre bei Luther," " Vierteljahr-

as the chief end of men, of absolute predestination, of original
sin, of the slavery and impotence of the will, of the consequent
impossibility of meritorious works, of justification by faith
alone through the imputation of the righteousness of Christ,
of sanctification as the fruit of faith, reappears in the
" Institutes." Calvin learned much in the school of Luther,
and, unlike Zwingli, frankly acknowledged his indebtedness to
him as well as to Bucer. At the same time he is no mere echo
of Luther. While he assimilates from him and other theologians, in the working out of his theology he is his own master.
Absolute predestination in virtue of God's sovereign will
occupies the fundamental place in his thought, whereas the
" gracious God," whom Luther had long sought and at last
found in " the Gospel of Christ," stands at the centre of his.
He did not follow him in his rather free handling of the
Scriptures, or in his evaluation of the Old Testament, which
was not for him, as for Calvin, equally binding for the legal
regulation of the Christian life. As we have seen, though he
signed the Augsburg Confession he did not share his conception
of the Lord's Supper, and sided with Zwingli and the Swiss
theologians in rejecting the ubiquity of Christ's body. Nor
did he hold his view of the necessity of baptism for salvation,
whilst agreeing with him in denying any magical effect to
either sacrament, and emphasising the efficacy of faith. The
influence of Bucer appears in regard to the characteristic
doctrine of the sovereignty of God and of the Sacrament
of the Lord's Supper. " Bucer's theology," says Loofs, " is
a preliminary stage of Calvinism, into which it flowed and was
absorbed by it." [5] Zwingli's influence, on the other hand, was
more limited. In spite of the humanist sympathy which, in
his earlier period, he shared with him, he seems ultimately to
have conceived a rather depreciatory opinion of the Zürich

schrift der Luthergesellschaft," 1936, 46 f. On Luther's influence see also
Loofs, " Dogmengeschichte," 897 f. He made use in the first edition of the
" Institutes " of Luther's " Catechism " and " The Babylonian Captivity
of the Church." Lang, " Calvin," 61, 94 (1909).

[5] " Dogmengeschichte," 879. He drew upon his Commentaries on the
Four Gospels and the Epistle to the Romans in the composition of the first
edition. Lang, quoted by Doumergue, iv. 424 (1910). Butzer war der
geistliche Vater Calvins. Lang, " Zwingli und Calvin," 108 (1913). Holl,
on the other hand, questions his dependence on Bucer, and emphasises that on
Augustine and Luther, " Aufsätze," iii. 263 (1928).

Reformer, and to have made no secret of his sense of the decided superiority of Luther.[6] Like all the Reformers, he owed much to St Augustine, with whose works he shows the utmost familiarity, and whom he constantly quotes and but rarely controverts. His indebtedness to Duns Scotus in his doctrine of the absolute unconditioned will of God is a disputed point. Ritschl, Seeberg, and others affirm it. Doumergue and Warfield [7] deny it.

The " Institutes " afford ample evidence of the influence of the humanist interest in Biblical study. Calvin has learned from Erasmus, Lefèvre, and Reuchlin the method of resorting to the sources for the knowledge of original Christianity. That he was a votary of the new culture before he became a convert to the new theology is not without its significance for the Biblical character of his work, though the spirit in which he writes it is not that of the humanist,[8] but of the convinced adherent of the evangelical Reformation. He accordingly shares in the reaction against the speculative scholastic method. If he has not emancipated himself entirely from scholastic ideas, he has, in the spirit of the humanist scholar, thrown overboard the scholastic method. His interest is, in fact, not in the speculative or philosophical, but in the practical and moral side of religious thought. He has always in view the nurture of the practical religious life by means of sound doctrine, based on the Word of God. Like Erasmus, he eschews scholastic speculation, though not in the Erasmian spirit, for the study of the sacred writings, of the Word as the grand norm of the knowledge of God and the spiritual life. He is thus pre-eminently the Biblical theologian of the Reformation period. His theology is the systematised expression of the religious conceptions of the sacred writings which, in virtue of the inspiration of their authors, are absolutely authoritative and final pronouncements in matters theological. For him the fact " It is written " is sufficient to settle any point in question. His view of the Word as the infallible voice of God precluded the

[6] " Opera," xi. 24, 438. See also Lang's article on the sources of the " Institutio " in *Evangel. Quarterly*, 1936.
[7] Seeberg, " Dogmengeschichte," iv. 576 (1917) ; Doumergue, iv. 120 f. ; *cf.* 431 f. Warfield, " Calvin and Calvinism," 155 f. (1931).
[8] On his attitude to humanism see Hauser, " De L'Humanisme et De La Réforme en France," *Revue Historique*, 1897, 289 f.

free exercise of the critical faculty, though he lays stress on the
necessity of adequate grammatical and historical knowledge to
its right understanding, and would not, like the later literalists,
vouch for the accuracy of every word in the text.[9]   A scholar
trained to exercise critical insight in accordance with the higher
standard, the exacting spirit of modern historic method finds
himself at times at variance with his assumptions and
conclusions.   His theology is thus no longer authoritative
in some respects for modern thought, in consequence of a
dogmatic view of revelation, of the limitation of his knowledge
judged from that of a more scientific age, of his dogmatic
prepossessions, of the characteristic texture of his mind and
temperament.

Allowance made for the influence of others in shaping his
thought and for his limitations from the point of view of scientific
method, the " Institutes " is undoubtedly the product of a
master mind.   He works with ideas that Luther and others had
preceded him in enunciating.   But he is no mere compiler of
other men's thoughts, no mere systematiser.   Not one of them,
not even Luther, could have written the " Institutes."   He is
less mystic, more logical and lucid, more constructive than
Luther or Melanchthon.   He gives, too, at times a new content
to the ideas with which he works, and the massive, masterly,
and monumental synthesis which, in its final form, he created
shows a wealth of reasoning power, a mental strength and
acumen, a moral and spiritual elevation and earnestness that
almost merit the title of genius.

His erudition is remarkable.   He knows some of the
schoolmen and many of the Fathers, and is steeped in the
literature of classical antiquity—its philosophy as well as its
more purely literary products.   The numerous citations from
the ancient writers—Christian and non-Christian—are not
merely ornamental or far-fetched, but evidently come voluntarily
from the store of a richly filled and highly cultured mind.
Among the ancient Fathers Augustine is his supreme teacher.
But he is familiar with Chrysostom and Jerome, whom he

[9] Clavier, whilst admitting that some passages in his writings seem to
imply the literal inspiration of the Bible, quotes others to show that he is
not, as a commentator, an extreme literalist of the later type, such as Seeberg,
Wernle, Tschackert, Viénot, and O. Ritschl represent him to be.   " Études
sur le Calvinisme," 26, 81 f. (1936).

quotes profusely and often critically, with Justin Martyr, Irenæus, Tertullian, with Lactantius, Origen, Eusebius, Hilary, Ambrose, Basil, Gregory Nazianzus. He knows Plato and Aristotle, Plutarch, Cicero, Seneca, and many more. He has studied St Bernard whom, next to Augustine, he quotes oftenest, and always with approval. He has studied Aquinas and Petrus Lombardus, and he usually subjects the Master of the Sentences to trenchant criticism. He knows the Bible in the original languages by heart, and is never at a loss for texts to support his contentions or conclusions. The " Institutes " is, in fact, largely the demonstration of such texts. It is very controversial in tone. He strenuously and intolerantly controverts the ancient philosophers; the heretics ancient and modern, the scholastic doctors, and though he adopts a very contemptuous attitude towards them and sometimes calls them " dogs " and " swine," his style, on the whole, is much more refined and chastened, much less explosive than that of Luther.

The French translation of the original Latin, made by Calvin himself, especially that of the edition of 1539, which appeared in 1541, is also, according to the unanimous testimony of distinguished French literary critics, of the highest importance in the history of the French language. " Calvin's French style," according to Paul Lacroix, " is one of the grandest styles of the sixteenth century—simple, concise, elegant, lucid, ingenious, animated, varied in both form and tone. He made a beginning in framing French prose, as Marot had done for French verse." [10] " The French translation of the " Institutes," says Nisard, " places Calvin in the rank of our greatest writers." [11] " It forms," according to Lanson, " along with the work of Rabelais, the greatest monument of our prose in the first half of the sixteenth century, and one may say that it is necessary to descend to Pascal and Bossuet in order to find an equally lofty and serious eloquence applied to religious and moral philosophy." [12] The judgment of Brunetière is equally explicit. " The ' Institutes ' is one of the great books of French prose and the first in date of which one may say that the proportions, the plan, the architecture

[10] Quoted by Durand in his preface to Baumgartner's edition of the translation of 1560 (1888).
[11] " Hist. de la Littérature Française," i. 272, quoted by Durand, *ibid*.
[12] " La Revue Historique " (1894), quoted by Doumergue, iv. 6.

are something truly monumental." [13]   From the literary point of view the translation of 1541 is preferred by the critics to that of 1560.   The 1560 version is also less exact and for the more important passages it should be compared with the Latin original.   Calvin dictated it and had not time to revise it sufficiently.   Even so, it may be regarded as the mature fruit of his religious thought.

THE KNOWLEDGE OF GOD

In the first of the four books into which it is divided, he treats of the knowledge of God as Creator and sovereign Governor of the world.   He begins with a theodicy.   His theology is theocentric.   His theme is God and His redemptive plan as revealed in Christ.   This knowledge also involves the true knowledge of self, since it is only in knowing God that we realise our own limitations and imperfections.   It is of the knowledge of God in the religious, not the intellectual, sense that he treats—of God in personal relation to man, from whom we derive all, to whom we ascribe all, and whom we thus learn to reverence and love.   It is not sufficient to realise that God exists.   " God is not known where there is

[13] *Revue des Deux Mondes* (1900), quoted by Doumergue, *ibid.*   See also Pannier, " Calvin Écrivain," 5 f. (1930), who places him in the very first rank of French writers ;   Bossert, " Calvin," 208 f. (1906).   The various Latin editions of the " Institutes " are in " Opera," i. and ii.   A recent edition of Books I.-III. of the Latin edition of 1559 in iii. and iv. of the " Opera Selecta," by P. Barth and W. Niesel (1926-31), contains valuable notes on the sources of the " Institutes."   The French translation (1560) of the Latin edition of 1559 in " Opera," iii. and iv.   Also edited by Baumgartner (1888).   The French translation of 1541 of the Latin edition of 1539, edited by Lefranc, Chatelain, and Pannier (1911).   English translation of the Latin edition of 1559, by Beveridge (1845-46).   The French translations are by Calvin himself.   On the literary history of the work, see Warfield, " Calvin and Calvinism," 373 f. (1931), and Autin, " L'Institution Chrétienne " (1929).   For a comparison of the Latin and French texts see Marmelstein, " Étude Comparative des Textes Latins et Français de l'Institution de la Religion Chrétienne " (1921).   The " Institutes " is the main source for his theology.   But his Commentaries and letters also contain relevant matter.   He worked the results of his Biblical studies in his Commentaries into the final edition of the " Institutes."   Recent works on his theology, Doumergue, " Calvin," iv. (1910) ;   Tschackert, " Entstehung der Lutherischen und Reformierten Kirchenlehre," 390 f. (1910) ;   Seeberg, " Dogmengeschichte," iv. 551 f. (1920) ;   Wernle, " Der Evangelische Glaube, III., Calvin " (1919) ;   O. Ritschl, " Die Reformierte Theologie," iii. (1926) ;   Mitchell Hunter, " Teaching of Calvin " (1920) ;   H. Weber, " Die Theologie Calvins " (1930) ;   Fenn, " The Marrow of Calvin's Theology," *Harvard Theol. Rev.*, July 1909.   A concise exposition without any criticism.

no religion, no piety, which consists in faith joined with a living fear of God." [14] This knowledge has a twofold source— natural and supernatural. Man has instinctively " a sentiment of divinity " in himself, " an innate persuasion of his existence," as Cicero says. Even the savage has, therefore, a certain seed of religion implanted in his heart. Idolatry itself is an evidence of the fact. It is, in truth, easier to destroy every affection of nature than to dispense with religion. It is therefore a silly notion to ascribe its origin to the craft and finesse of certain subtle men in order to establish their power over the simple people. Such devices are, indeed, not unknown. But they only succeed because of the seed of religion in the soul. Even those who deny the existence of God instinctively at times, he holds with Tertullian, betray this innate consciousness of Him. This knowledge has, however, been obscured by the super- stition or the perversity and arrogance to which man is liable. This arrogance shows itself especially in the tendency to speculate about God, which only leads men to substitute their own imaginations for the true knowledge of Him. In thus denouncing, along with superstition, the speculative quest of God, Calvin hardly shows an adequate sense of the value of rational reflection on this great question or of the striving to fathom the mystery of God, which is the legitimate consequence of the innate sense of divinity, on which he lays such stress.

In addition to the sense of divinity within, all nature bears witness to the majesty and glory of God—a witness so con- vincing that even the simplest has only to open his eyes to be conscious of it. The more we study this marvellous work of God in all its exquisite beauty and art, especially the mechanism of the human body and the process of the human mind, the more we may realise His power, goodness, and wisdom. Some, indeed, deify nature, make it its own creator, or regard it as independent of God. He utterly rejects such pantheistic and deistic notions and maintains the theistic conception of a God who creates, maintains, and governs the universe, which is alone adequate to the religious nature of man and worthily

[14] " Institutes," 19 f. I quote from the French translation of 1560, edited by Baumgartner (1888), cf. Latin edition, 1559, Lib. I., cap. ii. 1. " Opera," ii., and " Opera Selecta," edited by P. Barth and W. Niesel, iii. In translating, I have on occasion modified the text as the result of com- parison with the Latin.

expresses the fact of God—God within us and beyond us, God alike immanent and transcendental. He enlarges in moving language on the evidence for this conception in the material world and in human history. At the same time, he does not take sufficient account of the mystery of God in relation to a world in which evil as well as good seems to work unhindered its maleficent will in the forces of destruction and death, of which the world is also the arena. He is the confirmed optimist, who does not seem to realise the urgency of this grim problem.

Despite these testimonies, internal and external, to the being and attitudes of God, they are insufficient to enable man to apprehend Him, as the superstitions and errors that blind him conclusively show. Witness not merely the fantasies of the common people, but the vagaries of the philosophers, including even Plato, on this subject. Hence the necessity of a Divine revelation, of the Word spoken by God Himself, which contains the clear knowledge of God the Creator and God the Redeemer in Jesus Christ. This revelation, in the form of the Old Testament, was made by God to man in visions, or oracles, or through his ministers, Moses and the prophets, in whose hearts He imprinted such a certainty of doctrine that they were fully persuaded that what they revealed proceeded from the true God. To know what God is we must learn in the school of the Scriptures. Their authority is absolute. We must start with the conviction that " they have come from heaven, as if in them the living voice of God Himself is heard." [15] It is a pernicious error to make their authority dependent on the common opinion of the Church, as if the eternal and immutable truth of God were based on the fantasy of men. There can be no certainty in matters of faith if we have only so fallible a warrant to rest on. The Word, as proclaimed by the prophets and apostles, on which the Church is founded, preceded the Church. The conviction of its truth is based, he distinctively insists, on the internal testimony of the Holy Spirit, which is the most convincing of all reasons for receiving it as God's own message to man. It is as the Spirit creates this conviction in our hearts that we have the assurance that God has spoken by the mouth of the prophets. It is not the result

[15] " Institutes," 34; Latin ed., I., vii. 1.

of our own judgment or that of others, but of faith inspired
by the Spirit. It is " a thing elevated above the necessity of
being judged " [16]—a thing of individual spiritual experience,
not of reason, nor standing in need of arguments based on
reason. " The mysteries of God are only comprehended by
those to whom it is given." [17] Whilst subjective, it is a supernatural insight, superior to reason as a test of truth. Only on
this understanding is Calvin prepared to sanction the application
of reason to Holy Writ—on the understanding, that is, that
reason shall confirm its infallible truth and receive it un-
questioningly. Given the initial conviction, inspired by the
Spirit, of the Divine authority of Holy Writ, reason may be
very serviceable in thus confirming its authority. To this end
he proceeds to expatiate on certain characteristics of it as a
Divine revelation. For instance, the simplicity of its style,
which has no trace of mere literary artifice, mere rhetoric, and
yet fitly gives expression to the majesty of its contents, and
possesses beyond all other writings the power to move the soul.
Whether the Spirit makes use of the rustic language of Amos, or
the flowing and sweet style of a David or an Isaiah, we instinctively feel that this is no merely human utterance. Or
consider its antiquity, in which respect no other writings can
compare with those of Moses, whom he regards as the author
of the whole Pentateuch, or the miracles which are reliable
" approbations " of the law promulgated by him, which cannot
be explained as the mere tricks of a magician, and which the
people had ample means of putting to the test. Or take the gift
of prophecy, the verity of which appears in the fact that the
predictions made by the prophets were exactly fulfilled. Unfortunately the examples cited—Isaiah and Daniel—do not
bear out his contention that Isaiah predicted the advent of
Cyrus a hundred years before the event, and Daniel foretold
the things that came to pass centuries later. He is unaware
that Isaiah is a composite book, partly written in the age of
Cyrus, and that the Book of Daniel belongs to the second
century B.C. This method of proving the infallible authority
of the Divine revelation clearly shows the danger of postulating
a dogmatic theory of inspiration and refusing to test it by
critical historic inquiry.

[16] " Institutes," 37 ; Latin ed., I., vii. 5.　　　　[17] *Ibid*.

Such arguments adduced by reason in support of the Divine inspiration of the Scriptures are, however, of secondary importance. The conviction of their inspiration is fundamentally an act of faith wrought by the Holy Spirit. For faith the Bible is thus infallibly the very Word of God from the first chapter of Genesis to the last chapter of Revelation. As such every part of it has its validity, though it may not represent an equal degree of Divine knowledge. He rejects and denounces any claim, such as that of the Spirituals, to an individual inspiration of the Spirit, an inner light apart from the written Word, and, on the strength of this revelation, propound the aberrations of their own fancy as the dicta of the Spirit. There can be no Divine illumination of the mind apart from the Spirit acting through the Word. " The Word is the instrument by which the Lord dispenses to believers the illumination of His Spirit." [18] The inspiration which these seducers claim is the inspiration of the devil. He is equally denunciatory in his uncompromising antagonism to the Biblical critics of his time. For him such criticism is a crime against " the truth of God," and the critics are " canailles," contemptible cavillers, snarling dogs, calumniators. He has not an adequate sense either of a progressive revelation in accordance with the increase of knowledge, the development of the moral and spiritual life, or of the anthropomorphic elements in the Jewish conception of God, for instance, which might well provoke the strictures of the critics.

He accepts the canon of Scripture as it stands, though he examines the various works in order to ascertain whether, in the case of the New Testament, each book is of apostolic origin, and whether it has the support of the testimony of the universal Church to its canonicity. A number of critics have inferred that he rejected the Second and Third Epistles of John, since he never quotes them, and in quoting First John speaks of it as " the Canonical Epistle of John." But the term canonical was applied generally to the seven Catholic Epistles, and to speak of the canonical Epistle of John does not necessarily imply that he regarded the other two as non-canonical. Nor did he seriously question the Petrine authorship of Second Peter, in spite of the difference of style, which he explains away by saying that it was dictated by Peter in his old age to a

[18] " Institutes," 45; Latin ed., I., ix. 3.

disciple, to whom the difference of style is due. Again, he is said to have rejected the Apocalypse, and he certainly refrained from commenting it. Whilst he evidently had no relish for the task, he quotes it in the " Institutes " and other writings as authoritative. We may, therefore, safely agree with the contention of Dr Warfield that " he represents the evidence for the canonicity of the books of the Bible as sufficient in all cases, and declares with confidence his conclusions in favour of the canonicity of the whole body of books which make up our Bible, and in all his writings and controversies acts firmly on this presupposition." [19]

The knowledge of God unfolded in the Scriptures, which depict Him in relation to man, has been falsified by the superstition, which, in the ancient world, found universal expression in idolatry. Such superstition not only dishonours Him by robbing Him of his ineffable majesty. God is only known spiritually, since in His essence He is infinite and spiritual, and this fact forbids us to associate Him with anything carnal and earthly. " I do not think that it is lawful to represent God under a visible form, because He has forbidden us to do so, and also because His glory is so much the more disfigured and His truth falsified." [20] He is specially severe on " the papists," who are no better in this respect than the pagans. Besides the emphatic prohibition of the Scriptures, this superstition is expressly condemned by the testimony and example of the ancient Church. " If the authority of the ancient Church has any weight among us, let us observe that, for the space of five hundred years or thereabout, during the period when Christianity was in its greatest vigour and there was the greatest purity of doctrine, the Christian Churches were in common clean and exempt from such pollution." [21]

THE TRIUNE GOD

In God there are three hypostases or subsistences—Father, Son, and Spirit—which the Latins and, by way of accommodation, the Greeks expressed by the term persons. This conception of a Triune God he finds not only in the New, but

---

[19] " Calvin and Calvinism," 52 (1931).
[20] " Institutes," 51 ; Latin ed., I., xi. 12.
[21] *Ibid.*, 52 ; Latin ed., I., xi. 13.

throughout the Old Testament. He is, however, conscious of the riskiness and the difficulty of applying terms like substance and person to express this conception, though he defends them against the heretics as legitimate and orthodox, and implicitly believes in a metaphysical Trinity. He finds evidence of the eternal existence of Christ the Word, as a distinct Divine subsistence, in the story of the creation. Moses had, therefore, a clear consciousness of the Second Person of the Christian Trinity. He cites proofs equally forced from the Psalms, the Book of Proverbs, and the Prophets, in spite of Jewish objections and explanations and the cavillings of a Servetus. It is, however, clear that he interprets the Old Testament from the standpoint of the later developed doctrine of the Trinity and not in the light of its actual teaching. He is on firmer ground in quoting passages from the New Testament in support of the Divinity of Christ. At the same time he fails to realise the development of the evaluation of Christ from the adoptionist conception of the primitive apostolic preaching, through Paul and the writer of Hebrews to the enhanced Johannine conception, in consequence of the application of the Logos theory to the historic Jesus. He does not seem to be aware of such development under this problematic influence and thus treats the testimony of the New Testament indiscriminately. Other proofs on which he lays stress are the miracles which He wrought, the miraculous powers which He conferred on His disciples, and the experience of the individual Christian, who is conscious of His divine power in the salvation and sanctification of the soul. Similarly, in proof of the conception of the Spirit as the third hypostasis of the Godhead, he quotes a number of passages from both Testaments and appeals in addition to the experience of His working in the soul. Here, again, the appeal to Scripture is lacking in the historic sense. In the Old Testament the Spirit appears generally as a Divine effluence, and even in the New this conception persists before the Spirit becomes definitely personal in the Johannine writings.[22] " Therefore," he concludes, " it follows that there are three persons residing in the essence of God, in whom (the one) God is known." [23]

At the same time, he contends, with the ancient Fathers,

[22] See my " Gospel in the Early Church," 83 f., 224 (1933).
[23] " Institutes," 64; Latin ed., I., xiii. 16.

that though there is a distinction there is no division in the Divine essence. How there can be real personality without division as well as distinction of one person from another, he does not satisfactorily explain, since personality in any intelligible sense involves individuality. He hesitates, in fact, to involve himself in such an explanation, insists on prudence in the use of technical theological terms, and takes refuge in the teaching of the Scriptures. " If the distinction of the persons, which is difficult to comprehend, torments some with scruples, let them remember that, if we give rein to our thoughts to make curious discourses, they enter into a labyrinth, and though they do not comprehend the elevation of this mystery, let them suffer themselves to be guided by the Holy Scriptures." [24] It is, however, the Holy Scriptures envisaged through the medium of the later Greek and Latin orthodoxy which he reads into them, and which he defends against the anti-Trinitarian heretics, ancient and modern. Hence he adds little that is new to the discussion except that he emphasises the argument from individual spiritual experience, eschews metaphysics for the method of Biblical proof, as he understands it, and marshals it in a lucid and vigorous style.[25] For the modern reader he rather spoils his case by his persistent tendency to impute " impiety " and other personal offences to his heterodox opponents. It is as impossible for him, as for his fellow-Reformers, to consider such questions on their merits.

MAN

From the knowledge of God, he passes to the knowledge of man. He understands literally the story of the creation of the world and man as related in Genesis. His treatment of the subject strikes one as very naïve in the face of the advance of scientific research in the long interval since he wrote. We cannot, however, reproach him for his lack of scientific insight, which was only beginning, in isolated cases, to feel its way towards a truer view of the working of God in nature. Darwin

[24] " Institutes," 67; Latin ed., I., xiii. 21.
[25] Doumergue insists on the originality of his doctrine of the Trinity. But he adduces little in support of his contention, iv. 101 f. For a more detailed discussion of his teaching on the subject, see Warfield, " Calvin and Calvinism," 189 f.

would undoubtedly have been for him as great a heretic as
Servetus, because in this respect he only possesses the conventional type of mind.   Man, he explains, consists of soul or
spirit and body, the soul being an essence distinct from the
body.   The soul is essentially immortal and not a mere force
energising the body.   Conscience, which points to a future
judgment, is an infallible indication of its immortality.   Another
is the capacity of knowing God which elevates us above the
world to the fountain of life.   In short, in its moral and rational
nature, the soul is an immortal essence distinct from the body.
In this nature consists mainly the image of God in which man
was created, and which " comprehends the whole dignity by
which man is eminent above every kind of animal." [26]   The
faculties of the soul are intellect—the faculty of discerning
between things, of judging, approving, or condemning—and
will—the faculty of following or rejecting the things which
the intellect thus approves or condemns.   In man's primeval
condition there was harmony in the exercise of the intellect
and the will—the discernment in all things necessary not only
for the regulation of his earthly life, but for attaining to God and
perfect felicity, coupled with the necessary conformity of the
will to the direction of reason.   His will was perfectly free, so
that if he had willed it, he could have attained to eternal life.
Primeval man was thus created in " a state of integrity," of
" perfect rectitude " both in intelligence and will.   He had
only to persevere in order to remain in this state.   But Adam
by the misuse of his will fell and thereby ruined and corrupted
not only his originally good nature but all his posterity.   The
beginning of man's history is thus the beginning of a descent,
not of an ascent.   The theory is based on the mythical story of
the creation, which Calvin, with his age, naturally accepts as
historical, and which conditions his doctrine of man and his
salvation.   We cannot blame him for his ignorance of modern
scientific anthropology which has revealed to us the gradual
evolution of man and his mental and moral faculties.   In view
of the results of modern scientific research the theory of an
original perfect state, followed by a complete collapse of human
nature, seems quite untenable, and is not in accord with the
Divine order of the world.

[26] " Institutes," 86 ; Latin ed., I., xv. 3.

PROVIDENCE

The creation of the world and man involves their providential government by God.   God did not create the universe
and leave it to its natural course.   He is ever present to sustain
and rule it by His providence.   Calvin strenuously controverts
the deistic notion that God imparted a certain constitution to
the world, in virtue of which it subsists apart from Him.   He
will not hear of a *Dieu fainéant*, an inactive God, or allow
any part to what is called chance and fortune.   The world is
the revelation of a supreme and sovereign paternal Intelligence,
who has not only marvellously adapted it to realise His purpose,
but ceaselessly directs all things to this end.   " For we recognise
God as almighty, not because He is able to do all things and
nevertheless remains in repose, or because by a general inspiration He continues the order of nature such as He has disposed
it from the beginning ; but rather that in governing heaven
and earth by His providence, He so compasses all things
that nothing can happen except as He has determined it in
His counsel." [27]   His providence is, therefore, not, as the
philosophers opine, to be understood in the sense that He is
the first cause of all things.   It is not limited by the course of
nature.   It means for the Christian that everything happens
by His direct ordinance and command according to His good
pleasure, and not by the counsel and will of man.   There is
not only a general providence inherent in the Divine constitution
or course of nature, but a particular and ever-active providence
in the actual direction of the world, as the Scriptures abundantly
testify.   There does not fall a single drop of rain without
God's particular ordinance, and the ways of man are ordered
by His counsel, decree, and determination, not by his own
independent volition or inclination.   But is not this to teach
the Stoic doctrine of necessity or fate ?   He denies the inference
by saying that God, not a necessity of nature, is " the master
and moderator of all things." [28]   He rejects a pantheistic as
well as a deistic conception of providence.

The providential activity of God does not, however, preclude
human activity or lessen human responsibility.   God makes

[27] " Institutes," 91 ; Latin ed., I., xvi. 3.
[28] *Ibid.*, 95 ; Latin ed., I., xvi. 8.

use of means to attain His ends and man co-operates in the
realisation of these. "The eternal decree does not prevent us
from providing for ourselves under His good will and ordering
our affairs, the reason being that He, who has limited our life,
has also committed to us the care of it and has given us the
means of conserving it." [29] Man must, for instance, consider
the dangers to which he is liable and the remedies for them.
There must be no reckless and haphazard confiding in
providence. God Himself has inspired us with the instinct
of self-preservation by which we serve His providence. But
what about the use of evil instruments? If God wills all
things, does not the murderer do what He wills? And why,
then, punish the criminal for the crimes he commits? God,
he replies, indeed makes use of evildoers to execute His judgments. But the evil is not in God, but in the evildoer, as his
conscience clearly testifies. The sun's rays may cause putrefaction, but the putrefaction is in the thing putrified, not in the
ray that works it. Thus, too, "God makes a good and legitimate
use of their malice." [30] This is the doctrine of Scripture, to
which he constantly appeals, and it alone gives due glory to
God by recognising His sovereign will as the disposer of all
things. It alone affords adequate consolation and strength
amid the trials and mysteries of life, since it furnishes the
assurance that all that happens to us is ordered by His will
and determination, as it pleases Him so to do. It begets a
splendid optimism, in spite of the grimmer aspects of it, and
Calvin rises to real eloquence in depicting the supreme felicity,
power, and strength of the life that is rooted in this faith and
rises superior to the miseries and dangers that encompass it.
Here, again, it is the religious rather than the philosophic side
of the doctrine that weighs with him. It is taught in Scripture
and it is of the highest practical value for the religious life.
Hence the earnestness with which he defends it against its
impugners, whether ancient or modern. It has, of course,
its difficulties, which, with all his pious reasoning, he does not
succeed in clearing away, and he is fain to confess the partial
obscurity of the subject, though he does not doubt for a moment
that his view of providence is the right one. His contention,

[29] " Institutes," 99; Latin ed., I., xvii. 4.
[30] *Ibid.*, 100; Latin ed., I., xvii. 5.

for instance, that God governs according to His good pleasure suggests an element of arbitrariness in the Divine government of the world, and though he insists that everything that God does is good and right, the emphasis laid on His good pleasure as an explanation of His working in nature and history rather detracts from the consolation which he finds in the doctrine. How God's will intervenes in all action, good and bad, just and unjust,[31] he does not satisfactorily explain, though he argues the point at length, more especially as he rejects all distinction between the permission and the will and decree of God.

TOTAL CORRUPTION OF HUMAN NATURE

In the Second Book he treats of the knowledge of God as Redeemer in Jesus Christ, which was first revealed under the Law and has been manifested in the Gospel. He starts with a very pessimistic view of human nature. The true knowledge of God can only induce the feeling of self-humiliation. The remembrance of man's original dignity is, indeed, legitimate in so far as it may incite the effort to regain it. But it only accentuates the consciousness of his miserable state in consequence of the fall of Adam. This fall was the result of an act of disobedience, revolt against God, springing from unbelief, infidelity. It dishonoured God, brought death and moral ruin not only on Adam but on the whole human race. And Adam not only corrupted his posterity in corrupting himself but made it the participant of his guilt. The curse of God descended on both alike. Calvin had evidently not read the story in Genesis objectively, for it says nothing of this communication of guilt from him to his posterity. Nor had he read it critically, since death is a physiological fact incident to all living beings, and not the consequence of an act of sin like that delineated in the third chapter of Genesis. It is myth and not history that the writer records. It is dogma, the dogma of original sin, not science, that Calvin teaches. Original sin he defines as " a corruption and hereditary perversity [pravity] of our nature, which, embracing every part of the same, makes us guilty in the first place of the wrath of God, and then produces

[31] On this point in greater detail see Seeberg, " Dogmengeschichte," iv. 572 f. ; Mitchell Hunter, " Teaching of Calvin," 130 f.

in us the works which the Scriptures call works of the flesh." [32]
This corruption of our nature is so complete that with good
reason " we are damnable before God." Human nature is in
consequence, he holds with Luther, absolutely and actively
bad, completely dominated by evil. It is naturally vicious.

It follows that, like Luther, he depreciates reason and
denies the freedom of the will. He rejects the teaching of the
philosophers that man can by his reason discern between good
and evil and live in accordance with reason by keeping in
subjection the sensuous element in his nature, and that the
freedom of the will consists in the power thus to live in
accordance with reason, or not, though it may be difficult to
establish its rule. He rejects, too, the opinion of the early
Fathers who, in order to guard against the danger of inducing
slackness in welldoing, taught that the will is free to choose
between good and evil, whilst recognising the necessity of
Divine grace in realising the good. For him the term free
will is a misnomer, and he thinks that the use of it in theological
discussion has only tended to error, and that the Church would
do well to abolish it. He seems haunted by the fear lest man,
by " attributing to himself a single grain of good beyond measure,
should ruin himself by a vain confidence and render himself
guilty of sacrilege in usurping the glory of God." [33] To
belittle reason and its concomitant free will is for him, as for
Luther, alone compatible with God's glory and with the
humility which is an essential principle of religion. The
one-sided insistence with which he labours this point can only
be described as doctrinaire and even morbid, though happily
he refrains from the gross violence with which Luther expressed
himself on the subject, and recognises the operation of the gift
of reason and will outside the moral and religious sphere, *i.e.*,
in regard to what he calls " things inferior." With Augustine
he distinguishes between " the natural gifts " of intelligence,
judgment, volition, and " the supernatural or spiritual gifts "—
the things pertaining to the kingdom of God and his eternal
felicity—which were both conferred on man by God at his
creation. The former were corrupted by the sin of Adam ;
the latter wholly destroyed in us. In consequence of this

---

[32] " Institutes," 115 ; Latin ed., II., i. 8.
[33] *Ibid.*, 122 ; Latin ed., II., ii. 10.

corruption, the natural gift of reason has been darkened, though its light has not been completely extinguished. Similarly, volition, which is inseparable from reason, remains. But the will " has been taken captive to such a degree and, as it were, bound by evil desires that it is incapable of desiring anything good." [34]   In order to elucidate these assertions he enters into a lengthy examination of the powers of reason and will.   He admits that reason has a certain " taste " for the truth and is impelled by the search for it.   In things mundane— in political government, the arts, etc.—man shows remarkable ingenuity.   He is endowed naturally with many gifts of God, as his achievements in law, medicine, science, philosophy, and the arts show.   All these are inspired by the Spirit of God, in spite of the original corruption of his intelligence by the fall, and are to be thankfully recognised as gifts of God.   At the same time, they are only of very limited value in His sight, and as if he had conceded more than his dogma of human corruption would allow, he proceeds to belittle what he had first extolled.   " Nevertheless, in order that no one may esteem man to be very happy in that we concede to him so great a virtue in comprehending things inferior appertaining to this corruptible world, it is necessary to bear in mind that this faculty of understanding, which he possesses, and the intelligence which results from it, is a fleeting thing and of no importance before God, when there is no firm foundation of truth to rest on." [35]   In the moral and religious sphere reason is incapable of knowing God and regulating the conduct of life in accordance with His law.   " Human reason can never approach or address itself to the truth in understanding what is the true God and what is His will towards us." [36]   The natural man, he insists, quoting St Paul and other Scripture passages, cannot discern spiritual things.   Such discernment comes from God alone, who must open our blind eyes.   " How, then, some one may object, is all our industry, wisdom, knowledge, and solicitude so depraved that we cannot think or meditate anything good before God.   This may seem a very hard saying, but it is a very equitable one to the Holy Spirit,

[34] " Institutes," 123 ; Latin ed., II., ii. 12.
[35] *Ibid.*, 125 ; Latin ed., II., ii. 16.
[36] *Ibid.*, 126 ; Latin ed., II., ii. 18.

who knows that all the thoughts of man are vain and pronounces
that all that the heart of man conceives is wholly bad." [37]
So, too, of the will.   By the fall man has become the servant of
sin and can only will evil.   He has entirely lost the power to
will the good and his will is, therefore, not free.   He has,
indeed, a certain inclination or appetite, in common with the
animals, to seek what is advantageous.   But such a desire is
distinct from will.   The question is not one of desiring, but of
discerning, choosing, and following the good, and this freedom
man does not possess.

How, then, explain the fact that so many, in their natural
condition, have lived a life of virtue and earnestly striven to
realise the good ?   Is a Camillus to be placed on the same level
as a Catiline ?   This, he replies, is due to the special grace of
God and not to their own innate goodness.   Without inspiration
by the Spirit, there can be no real goodness.   Man is under the
necessity of sinning, and yet this necessity is not to be taken
in the sense of constraint; but is due to his own act, the
consequence of the fall being that he wills to do evil but not
to do good.   This is, however, more a distinction than a
difference, for if we cannot but will to do evil, necessity becomes
practically constraint.   The deliverance of the will from this
necessity is the work of God's Spirit alone.   Conversion is
purely a work of grace, not of co-operation.   It is a second
creation by God's Spirit.   There is no synergism in the work
of conversion or even in the Christian life that ensues.   He
will not hear of the perverse distinction between operating and
co-operating grace in the sense that man of his own accord
can co-operate with the grace of God.   " From the first movement even until the last perseverance the good we do is of
God in all its parts." [38]   Man has thus no merit in God's sight
and God's glory requires that all should be attributed to Him.
Like Luther, he carries the dogma the length of saying that
even the evil that man does he does not merely by the permission
or prescience, but by the power of God.   He works His will
in the devil and the wicked in accordance with His good
pleasure, though He also holds that His justice in so doing is
irreproachable.   He closes the discussion in a chapter in which

---

[37] " Institutes," 130; Latin ed., II., ii. 25.
[38] *Ibid.*, 136; Latin ed., II., iii. 6.

he takes notice of the arguments—logical and scriptural—on the other side, such as the futility of all exhortation and admonition to do good, of the reprehension of doing evil, of the conditional promises of God, etc., if the will can effect nothing. He does so, however, only to refute them with the aid of Scripture and St Augustine, in accordance with the dogmatic conviction that he has thus developed, and he certainly does not sufficiently realise their force.

Throughout the whole discussion he tends to exaggerate, in deference to this dogmatic conviction, which starts from a literal and even erroneous interpretation of the story of the fall, the moral and intellectual impotence and degradation of man. His standpoint is, of course, the religious one, and from the religious point of view the attitude of self-humiliation before God, a keen sense of the limitation of reason, the imperfection of the moral life even at its highest is the right attitude. But even religious feeling does not necessitate a one-sided, exaggerated, and even a morbid view of facts in deference to a preconceived dogma, and Calvin distorts the actual state of the case in maintaining that reason cannot discern between good and evil and that the will can do nothing but evil. To say that true religious feeling demands this belief as an essential element is extreme and misleading. Man can honour and serve God all the more earnestly the more he realises the capacities and dignity, in its more developed state, of his nature as a moral and rational being, and the possibilities and obligations which this involves. To belittle his nature and harp on its total depravity is, on the other hand, to deprive him of the religious impulse which instinctively seeks its highest object in God, apart from any dogma of a primeval fall and a consequent state of utter alienation from Him. The moral and religious life, in other words, is inherent in man's moral and rational nature, and the higher this nature is developed by the advancing knowledge and spiritual experience of humanity, the more the Divine life becomes a necessity and a fact of our nature. His theory that, no matter how developed this nature, there can be no true life of the soul in communion with God unless God alone, through His Spirit supernaturally, by the exercise of His omnipotent power, operates the good in us, is merely a theological assumption. The very fact of reason and the moral sense, as thus developed, involves the consciousness of God and the impulse to know Him and live in accordance with this knowledge. This is in itself a truly religious mood and this mood does not exclude the feeling of the imperfection of both knowledge and life. There is room for this feeling even in the most developed state of both. But that there must be in addition in every truly religious mind a sense of utter moral impotence and estrangement from God does not necessarily follow unless, like Calvin, we are prepared to prejudice our judgment by a preconceived dogma of the absolute corruption of human nature in virtue of the supposed complete moral collapse in the Garden of Eden. Moreover, he only succeeds in maintaining his theory by a persistent *ex parte* view of Scripture. He adduces passages that seem to make for his view of the absolute ignorance and impotence of human nature in the religious sense. He ignores or refuses to give due weight to others which make for the opposite view, and he certainly fails to do justice to the teaching of Jesus who cherished a more optimistic conception of man as the child of a heavenly Father. Nor is it true, as he insists all through, that it is necessarily derogatory to the glory of God to assert that man can of himself do any good. This additional assumption tends to beget the impression of an egotistic God, who seems to be jealous of the very nature that He has conferred on him. Calvin's God is too much the jealous anthropomorphistic God of the Old Testament.

Its Redemption by Christ

The hopeless corruption and degradation of human nature have rendered necessary the redemption of Jesus Christ, through whom alone salvation is possible. Hence the exposition of the Divine plea of salvation to which the remainder of the Second Book is devoted. He finds this plan unfolded throughout the Old Testament in which the historic Jesus Christ is already known as the Redeemer, though this knowledge is not so clearly expressed in Moses as in the later writings. He finds it, for instance, by a questionable exegesis in the song of Hannah and the prophecy of Eli as well as in the Psalms and the Prophets. " The hope of the faithful has never reposed

on any other than Jesus Christ." [39] " From the beginning of
the world Jesus Christ has been put forward (*mis en avant*) to
the elect in order that they might fix their eyes on Him, and
that their confidence might repose in Him." [40] The Law
(and by this term he means the form of religion given to the
people of Israel through Moses) was not meant to supersede
the promise which was given to Abraham and his race, and
pointed to the coming of Jesus Christ. This religion, with its
complicated sacrifices and ceremonies, had a purely spiritual
significance. In themselves sacrifice and ceremony were of
no validity. They were merely figurative of Christ, though
he admits that the Jews had only a very imperfect sense
of the spiritual character of the religion they professed,
as the utterances of the prophets show. The Law in its
narrower or moral sense it is impossible to observe. It reveals
the righteousness of God and at the same time the unrighteous-
ness and condemnation of man. It serves to bridle the wicked
by the fear of punishment. It makes known to the believer the
Divine ideal of the moral life and acts as an incentive to its
realisation. The Law in this narrow sense retains its validity.
Only the ceremonial law was abolished in Christ, though he
omits to point out that Jesus Himself observed it. Although
under the Law Christ was known to the Jews, it is only in the
Gospel that He has been plainly revealed. The Gospel is,
indeed, to be understood of all the testimonies that God has
given of His mercy and His paternal favour. But though the
old covenant was substantially the same as the new in the
realisation of eternal life solely by the mercy of God in Christ,
the new differed from the old in respect of greater spirituality,
directness, freedom, and universality. Under it we have the
clear and concrete manifestation of God's grace in Christ,
which was only shadowed forth under the Law and was delayed
till His coming. This is the Gospel *par excellence*.

In order that Christ should become the mediator between
God and man, it was indispensable that He should become
man. He marshals against the heretics the arguments drawn
from Scripture and the orthodox patristic theology in support
of the incarnation and of the twofold nature and the single

[39] " Institutes," 157; Latin ed., II., vi. 3.
[40] *Ibid.*, 158; Latin ed., II., vi. 4.

person of the God-Man with great verve and skill. As God-Man He performed the threefold office of Prophet, King, and Priest. As Prophet He completed the revelation of the grace of God made known by the ancient prophets and thereby also fulfilled their prophecies. Beyond His Gospel we cannot go, since it contains all the treasures of wisdom and knowledge. As King He rules the spiritual kingdom and the Church, which He has established as the continuation of the old kingdom of God, and directs and succours from His eternal throne amid the tribulation to which its members are exposed in the struggle with the devil, the world, and the flesh. He will thus direct and succour it till the time when every knee shall bow before Him and acknowledge His kingship. As Priest He has offered Himself a sacrifice to God and made the only possible and adequate satisfaction for sin by His death, and He continues His priestly function in the work of intercession.

In order to realise what His work as Redeemer means for us we must first realise our lost and miserable condition—subject to the wrath and damnation of God because of sin, enemies of God and God the enemy of us. God's sovereign justice demanded expiation and satisfaction for sin, and without this satisfaction we could not become the objects of His grace and benevolence. Nevertheless, He did not cease to love us as His creatures, though He hated us as sinners, since He created us for life, not for death. Hence the cardinal importance of the satisfaction made by Christ to the Divine justice which enabled God, by imputation, to regard us as righteous, in spite of our sin, and made reconciliation possible. The grand act of redemption consists in the voluntary subjection of Himself to the death that we had merited. His death is not merely a bodily one. It involved the most awful spiritual suffering, the consciousness of the pains of hell, which He thinks the phrase, " descended into hell," means. In this intensive sense He paid our penalty and thereby delivered us from it. The legal character of the action is strongly emphasised. At the same time, by His death He not only bore the death sentence for us, but destroyed the power of death and bequeathed to us the power of a new life in the death of the old man, the mortification of the flesh.

His work on earth finds its adequate conclusion by His

resurrection, which affords the crowning proof of His victory over the power of death, and is not only the emblem of the new life of the soul, but the guarantee of our own ultimate resurrection after death. Finally, He is enthroned by His ascension at the right hand of God as the possessor of all power in heaven and earth and our Advocate with the Father, whence by the Spirit He makes His power felt in the hearts of His followers, and shall reappear as Judge.

CHAPTER XVII

CALVIN AS THEOLOGIAN—*Continued*

FAITH

CALVIN proceeds in the Third Book to treat of the appropriation of the benefits of the work of Christ by the individual believer through the operation of the Holy Spirit. The ministry of the Spirit, on which he lays great emphasis, is essential for the salvation and the sanctification of the soul. " As we have said that the whole perfection of salvation is found in Jesus Christ, He also, in order to our participation in this salvation, baptizes us with the Holy Spirit and with fire, illuminating us into the faith of His Gospel and regenerating us so that we become new creatures, finally purging us of all our pollution and filth in order to be consecrated to God as holy temples." [1] The Spirit operates in us faith by which we apprehend and lay hold of the Gospel. Faith " is the principal *chef d'œuvre* of the Spirit "—faith in the evangelical, not in the speculative or intellectual sense, personal faith in Jesus Christ, the Revealer of God and the Redeemer of man. It is not mere belief in certain doctrines on the authority of the Church, nor is it the labyrinthian thing that the scholastic theologians have made of it. " Faith consists in the knowledge of God and of Christ, not in reverence for the Church," which results in error, ignorance, blindness. He will not hear of such " implicit " faith. Faith rests on the Word, which must be received as it stands, as literally and infallibly the voice of God. Without this indispensable preliminary conviction, faith is impossible, though he admits that there are many things which, owing to the limitation of this mortal state, we cannot clearly understand and shall never fathom till we have been delivered from this mortal body. Even Scripture has its enigmas.

[1] " Institutes," French ed. (1560), 249 ; Latin ed. (1559), III., i. 4.

Faith is the assured knowledge of salvation by Christ, revealed to our understanding and sealed in our hearts by the Holy Spirit. But it is not knowledge in the ordinary sense, knowledge which can be taught by demonstration and argument. It is the firm conviction or persuasion of what surpasses the capacity of human intelligence to grasp, since it deals with things infinite. For Calvin it is of the nature of an intuition supernaturally inspired by the Holy Spirit. Nevertheless, it may be called knowledge in the sense that believers know for certain that they have become the children of God through Christ, though it consists more in certitude than in apprehension. Certitude, confidence in the face of doubt and anxiety, is an essential of it. It is not, indeed, absolutely free from doubt, and the trials to which it is subject show that confidence is not to degenerate into presumption and pride. But the struggle with doubt providentially tends to strengthen it and to lead us more and more to distrust ourselves and place our trust in God. It is like a spring which resists every burden placed upon it and invariably reacts upwards. Here Calvin is the most thoroughgoing optimist. This inexpugnable optimism of faith is the secret of the strength and the militant spirit of Calvinism. If he debases and humiliates man by the dogma of his corruption and moral impotence, he exalts, inspires, energises him by his doctrine of faith. It imparts to him the absolute certainty of salvation, eternal life, and the power to triumph over all the afflictions, temptations, and struggles of this life. "The end of the struggle is always such that faith surmounts these difficulties by which it is besieged, and which seem to imperil it." [2] It is, however, questionable whether he has a due sense of these difficulties—of those, for instance, which spring from such a conception of the Word as he insists on.

REPENTANCE AND REMISSION

Faith produces in us repentance, which he defines " as a true conversion of our life to follow God and the way which He shows, proceeding from a right and unfeigned fear of God,

[2] " Institutes," 260; Latin ed., III., ii. 18. On his conception of faith in greater detail, see Pieter Dee, " Het Geloofsbegrip van Calvijn " (1918); P. Brunner, " Vom Glauben bei Calvin " (1925); Seeberg, " Dogmengeschichte," iv. 590 f.

and showing itself in the mortification of the flesh and the old man and a vitalising of the spirit." [3] It involves, more particularly, a change of life Godwards, the consciousness and hatred of sin, complete self-renunciation, the resurrection through the death of self to new life—in a word, a spiritual regeneration, by which the image of God is restored in us. This regeneration, he holds with Luther, is not the work of a moment, but continues throughout our earthly life in the conflict with sin, since the fact of sin remains in manifold concupiscence, though its guilt has been removed. He attacks the antinomian teaching of certain Anabaptists, who maintain that for the regenerated Christian sin no longer exists, and that, being led by the Spirit, the desires of the flesh are matters of indifference, as if regeneration abolished the distinction between good and evil, virtue and vice! Against the perversions of this "popular philosophy" he emphasises the fruits of the Spirit, the imperative obligation of Christian morality. He combats, too, the scholastic doctrine of repentance which makes regeneration an external discipline, instead of an internal renovation of the soul, and requires on the part of the penitent contrition, confession, and satisfaction for the remission of sin. The question is of the most vital importance, since the issue at stake is how and under what conditions sin is remitted. Contrition, he grants, is a necessary element of true repentance. But the teaching of these theologians is misleading and mischievous, inasmuch as they make contrition not only a condition but the cause of the remission of sin. They thus deprive the penitent, who can never be sure that he is sufficiently contrite, of the assurance of remission, which, he insists, is due not to his contrition but to the mercy of God. He denies further that ecclesiastical confession is a Divine ordinance, as these theologians also teach, and that it was commanded by Christ. The mutual confession, of which St James speaks, and which he approves, was a very different thing from ecclesiastical confession to a priest. Priestly confession, as a universal ecclesiastical ordinance, is, he holds, not older than the constitution of Innocent III. It is merely the usurpation of

[3] "Institutes," 275; Latin ed., III., iii. 5. On his teaching in greater detail, see Strathmann, "Die Entstehung der Lehre Calvin's von der Busse," "Calvinstudien," edited by Bohatec (1909), and "Calvin's Lehre von der Busse in ihrer späteren Gestalt," *Stud. und Krit.* (1909).

an authority for which there is no warrant in Scripture and
the exercise of which is detestable on both moral and religious
grounds. The power of the keys in the evangelical sense,
which consists in declaring remission or damnation in accordance with the Word, and of which he made use in his liturgy
at Strassburg, but was fain, for reasons of expediency, to discard
at Geneva, is something very different from this priestly
usurpation in virtue of an arrogated ecclesiastical authority.
It is a tyrannical device in order to subject the laity to the
priesthood, and it is sacrilege against God, to whom alone it
belongs to pardon sin. The imposing of satisfaction in the
form of fastings, oblations, etc., as a condition of remission,
is an additional device by which the priest interposes himself
between God and the sinner and deprives him of the benefit of
God's free grace. It is based on the erroneous notion that
although the Lord by His mercy remits the guilt of sin, He
retains the penalty for which we have to make satisfaction by
the merit of works. To this erroneous notion he opposes the
conception of remission as the gratuitous gift of God, which
is alone in keeping with the clear testimony of Scripture.
The subterfuge by which the Roman theologians defend it,
viz., that in baptism we receive remission by the grace of
Christ, but for sin committed after baptism satisfaction is
necessary, is equally incompatible with the scriptural doctrine
that Christ is the propitiation for our sins. Otherwise, who
could be sure of his salvation ? He adds a scathing criticism
of the practice of indulgences and the belief in purgatory.

JUSTIFICATION

After treating of the nature of the Christian life, whose
main characteristic is complete self-renunciation, he proceeds
to expound the doctrine of justification by faith, which " is
the principal article of the Christian religion." He is said to
be justified before God who is esteemed not as a sinner, but
as just and righteous in His sight. To this just status in
God's sight the sinner attains who lays hold by faith of
the righteousness of Christ, so that, being clothed therewith,
he appears before God not as a sinner but as just. He
thereby obtains acceptance by God, who graciously receives

us as righteous and remits our sins by the imputation
to us of Christ's righteousness. To justify in this sense is
simply to absolve an accused person as innocent, though
it is not because he is really innocent, but because, by
gratuitous imputation, he is held to be so in Christ. Calvin
lays stress on the legal aspect of the transaction. Justification is a judicial act by which God, as judge, absolves the
accused. The actual process consists in gratuitous remission
or absolution by the supreme Judge. He controverts at length
Ossiander's contention that God does not merely repute us
righteous in Christ, but infuses into us the Divine righteousness
and justifies us on account of this infused righteousness. Nor
will he listen to the objection that his view of justification
leaves the sinner without any change of nature, or that it is
dishonouring to God to assume that He would justify those
who perforce remain in their sinful state. Such objections
arise from the confusion of justification with regeneration,
which it involves as a necessary consequence, but which is
not the ground on which we are justified before God. The
gratuitous acceptance of the sinner in virtue of Christ's
righteousness is a different thing from regeneration, which is,
indeed, the inseparable result of it, but is a lengthy and laborious
process. The two are conjoined as cause and effect, yet
distinct. The neglect of this distinction renders the conviction
of our salvation impossible, leads to constant doubt, destroys
peace of conscience by making us dependent, not on the
gratuitous gift of God in Christ, but on the works of the law,
in which even the greatest saints on earth are unable to confide.
In justifying, God has no regard to anything in man. Even
faith is only the instrument of justification, of which God in
Christ is the Author. What renders this justification possible
is the obedience of Christ, who took upon Him the form of a
Servant for our sakes, to God His Father. We owe it solely
to His obedience in becoming flesh and suffering that His
righteousness might become ours in God's sight.

Justification is thus not a mixture of faith and works. We
must utterly abandon our own righteousness, if we would
obtain the benefit of that of Christ. It will not do to compromise in this matter and distinguish between works in our
unregenerated state and works wrought in the believer by

the Holy Spirit. This distinction is an invention of the scholastic theologians, who hold that man is justified by the works which are produced by the Spirit as the fruits of regeneration. They forget that St Paul excludes all works whatever and attributes justification solely to the agency of faith in Christ. There are only two alternatives—justification either by way of the perfect observance of the Law, which is impossible, or by way of faith in the grace of God, which is thus the only possible way. The scholastics have entirely obscured the meaning of faith and grace by pretending that faith is the certainty of attaining the reward by God of the merits acquired in our regenerate state, and that grace, instead of being the gratuitous righteousness which God confers on us, consists in the aid of the Spirit in living a good and holy life. These mediæval doctors have gone from bad to worse until finally they have landed in Pelagianism and ignored the radical Pauline differentiation between the Law and the Gospel. They cavil at the phrase of Luther and his fellow-Reformers, " by faith alone," on the ground that this adverb is not in Scripture, ignoring the fact that it is undoubtedly involved in the Pauline teaching of justification by faith and not by works. If justification is not possible by works, it can only be possible by faith. But does not St Paul join faith with charity? It is, indeed, true that there can be no faith in any efficacious sense that is not joined with charity. But faith does not derive from charity the virtue of justification.

It is absolutely necessary, in this matter, to bear in mind what constitutes righteousness in God's sight, in order to eschew this doctrine of justification by works. Before God's judicial throne as depicted in Scripture no human righteousness can avail. What mortal can approach this throne confiding in his own works or without the overwhelming sense of his guilt and unworthiness? Gratuitous justification (which ascribes all to Him) is alone compatible with the glory of God and with peace of conscience. He even (with Augustine) hazards the assertion that pagan virtues, as in the case of a Vespasian and a Trajan, are not good *per se*. They are really vices (*vitia*), because of the corruption of human nature underlying them, even if they are to be regarded as gifts of God and are not to be placed on the same level as the vices of a

Caligula or a Nero. Apart from faith, they have no validity for salvation, but merit certain damnation. Such, he holds, is the verdict of Scripture, which teaches the natural corruption of the children of Adam, and any other view implies the falsification of its testimony. The whole doctrine of human merit in God's sight is a perversion of the Gospel as interpreted by Paul and the best of the Fathers—Chrysostom, Augustine, Bernard, for instance. It is incompatible with both the glory of God and the certainty of salvation.[4]

A necessary fruit of justification is Christian liberty. This liberty consists, in the first place, in deliverance from subjection to the Law as a means of salvation, though not from its moral sway as a guide and stimulus to the practical Christian life. It is not merely deliverance from the ceremonial law, but from the principle of salvation by meritorious works. It consists, in the second place, in the substitution of voluntary obedience for the constraint of the Law—the obedience not of slaves to a master, but of children to a gracious Father. It frees us, in the third place, from the bondage to things external, from scruples of conscience in regard to things in themselves indifferent, and from the superstition from which these things spring. It allows a large latitude for the exercise of individual discretion. At the same time, it is to be used with due consideration for weaker brethren. Liberty is not to be mistaken for licence. It does not, for example, legitimate a life of luxury or intemperance unbefitting a Christian spirit. We are always bound to have regard to the edification of our neighbour and to avoid not only the giving but the taking of offence. Liberty must thus also be limited by expediency. His observations on this subject are marked by prudence and common sense and are free from the puritanic narrowness of his Genevan practice. The grand rule applicable to the exercise of our liberty is conscience and consideration for others.

Calvin's doctrine of justification by faith is derived from Paul, though, in the emphasis laid on its forensic character, he seems to lose sight of the Pauline aspect of it as the means of deliverance from the power as well as the guilt of sin. He

[4] On his teaching in greater detail, see Lüttge, " Die Rechtfertigungslehre Calvin's und ihre Bedeutung für Seine Frömmigkeit " (1909) ; Wernle, " Der Evangelische Glaube," iii. 276 f. ; O. Ritschl, " Die Reformierte Theologie," iii. 199 f.

follows Paul, too, in the tendency to read the Christian doctrine into the Old Testament. He does not realise that there is any difference between the teaching of Jesus Himself and that of Paul. He does not, in fact, seem to have considered the question, which has troubled modern theologians, whether the developed Pauline teaching on the subject is quite compatible with that of Jesus Himself. Jesus, indeed, emphasised the complete dependence of the sinner on God's forgiving mercy in the parable of the Pharisee and the publican. But, unlike Paul, he was no adept in the rabbinic theology, in terms of which Paul worked out his theory of justification by faith from his own personal experience of God's mercy in Christ. He, indeed, regarded His death as a ransom, a deliverance, a sacrifice for many. But it is hazardous to assume or dogmatically assert that in so doing He had in mind the developed theory of justification in virtue of a blood offering for sin to a wrathful God, and that in the few references to His death on behalf of man's salvation, He foreshadowed this full-fledged Pauline doctrine. The publican is " justified " in virtue of his appeal to the mercy of God, apart from any blood offering for sin. The prodigal is freely received back into sonship by the Father in virtue of his repentance, and the Father in his spontaneous love and mercy stands in striking contrast to Calvin's inexorable Judge. Such questions [5] do not seem to have occurred to him. At any rate they are not grappled with.

ELECTION AND PREDESTINATION

In the last chapters of the Third Book he discusses the question why the Gospel is not preached equally to all the world and why, even where it is preached, it is not equally received by all. This, he thinks, is ascribable to the good pleasure of God, and this view in turn leads him to the doctrine of election and predestination, which he holds in its most extreme form. This doctrine is absolutely necessary in order that we may be fully persuaded that our salvation is wholly due to God. It alone is compatible with due humility and with God's glory. In this matter we must eschew the temerity and curiosity of reason and keep strictly to the Word, which, he holds, contains

[5] See my " Gospel in the Early Church," 95 f.

all that it is legitimate to know on the subject. At the same time,
just because this doctrine is taught in Scripture, we should not
ignore it on account of its difficulties and for fear of troubling
the minds of the faithful or incurring the gibes of the wicked.
He certainly states the doctrine in the most uncompromising
fashion. " We say, therefore, as Scripture evidently shows,
that God has once decreed by His eternal and immutable
counsel those whom He willed to take for salvation and those
whom He willed to devote to perdition. We say that this
counsel, in respect of the elect, is founded on His (free) mercy
without any regard to human worth ; that on the other hand,
the entry into life is foreclosed to all those whom He wills to
deliver over to damnation, and that this happens by His just
and incomprehensible, but irreprehensible, judgment.⁶ " The
election of some, the reprobation of others, are thus alike due
solely to the eternal decree and predestination of God. They
are not actuated by any consideration outside His omnipotent,
arbitrary will and good pleasure. They are not merely a
matter of the Divine prescience in the sense that He elects
or rejects in accordance with what He foresees will happen.
They are due solely to His eternal decree, apart from any consideration of human character and conduct. Calvin founds
this conclusion on the election of a chosen people from the
race of Abraham for no other reason than His good pleasure,
and not because of any merit in this race. Similarly He
arbitrarily rejected part of this race in favour of the line of
Jacob as well as the nations outside the lineage of Abraham.
Even within this chosen people not all but only a remnant
are really elect. He accordingly distinguishes between a
general or external election and an efficacious election, due to
the secret operation of the Holy Spirit, who gives to the truly
elect the grace of perseverance to the end. This difference is
applicable under the new as well as the old dispensation. He
silences all objectors who ask why some should be preferred to
others, if election is in no way affected by human character and
action, by adducing the good pleasure of God and quoting
Scripture in support of his contention. He lays special stress
on the cardinal testimony of Paul to the Ephesians that God
chose us in Christ before the foundation of the world, having

⁶ " Institutes," 431 ; Latin ed., III., xxi. 7.

predestined or foreordained us to adoption as sons through Him, according to the good pleasure of His will and to the praise of the glory of His grace.[7] Paul certainly teaches the predestination of the believer by God's eternal decree. But this election, if due to an act of God's will, is also conditioned by its moral purpose—" that we should be holy and without blemish before Him in love." It is also the evidence of God's grace, as shown in the redemption of Christ, and in the sequel Paul makes it perfectly clear that this grace is open to all, Jews and Gentiles alike. It is thus not really the Calvinist conception of a God arbitrarily consigning by a *decretum horribile* some to salvation, others to damnation, in accordance with His fiat, that Paul sets forth. In the ninth chapter of the Epistle to the Romans he seems, indeed, to teach the Calvinist doctrine of both election and reprobation by the Divine decree, in the case of Esau and Jacob respectively, in vindication of the fact of salvation by the mercy of God, not by works. Like Calvin, he meets objections by emphasising the will of God as a sufficient reason for acquiescence. He does not, however, enter into the problem, and he emphasises the fact that the Jews have been rejected by their own fault in seeking salvation by works and not by faith, and that the Gentiles have been accepted because they sought it by faith and not works. The element of human responsibility is there alongside the Divine will, and the universality of salvation is certain. " For there is no distinction between Jew and Gentile, for the same Lord is Lord of all and is rich unto all that call upon Him, for *whosoever* shall call on the name of the Lord shall be saved." [8] There is a different note here from that of the Calvinist contention that God elects some and damns others solely according to His good pleasure. The apostle may be illogical, but he is human. Calvin's logic is too much for his humanity and obscures the Gospel of God's mercy, available for all, by the Hebraic conception, in its older, narrow form, of God as the God of a small chosen people, who is, in reality, only a tribal or national God. In keeping with the later universalism of the Hebrew prophets, Paul, while retaining the idea of election and predestination, discarded this narrow conception and substituted for it that of the Father-God of humanity, who,

[7] Ephes. i. 4-5.   [8] Rom. x. 12-13.

as revealed by Jesus Christ, seeks and gratuitously saves all,
Jew and Gentile alike, who turn to Him in faith.[9]

At bottom, in spite of his repellent dogmatism, Calvin's
interest in the problem, like that of Paul, Augustine, and
Luther, is the practical one. Moreover, while asserting and
defending predestination as a cardinal dogma, which may not
be ignored or evaded, he cautions against its inconsiderate
proclamation from the pulpit, and, in view of our ignorance of
the inscrutable will of God, the assumption that any one in
particular is doomed to damnation, unless it can be proved from
Scripture that he is manifestly a castaway. Even so, such
proof is rarely available, and the Gospel should rather be
preached to all on the assumption that their salvation is both
desirable and possible. We may not anticipate the final
judgment of God. There are not a few passages in the
" Institutes " in which he sets forth the more human side of
the Gospel—the mercy and love of the Father-God in Christ.
At the same time, he himself does not shrink from the categoric
assertion, in the pulpit and through the press, of the dogma of
predestination in its extreme form, which, he holds, is the only
scriptural one and is alone compatible with the glory of God
as absolute Sovereign of the universe. In so doing he went
beyond Paul and Augustine, if not Luther, and found himself
at variance with Melanchthon, Bullinger, and other fellow-
Reformers as well as with opponents like Bolsec and Pighius.
Practical reasons as well as logic seemed to him to demand the
absolute exercise of the sovereign Divine will in the matter of
salvation and damnation. Only by placing the issue solely in
this sovereign will could the believer be freed from the uncertainty of depending on works, human merits for salvation.
Only thus could the papal claim to domination over soul and
conscience be invalidated. All mortals are abject and impotent
before God and none may presume to usurp His function as
supreme dispenser of the fate of man, is the thought that such
a conception begets. It was equally serviceable in giving an
absolute assurance to the evangelical believer, who might be

---

[9] For a critical review of the doctrine of predestination in detail, see
H. Bois, " La Philosophie de Calvin " (1919). See also Hunter, " Teaching
of Calvin " ; Scheibe, " Calvin's Praedestinationslehre " (1897). Scheibe's
contention that Calvin got his doctrine from Lefèvre is forcibly controverted
by Dörries, " Z.K.G.," 1925, 544 f.

troubled by the scruple that salvation depended on the intervention of a divinely commissioned hierarchy, and who could triumphantly retort that it depended on nothing but the Divine decree. From this point of view, we might almost say that predestination was a necessity for the Reformation in its struggle with a system that could command all the prestige of a long history and all the force of the civil power. It undoubtedly communicated to the movement in Western Europe a tremendous strength in the days of stress, and thus served a great historic purpose. Calvin might, of course, have substituted for such reasoning the plea for liberty of conscience on Divine and human grounds. But he did not really believe in liberty of conscience in any large and impassioned sense, and if he had, the age would hardly have responded to it, as it did to his grim doctrine of the absolute Divine sovereignty.

THE CHURCH

There remains his doctrine of the Church and the sacraments, which God has instituted as aids to faith, and of which he treats in the Fourth Book. The basis of the Church is the secret election of God and the internal calling by which He draws His elect to Himself. Since election is His great secret, the Church in the sense of the universality of the elect is manifest to the eye of God alone. Hence the distinction between the invisible and the visible Church, which he shares with Zwingli. The former consists of the elect of all the ages from the beginning of the world, who are known to God alone. The latter, with which he is more particularly concerned, of all professing Christians scattered throughout the world, who form the Church in the concrete sense. In this concrete sense it contains a very large proportion of hypocrites, who have nothing of Christ but the name and the appearance, and who are tolerated for a time either because their guilt cannot be legally established or because of the slackness of ecclesiastical discipline. All the elect form a unity under Christ their Head. Hence the designation, the Catholic or Universal Church, in which the elect are knit together and made truly one under the same Spirit of God in one faith, hope, and charity. This unity involves further the maintenance of brotherly fellowship

in Christ, " the communion of the saints," the mutual com·
munication of all the blessings bestowed by God on them, as
in Pentecostal days when the multitude of them that believed
were of one heart and one soul (Acts iv. 32). To the consciousness of this unity and communion it is not necessary
that we should be able to distinguish between the elect and the
reprobate within the Church, which is the prerogative of God
alone. It is sufficient to rely on faith, " the certitude in our
hearts that all those who by the clemency of God the Father,
through the power of the Holy Ghost, have attained to participation in Christ, are set apart for the particular and proper
possession of God, and, as they are of this number, are partakers
in common of this grace." [10] As the community of the elect,
the Church is rightly called our mother, and there can be no
entry into eternal life unless we are conceived, nurtured,
guided, and governed by this mother. In other words,
outside the Church there is no remission of sin, no salvation.
Hence the fatality of abandoning it, though he is fain to admit
with Augustine that " by the secret predestination of God
there are very many sheep without and very many wolves
within it." [11] At the same time, he does not explicitly go so
far as Zwingli, who large-heartedly included Plato and the great
teachers of pagan antiquity among the saints. Moreover, his
admission does not amount to much. As the elect are only a
small number, " like a few grains of wheat among a heap of
chaff," the reader is left with the desperate inference that, in
accordance with the Divine decree, only a small minority of
mankind is capable of salvation.

To the Church Christ gave a ministry when He instituted
apostles, prophets, evangelists, pastors, and teachers for the
work of preaching the Gospel, edifying, and perfecting the
saints. Hence the supreme religious importance of the
ministry, thus divinely instituted and invested with the power
to preach the Gospel, govern, and dispense the sacraments.
It is, indeed, God who inspires and maintains faith. But
faith cometh by hearing, i.e., by the preaching of those through
whom God speaks to man, as by the prophets of old, though he
is careful to emphasise the fact that it is only as God gives the

[10] " Institutes," 471 ; Latin ed., IV., i. 3.
[11] Ibid., Latin ed., IV., i. 8.

increase that the ministry of man is effective and authoritative, and that every member is entitled to edify others, according to the grace given him, as long as it is done decently and in order.[12]

Calvin has a keen sense of the constitutional aspect of the Church as the organ and nurse of the religious and ethical life of its members. In this respect he is more ecclesiastically minded than Luther, who showed no great appreciation of the Church in the constitutional sense. For Luther the Church is the community of believers, who are bound together by their faith in the Word of God. Faith being spiritual the Church is essentially invisible, though it takes perforce a visible form in so far as it exists for the preaching of the Word and the dispensation of the sacraments. For Calvin it is not only invisible as the community of the elect of all the ages, known to God alone, but the visible, divinely instituted organisation, in which the elect and the non-elect assort together and through which God mysteriously works out His redemptive and educative purpose by means of the ministry of the Word and sacraments. Luther was the prophet of a religious revolt and renewal, forged out of his own thought and experience. He was not a constructive genius with the power to systematise his thought and organise the movement which he created. Calvin was no prophet. But he was a constructive genius, both in thought and action, of the first rank. Luther gave up the study of law after a few weeks' trial to enter the monastery at Erfurt and struggle out a new conception of religion, apart from the actual world around him. Calvin pursued his legal studies to a successful conclusion, and after his conversion forthwith grappled with the task of systematising the content of his evangelical faith, and erelong, albeit reluctantly, of organising the evangelical movement as a religious and ethical force at Geneva and elsewhere. For this task the prophet of Wittenberg was unfitted, though he did attempt, in the " Address to the German Nobility," to suggest a reconstruction of the German Church on evangelical lines, which never matured. In his earlier period, at least, he naïvely advocated the method of leaving the Word, the Gospel, to work its own way in the world in virtue of its Divine power, while he wrote and preached

[12] " Institutes," Latin ed., IV., i. 6, 12.

on its behalf in his own prophetic fashion.   Ultimately, under
the direction of Melanchthon, the organisation and administration were given over to the State and its consistorial régime,
under which the Church became a mere State department.
Calvin, on the other hand, gave it a constitution based on
its inherent Divine rights and powers, whose exercise, in
co-operation with the State, transformed it into a religious,
moral, social, and even political force of far-reaching effect in
modern history.

Although the Church in its concrete form contains a
promiscuous multitude of professing Christians, who are not
all in reality elect members of the body of Christ, this Church
may be known by certain tangible proofs or signs.   These he
finds in the effective preaching and hearing of the Word, the
administration of the sacraments in accordance with Christ's
institution, and (inferentially if not explicitly) in the effective
maintenance of discipline.   Wherever this takes place, the
Church exists, whatever the diversity of nation, the distance
of the region, the smallness of its local members.   Whether
its members are all truly Christian or not, they are to be esteemed
as brethren, participating in the common benefit of the Word
and sacraments, unless any of them is proved by public judgment
to be unworthy of the title.   Estrangement or separation from
this Church is not permissible.   Whoever is guilty of this,
renounces God and Jesus Christ and sins against the Divine
unity and authority of the Church.   " Revolt from the Church
is denial of God and Christ." [13]

These signs are indispensable tests of the true Church,
though he thinks that absolute identity in all doctrinal articles
or in the manner of administering the sacraments is not necessary
to the maintenance of communion with any particular Church.
Agreement in essentials—the existence of one God, the deity
of Christ, salvation by God's grace, for instance—there must
be.   But he does not approve of contention and division on
less important points which do not endanger salvation.   He
warns, too, against the extreme puritanism that would exclude
all from the Church that do not come up to its standard of
holiness, as in the case of the ancient Cathari and Donatists
and the modern Anabaptists, who deny that there can be a

[13] " Institutes," Latin ed., IV., i. 10-11.

Church where there is not perfection of the Christian life. They forget the parable of the tares and the wheat. Men of evil life ought certainly to be cut off from the body of the faithful. But this is a different thing from saying that a true Church cannot exist which harbours in its midst imperfect members, and that separation from such a Church is imperative. This extreme view springs merely from spiritual pride and a false estimate of one's own righteousness, and from ignoring the fact that the best Churches are very imperfect in the sight of God, whose judgment is to be preferred to that of man. The remission of sin is only possible in communion with the Church, whether at our entrance into it or during the whole course of our life. We participate in this grace of remission through the Church, to which the keys were given, and whose ministers are empowered to declare the promise of the Gospel and certify this remission to the faithful. It is only a fanatic fancy of the ancient Novatians or the modern Anabaptists that we are regenerated once for all from sin and that we have no need daily or hourly of God's pardon.

The Papal Church

It is, however, imperative to distinguish between the true and the false Church. When the cardinal doctrines and the sacraments of the Christian religion are falsified, the ruin of the Church ensues. " There can be no doubt that there is no Church where falsehood and lies reign." [14] How, then, does it stand with the Church of the papacy from this point of view ? The papacy has substituted for the ministry of the Word a perverse and lying system which has extinguished the pure light of doctrine. It has made an execrable sacrilege of the Lord's Supper. It has disfigured the worship of God by diverse superstitions, and its religious services are schools of idolatry and impiety. Separation from it is not separation from the communion of the Church, which was not instituted to nurture idolatry, impiety, and ignorance of God. The papacy brands its opponents as schismatics and heretics. It claims to be the true Church in virtue of its descent from the early Church of the West and the unbroken succession of its bishops from the

[14] " Institutes," 483 ; Latin ed., IV., ii. 1.

apostles. But what of this unbroken succession in the case of the Greek Church ? If succession makes the true Church in the one case, why not in the other ? The Greeks, say " the papists," are schismatics, because they have revolted against the papal authority. Are not they, then, much more schismatics who have revolted against Jesus Christ ? The papal Church is in the same case with the Jewish Church in the days of the prophets or of Paul. It has departed from the truth of God and corrupted it by its externalism, its superstition, its lying pretensions. It adduces the argument from succession to cover its abominable errors, forgetting that this argument is used by the Fathers only as a testimony that the primitive doctrine had been preserved intact, and not because of any validity which mere succession in itself possesses. Tried by this testimony, the papal Church has no claim to be regarded as the Church founded on the prophets and the apostles, of which Christ is the chief corner stone.[15] Where the mind of Christ is not, there can be no Church. " Everyone that is of the truth heareth my voice." [16] The papacy is, in short, an alienation from the Gospel, and " the papists," not the Protestants, are, he holds with Luther, the real heretics and schismatics. They are more alien from the true Church than the Jews in the time of the prophets. The Pope is the Antichrist.

At the same time, he will not deny that some portion of the true Church remains even under the tyranny of Antichrist— in the sacrament of baptism, for instance. " We do not deny that the churches which Antichrist dominates by his tyranny remain churches. But we say that he has profaned them by his sacrilegious impiety, that he has afflicted them by his inhuman domination, that he has poisoned them with false and wicked doctrines, and that he has corrupted and, as it were, put them to death, so much that Jesus Christ is half buried, the Gospel strangled, Christianity exterminated, the service of God almost abolished. In short, all is so disfigured that there appears rather an image of Babylon than of the holy city of God." [17] This is a harsh judgment which the declension of the late mediæval Church and the fierceness of contemporary

---

[15] Ephes. ii. 20.   [16] John xviii. 37.
[17] " Institutes," 488 ; Latin ed., IV., ii. 12.

theological controversy may tend to explain. At the same time, it does not take sufficient account of the better side of the religious life of the papal mediæval Church. Nor does it show an adequate sense of the historic purpose which it served in preserving and maintaining Christian civilisation and vindicating, albeit very imperfectly at times, moral and spiritual verities and forces throughout the Middle Age. From this point of view Calvin's arraignment must appear to the judicial historian partial and lacking in due discrimination.

THE MINISTRY

He next treats of the ministry which God has instituted as His instrument and representative in the Church. The ministerial office is of the utmost importance for the conservation of the Church, and is to be held in the greatest reverence as Christ's institution. In the Church of the apostolic period the ministerial order consisted of apostles. prophets, evangelists, pastors, teachers (Eph. iv. 11). The apostles were universal functionaries, whose office it was to preach the Gospel at large. They were "the first architects of the Church" throughout the world. Evangelists, though inferior to them in rank, exercised the same function and might act as their substitutes. The prophets were the interpreters of the Divine will by special revelation. All three were only temporary and ultimately disappeared, or only reappeared in special circumstances. The function of the pastors and teachers or doctors, on the other hand, was perpetual. As permanent functionaries, the pastors are the successors and substitutes of the apostles (except that their function was limited to a particular community), the teachers of the prophets. To the former belonged the function of preaching the Gospel, administering the sacraments, and exercising discipline. To the latter the interpretation of Scripture for the preservation of sound doctrine. To the pastors the designation bishops or presbyters was indiscriminately applied in the New Testament, bishops and presbyters denoting the same functionaries. The single pastor or bishop of the local community was not yet developed in apostolic times. At Ephesus and elsewhere the community is under the charge of a number of bishops or presbyters. With them, he infers from Romans xii. 7 and 1 Corinthians xii. 28, were associated in the task of government a number of senior members selected by the people for this purpose, and these, together with the pastors or bishops, constituted the Council or consistory with disciplinary powers. Finally there was the office of deacon and deaconess, to whom was entrusted the care of the poor and the sick. The pastors or bishops might not assume their office without the personal assurance of a Divine call, followed by a public call, which is conditioned by their fitness to exercise it, their election by the people, and their ordination by the laying on of hands.[18]

This ministry, he holds, was instituted by Christ and is founded on the Word of God.[19] Here, as in his doctrinal teaching at times, he betrays an inadequate sense of the fact of development. Christ did not institute the apostolic ministry, which gradually developed in accordance with the needs of the nascent Church. Moreover, he rather overlooks the community itself as a brotherhood inspired by the Spirit of God, whose members freely exercised their ministerial gifts in a variety of service. This brotherhood, which is subject to apostolic direction, and in which the Spirit of God operates, and the " charismatic " ministry of the members finds free scope as well as in the ministry of certain specified functionaries —this is the original form of the Church in the apostolic period. From the strictly historic point of view, therefore, his diagnosis of the early apostolic ministry does not altogether correspond with historic reality.

In regard to the ministry of the succeeding three centuries, he notes the development of the episcopal system by which one of the pastors or presbyters of a church became, under the title of bishop, their president. It is on this development in the early second century, which ultimately produced the universal threefold ministry of the single pastor or bishop in each community, with elders or presbyters and deacons as his assistants, that he models the Reformed ministry. This innovation was the result of expediency, i.e., for the better maintenance of order in the Church. It can claim no higher origin, though the various functionaries of whom it is composed have the warrant of Scripture. For the purpose of efficient

---

[18] " Institutes," Latin ed., IV., iii. 4 f.   [19] Ibid., Latin ed., IV., iv. 1.

government the ministry was further developed in the following three centuries by the institution of archbishops and patriarchs. Of this ecclesiastical development in these centuries he gives, however, only a very meagre account. He has no adequate sense of the historic conditions by which it was influenced,[20] his aim being to show that it was far more in accord with God's Word, as well as of a much simpler character, than that which succeeded. He reminds the bishops of his own time, in the words of Jerome, " that they are greater than presbyters more by custom than our Lord's appointment, and ought to rule the Church for the common good." He lays stress on the continued observance of the rights of the people in the election of the clergy, though he shows a rather aristocratic disposition to distrust the democracy and to limit their right to that of consent and confine the actual election to the clergy.[21]

With the Church of the Fathers he contrasts the mediæval Church, with the object of showing the corruption and tyranny of which it was the victim under the papal régime, and of combating the papal primacy. He finds in this Church the total perversion of that of the apostles and the Fathers and condemns it in language hardly less sweeping than that of Luther himself. " If we look in the face the system of ecclesiastical government which is in vogue to-day throughout the whole papacy, we shall find no such excessive brigandage the world over. Assuredly the whole thing is so different from and so repugnant to the institution of Christ, and so remote from the ancient form, so contradictory to both nature and reason, that one could not do a greater injury to Christ than to claim His name as a colour for such a disordered and depraved régime." [22] He subjects the papal claim to primacy, in particular, to a searching historical criticism for the purpose of showing that it is a tyrannical and antichristian device for robbing the Church of its liberty, contends that the Word of God and not the Church is the standard of truth, and denies that the decrees of Councils are *ipso facto* to be received as infallible in matters of faith.

[20] On this subject, see my " From Christ to Constantine " (1936).
[21] " Institutes," Latin ed., IV., iv. 1 f.
[22] *Ibid.*, 507 ; Latin ed., IV., v. 13.

POWERS INHERENT IN THE CHURCH

There follow several chapters on the spiritual powers inherent in the Church, which under the papacy have been shamefully misused. These powers are threefold, according as they concern doctrine, the making of laws, and jurisdiction. They do not inhere in the persons of the ministers, but in the ministerial office, and their exercise is itself subject to the inspired Word of God, which contains the complete and final revelation in Jesus Christ. The Church possesses the power of declaring the truth of God as contained in the Law, the prophets, the writings of the apostles, to which inspiration is limited, but, as Luther had insisted before him, not to invent new articles of faith. Faith cometh of hearing and hearing by the Word of God. There is a cardinal distinction between the apostles, who spoke by direct inspiration of the Spirit, and their successors, who can only teach what they have been taught. For Calvin there is no possibility of progress beyond the Word in matters of doctrine, whether by way of individual spiritual illumination or through an official ministry and infallible councils. He is the staunchest of advocates of the Book religion theory. The Roman Catholic theory, on the other hand, is merely a device for augmenting clerical authority and attributing to this authority that of the Spirit, of substituting an ecclesiastical tyranny for the faith once delivered to the saints. In this respect he is the sworn enemy of ecclesiastical dogmatism, though he is in practice strongly influenced by its spirit in enunciating his own conception of the faith.

The legislative power is likewise strictly limited by the Word. Like Luther, he attacks the whole papal accretion of law, tradition, and usage, which militates against the spiritual liberty of the believer and burdens the Christian conscience with an intolerable tyranny. God is the sole legislator of His Church, and what goes beyond the enactments of His Word is a pernicious usurpation. Subject to this fundamental rule, he is disposed to allow considerable latitude of ecclesiastical practice. "The sum of the matter is, since God has faithfully comprised in His Word and has fully declared what is the whole true rule of justice, the whole manner of worshipping Him aright, and all that is necessary for our salvation, it is incumbent

on us to hear Him as our sole master in these things. As to
external order and ceremonies, He has not willed to ordain in
particular and, as it were, word by word what we are to observe,
since He foresaw that this depends on the diversity of the times,
and that one form would not be proper and useful for every age.
Therefore we must have recourse to those general rules which
He has given, so that whatever the necessity of the Church
may demand for the observance of order and decency may be
considered in accordance with them." [23]

On the other hand, unlike Luther, he lays great stress on
the utility and the necessity of ecclesiastical jurisdiction or
discipline by means of admonition, censure, and excommunication. In this consists the exercise of the power of the keys
committed by Christ to the Church, which he explains in the
Protestant in opposition to the papal sense, and its exercise is
essential to the preservation of its doctrine and life, as he
proceeds to show in the characteristic fashion with which we
are already familiar.

The Sacraments

He devotes several chapters to the discussion of the sacraments, which he reduces to two—Baptism and the Lord's
Supper. A sacrament, he briefly explains, " is an external
sign, by which God seals in our consciences the promises of
His goodwill towards us in order to sustain the weakness of
our faith, whereby we mutually render testimony to our piety
before Him and the angels as well as men." [24] He denies that
they have any secret magical effect in virtue of their celebration
by the priest. They are but the visible signs of the spiritual
verities contained in the Word, and their efficacy depends on
the apprehension of their significance by the recipient and on
his faith, which they nurture, confirm, and increase. It is due
to the inward operation of the Spirit of God. They do not in
themselves justify and confer grace, if there is no impediment
of mortal sin, as the " papists " hold. Salvation does not
depend on participation in them, but on faith in Jesus Christ
alone. They are, indeed, divinely instituted for a definite
purpose. But the grace conveyed through them is not in them,

[23] " Institutes," 556 f. ; Latin ed., IV., x. 30.
[24] Ibid., 589 ; Latin ed., IV., xiv. 1.

but comes from Jesus Christ, working in us by His Spirit, and is received by faith.

Baptism and the Supper are testimonies of the cleansing from sin and the ransom of the sinner by Jesus Christ, which the Spirit enables us effectively to believe and understand. They are not mere symbols, but in this spiritual sense channels of grace. In baptism we receive, as the result of faith, the assurance of the washing away of sin through the blood of Christ, and of regeneration by the Spirit, of which it is the sign and seal. The washing has reference not merely to the sins already committed, but to the sins of our whole earthly life, and there is, therefore, no need of the additional sacrament of penance, which the papacy has invented for the remission of these subsequent sins. Baptism is also a confession of Christ before men, by which we attest our enrolment among His people. By it, too, we participate in Christ's death and resurrection through the mortification of the flesh, and union with Him in a new life of the Spirit. He denies the contention of the Donatists and the Anabaptists that its validity depends on the character of the celebrating minister and that, if we have been baptized by men of heretical views or immoral life, rebaptism is necessary. Its validity depends on its Divine institution. We are not baptized in the name of any man, but in the name of the Father, the Son, and the Holy Ghost; not in communion with his ignorance and impiety, but in the faith of Christ. He denies, too, that baptism is vain if it does not produce real sanctification of life, as the fruit of a living faith, and must, therefore, be repeated when faith becomes really operative. It is sufficient that, without the repetition of the rite, we recur to the promise of remission which is offered in and signified by our baptism and of which we lay hold by faith. But should not baptism be by immersion and not by sprinkling? The method, he replies, is not of the least consequence although the former was usual in the primitive Church. Churches should be at liberty to adopt either according to the variation of climate. Should it not, further, be reserved for adolescents and not given to infants, if faith is essential to its efficacy? Baptism, he holds too hazardously, being the substitute for the rite of circumcision, is, therefore, applicable to infants. Jesus invited the little children to come to Him and they are thus enabled to participate in the new life, the regeneration He offers from their natural state as children of Adam. But does not faith come by hearing, and how can faith operate in those who are as yet incapable of it ? God, he replies, can secretly touch their hearts and we may not restrict His power. He does not, however, quite satisfactorily meet the objections of his opponents in view of his own insistence on the necessity of faith for the proper efficacy of the rite, though he displays a fine humanity in vindicating the participation of the children of at least Christian parents in its benefits.

Whilst his view of this sacrament is largely identical with that of Luther,[25] he differs markedly from Luther in his view of the Lord's Supper. His conception is far more spiritual. The bread and wine are visible signs of the spiritual nourishment which we receive from the body and blood of Jesus Christ, and of the sacrifice which He has offered for our sins. By these corporeal things we are led to things spiritual. They signify and confirm the promise of Christ that His flesh and blood are meat and drink unto eternal life to those who rightly partake of them. They are commemorative of the cross, the death for sin and of the resurrection unto life in which we participate. But the sacrament is not, as with Zwingli in his conflict with Luther, if not before, a mere commemoration. It is an energising experience in the soul analogous to that produced by bread and wine in the case of the body. We receive Christ not merely by the eye of faith as afar off, but as uniting Himself with us and making us His members. It is in this dynamic, mystic sense a real vitalising communion as well as a commemoration. He professes his inability fully to explain this mystic experience. He views it from the standpoint of the incarnate and exalted Christ as the living Word, the origin

[25] He differs, however, from Luther, who, whilst stressing the supreme factor of faith, maintained that baptism is essential to salvation in virtue of the text, "He that believeth and is baptized shall be saved." From this point of view, it is for Luther "the first of sacraments and the foundation of them all," "Werke," vi. 528 f., and see my "Luther and the Reformation," ii. 255 f. In making baptism an essential of salvation, he thus retained, in this respect, the Roman doctrine, whereas Calvin makes salvation the result solely of the faith of the baptized person, not of his participation in this sacrament. "How much error has been caused by the dogma, ill expounded, that baptism is necessary to salvation," iv. 15, 20. God, he further maintains, has certainly called and endowed many with the true knowledge of Himself by internal means, by the illumination of the Spirit, without even the intervention of preaching, iv. 16, 19.

and fountain of spiritual life, by whom we recover the hope of the immortality lost in Adam, and apart from whom we have no real life. He is the Bread of Life inasmuch as He manifested the Divine life in His incarnation, His humanity, which remained intact after His resurrection and ascension, and through which this life is communicated to us in real communion by faith with His flesh and blood, His human body now in heaven. This real communion, though incomprehensible to our understanding, is operated by the Spirit and is experienced by faith in this spiritual banquet. Calvin is more mystic and less rational than Zwingli, whose doctrine he at first regarded as imperfect, though he ultimately came to see in Zwingli's more mature statement of it, after the Colloquy of Marburg, an approximation to his own. He holds that the Supper is not merely symbolic of the death of Christ, but brings the true communicant into living and energising touch with His incarnate and resurrected body in heaven, though this experience is spiritual, not carnal. " I say that in the mystery of the Supper Jesus Christ is truly exhibited to us through the signs of bread and wine, which denote His body and blood, in which He has performed all obedience in order to procure for us righteousness. And this takes place, in the first place, in order that we may be united in one body, secondly, that being made participators of His substance we may feel also His power in the communication of all His benefits." [26] On the other hand, Calvin rejects the bodily presence of Christ in the elements, whether in the Romanist sense of transubstantiation, which transforms the bread and wine into His actual body and blood, or in the Lutheran sense of impanation or consubstantiation, which conjoins the body and blood with the bread and wine, on the theory of the ubiquity of Christ's body.[27] Christ's body is in heaven and we only have a spiritual, though real, communion with it through the Spirit. He totally rejects the

[26] " Institutes," 630; Latin ed., IV., xvii. 11. The roots of his doctrine are discernible in the pre-Calvin Swiss Confessions and other doctrinal statements, and in the works of Bucer, Brenz, and others, though he stamped on it his own mediating spirit. In his maturer, though not in his earlier teaching, Zwingli came nearer to what became the Calvinist view.

[27] On Luther's and Zwingli's teaching on the subject see my " Luther and the Reformation," iii. 306 f. (1929), and W. Köhler, " Zwingli und Luther," i. (1924). See also Barclay, " The Protestant Doctrine of the Lord's Supper " (1927); Mitchell Hunter, " Teaching of Calvin "; Niesel, " Calvin's Lehre vom Abendmahl " (1930).

Mass as a sacrilegious profanation and perversion of the Supper, as also the other five sacraments of the Roman Church.

CIVIL GOVERNMENT

Finally he treats, in the last chapter of the Fourth Book, of civil government. He enters a caveat against the tendency, on the one hand, to minimise the rights of the civil power in the interest of an excessive liberty, and, on the other, to unduly magnify them in the interest of absolutism. He distinguishes between the spiritual and the civil spheres. But he emphasises the religious and ethical function of the State, which consists in nurturing and maintaining the external service of God, the purity of doctrine and religion, the rights of the Church, equity as between its citizens, morality and tranquillity. If the reign of God on earth through His Church were perfect, this function would be needless. But as we live in an imperfect world, the régime of the State is imperative for curbing the wickedness of men. To belittle it, or refuse it obedience on the pretext of the liberty of the Gospel, is a perverse and unscriptural attitude. He quotes Paul in proof of the statement that political servitude can quite well consort with spiritual liberty, since the kingdom of Christ does not consist in such things. This certainly does not betray any adequate sense of the value of political liberty, as enlightened modern nations understand it. The remark is, however, only a rejoinder, though a rather questionable one, to the fanatics who, in the name of Christian liberty, deny the necessity and the legitimate function of civil government, on which he rightly lays stress. At the same time, he includes in this function that of suppressing idolatry, blasphemy against the name of God and His truth, and other offences against religion, and the general use of the power of the State in the interest of the Christian religion. He thus opens the door to religious intolerance and persecution, and, in this respect, makes the State the oppressive servant of the Church in the mediæval fashion. On the other hand, he will not admit its right to make laws as it pleases touching religion and morality. The State, it seems, must use its power for the benefit of the Church, but it must not encroach on its specific jurisdiction.

He is a firm believer in the co-ordination and co-operation of Church and State, and in this chapter we have the theory underlying the " Ecclesiastical Ordinances," by which he strove to realise it in the organisation of the Reformation at Geneva.

Civil government, as embodied in the executive (the magistrates or prince), he proceeds, is a Divine institution, as is proved by Scripture. The magistrates or rulers are the vicars or representatives of God, from whom they derive their power. He evidently has no adequate historic insight into the varied origin and rise of government. He merely explains its origin by saying, in his theological way, that God is the author of it. " Civil government is, therefore, a vocation, not only holy and legitimate before God, but also the most sacred and honourable among all others." [28]   It has, in a word, a religious sanction, and submission to it, even in the form of an absolute monarchy, which involves a common servitude to the domination of a single individual, is a religious duty.

In virtue of this Divine institution, the magistrates or rulers are responsible to God for the exercise of their power and ought to rule as His vicars and in His fear, as the instruments of His providence. He is not concerned about the form of government, which is for him a matter of secondary importance. He has no interest in discussions of this kind. The form depends on circumstances and each—whether monarchy, aristocracy, democracy—has an almost equal validity in its own sphere. Each has, too, its disadvantages. The monarch easily becomes a tyrant ; an aristocracy lends itself to the iniquitous domination of a few enterprising spirits ; a democracy to sedition. Speaking generally, however, he thinks that monarchy is less favourable to good government and liberty than government by an aristocracy. A monarch tends to substitute his own will for equity and right, and very rarely is he gifted with such prudence and alertness of mind that he discerns rightly what is good and useful for the State. He seems to have a distaste for the oppressive monarchic absolutism of his time, as exercised in France by the later Valois kings. He prefers an aristocracy, whose members act as a check on each other, and which experience has proved to be the most tolerable and the safest

[28] " Institutes," 682 ; Latin ed., IV., xx. 4.

form of government. Whatever the form, the best government is that which secures a tempered and stable liberty, on which he lays great stress, and in the case where the form is democratic, *i.e.*, where the people are free, this liberty should be jealously guarded by the executive. But he is no friend of innovation in the form of government, on the part of the subjects, in deference to a revolutionary spirit in the people. Whatever the form, the people ought submissively to render obedience to it as the ordinance of God. In this respect he is as emphatic on the duty of submission to the powers that be as Luther himself. It is, in fact, a misapprehension to speak of Calvin's political doctrine as, in principle, democratic. Calvinism ultimately developed democratic tendencies and, under the stress of persecution, showed a livelier sense of the identity of political and spiritual liberty. "Calvinism, but not Calvin," rightly observes Lang, "shows a predisposition for democracy." [29] Calvin himself, whilst favourable to the maintenance of liberty where it existed, was not inclined to assert it where the existing form of government did not admit of it. He is as little as Luther the champion of the self-assertive spirit in politics, though the sworn revolutionist against the papal mediæval Church.

Dealing next with the office of the executive, he energetically rebuts the contention that it should concern itself only with the maintenance of civil justice, of the material welfare of the subject, and insists that its primary duty is "to maintain the honour of God" in accordance with His Law. He takes as his model, in this respect, the Jewish theocracy and applies it to the modern State, whose rulers are to rule in its spirit and by its methods. He insists on its right and duty to maintain justice against evil-doers and defend and protect the innocent, to impose the death penalty to this end as the instrument of the Divine judgment and vengeance, to wage defensive though not aggressive war, and contract alliances for the same purpose, to raise taxes, though not to oppress and exploit the people for its own advantage. Its rulers are to exercise due severity in the repression of crimes, and he cites with approval the examples in the Old Testament, such as that of Moses killing 3000 people for idolatry, on the ground that he was only executing the Divine judgment, though he rather inconsistently cautions against excessive severity.

In regard to the administration of the Law, the Decalogue is binding on all rulers as " the true and eternal rule of justice, ordained for all men to whatever country they belong and in whatever time they live." He thus lays the greatest stress on political and public morality. In addition each nation may make laws as its situation requires. But these must be in consonance with the eternal law of God and with natural equity, which finds its fullest expression in this law. He emphasises, too, the duty on the part of the subjects of fostering and maintaining a Christian spirit towards their fellow-men, even in litigation, and of seeking the public good and not their own personal advantage. For this reason, also, they are to show due reverence and obedience to the civil power as divinely ordained. He condemns all attempts at forcible resistance, even to an oppressive government, or unauthorised interference in the government. Submission to government, whether it is good or bad, he maintains with Luther, is a Christian duty. He leaves no room for resistance or rebellion in case of misgovernment. Such, he holds, is the teaching of the Word, and this is sufficient to settle the question. " The Word of God requires of us obedience not only to the rule of princes, who justly and faithfully perform their office, but to all those who exercise power by whatever mode they do so, although there may be nothing they perform less than that which pertains to their office." [30] Rulers who are guilty of injustice and violence are equally to be regarded as the ministers of God to punish the iniquity of the people.

Certainly a very tame doctrine from the point of view of equity and political rights. Of political progress Calvin has no adequate conception. He looks at political institutions from the Biblical point of view and, as in his theology, he sets up his dogmatic interpretation of the Bible as the only permissible one. In politics Providence must work His will and the people evidently must not assist Him, but leave the wicked ruler to His judgment. It is folly and sedition to think that a king should be treated according to his merits, and that subjection depends on the character of the government. The

[30] " Institutes," 692 ; Latin ed., IV., xx. 25.

case is different when the constitution provides checks on
the arbitrary power of the executive, like the ephors among
the Lacedæmonians, the tribunes of the people at Rome, the
demarchs at Athens.   In such cases the limitation of the
executive power, in defence of the liberty of the people, is a
public duty, in accordance with the will of God, which is not
to be neglected.   This power belongs in modern States to the
Three Estates when they are in session, whose duty it is to
remedy the intemperance or cruelty of kings.   In any case,
to the people this power is not given.   Their duty is one of
absolute submission.[31]

There is, however, one grand exception.   The Lord is
King of kings.   Obedience to earthly rulers is conditioned by
obedience to the Supreme Ruler.   If they command anything
against Him, we are not bound to obey or pay any regard to
their dignity.   In ordaining rulers God has not abdicated His
Divine authority.   We must obey God rather than man.   He
does not say that we must resist, and he does say, like Luther,
that we must suffer all things.   But the refusal to obey might
lead to the right to resist, and Calvin's disciples in France,
England, Scotland, the Netherlands, if not Calvin himself,
were erelong, under the stress of persecution, to draw this
inference.   They were not content to refuse obedience and
suffer.   They drew the sword to strike down the oppressor
on political as well as religious grounds.   Calvinism, if not
Calvin himself, thus became a mighty force in the vindication
of both religious and political liberty, in moulding the destiny
of nations as old as England and Scotland, of nations yet
unborn like Holland and the United States.   " To trace the
course of political liberty among the modern nations (of
religious despotism, too, alas !) is partly at least to write the
history of Calvinism. . . . That terrible dogma of predestination was a dogma for strong men, a creed for stern fighters for
God and the right against all the world, and to it we owe some
of the most heroic chapters of human history.   To it we owe
the puritan drama in France, Holland, England, Scotland, and
America, if also some sad chapters in the history of human
bigotry.   Calvin gave the Bible and nothing but the Bible to

[31] On Calvin's attitude to the right of resistance in greater detail, see
Bohatec, " Calvin und das Recht," 133 f. (1934).

his followers—the Bible of the Hebrew prophet as well as the Christian apostle—and what this Bible in such hands accomplished in vindicating human rights against persecution we may read in the deeds of Huguenot, Sea Beggar, Puritan, and Covenanter." [32]

[32] MacKinnon, "History of Modern Liberty," ii. 155 f. (1906).

CHAPTER XVIII

AN EVALUATION

THE PASSING OF CALVIN

CALVIN'S last years were clouded by increasing ill-health. Early in 1564 it became apparent that his days were numbered. On the 6th of February he preached what proved to be his last sermon. On the 27th March he was carried to the Council Chamber to present Colladon, who had been re-elected Rector of the Academy, to the Council. His words came in gasps owing to his extreme breathlessness, and his moribund condition melted his auditors to tears. On Sunday, the 2nd April, he was carried to worship for the last time in St Peter's and partook of Communion. The Council, hearing of his intention to come and address it once more, insisted on waiting on him in his home on the 27th April in order to spare him the exertion. He thanked its members for their friendship and support in the past. If he had not been able to do more in the service of God and the republic, he prayed them to take the will for the deed. He further thanked them for bearing with him in his violent moods, which he regretted and which, he was assured, God had pardoned. He had preached the Word of God in purity, sincerity, and complete assurance that he had declared the truth, in spite of the perverting opposition of the devil and his minions. He admonished them to continue to govern in accordance with God's will and for His Glory and in His fear. In conclusion he shook hands with each of them, " who departed from him in tears as from a common father." [1]

On the following day (28th April) his fellow-ministers came to hear his valedictory exhortation. In order to strengthen them in the maintenance of the good work he had begun, he spoke in reminiscent vein of his early struggle on behalf of

---

[1] " Opera," xxi. 99 f., 166.

the Gospel. "When I first came here there was almost no organisation. The Gospel was preached and that was all. Everything was in upheaval. I have lived through many marvellous conflicts. I have been greeted in mockery in the evening before my own door with fifty or sixty shots. You may imagine how this affected a poor, timid scholar such as I am and, I confess, always have been. Then I was hunted out of the town, and on my return from Strassburg, I had as great difficulty as before in performing my office. People set their dogs on me, which caught at my robe and my legs. . . . When I went to the Council of Two Hundred to appease a tumult, I was greeted with cries to withdraw. 'I shall do nothing of the sort,' I replied. 'Kill me, you rascals, if you will. My blood will witness against you, and these benches will require it of you.' So it will be with you, my brethren, for you are in the midst of a perverse and unhappy people. However many persons of goodwill there be, it is a wicked and perverse folk, and you will have experience of its perversity when I am gone. But take courage and fortify yourselves ; for God will make use of this Church and maintain and preserve it. I have had many failings with which you have had to put up, and all I have done is worth nothing. The wicked will lay hold of this saying. But I repeat that all I have done is of no worth, and that I am a miserable creature. This, however, I can say, I have wished to do good and my failings have always displeased me, and the fear of God has been rooted in my heart. So that you can say that my intention has been good, and I pray that the evil may be pardoned me, and if there has been anything good, that you will conform to it and follow it.

"Concerning my doctrine, I have taught faithfully and God has given me the grace to write. I have done this as faithfully as possible and have not corrupted a single passage of Scripture, nor knowingly twisted it. When I have been tempted to subtlety, I have withstood the temptation and always studied simplicity. I have never written anything from hatred of anyone, but have always faithfully set before me what I deemed to be the glory of God." In conclusion he begged them to support Beza, his successor, to avoid contention, and beware of making changes and innovations, which were always dangerous and sometimes harmful. He finished with a parting thrust at the Bernese ministers, whose hostility rankled to the last. " They have always feared more than loved me, and I wish them to know that I died with this opinion of them." [2]

His last letter was written on 2nd May to Farel, from whom he had latterly been estranged owing to his marriage, at an advanced age, with a young girl,[3] and his old friend hastened from Neuchâtel to his bedside to renew their old friendship and bid him a touching farewell. Once more, on the 19th May, the ministers assembled in his house for their quarterly meeting for mutual correction. He was carried into their midst—" a pitiable entrance," says Colladon—to murmur a few sentences of fraternal greeting and even to spend a few minutes with them at the supper table before taking his final leave of them. Eight days later (27th May) he was peacefully relieved from his long suffering and passed into the unseen with the serenity begotten of an indomitable faith and hope. He was laid to rest in the common cemetery. The exact spot remains unknown, since, in accordance with his desire, no stone was placed on his grave.[4]

THE MAN

The impression we derive from his public career is that of an austere, inflexible, self-concentrated, harsh personality. The theologian, the controversialist, the party leader, the disciplinarian, the legist are ever in evidence. It is very difficult to get to know the *inner man*. He was by nature shy and reserved, and, as we have seen, was disposed to shun rather than court publicity. He had nothing of the outwardness of Luther, whose inner personality was an open secret. Seen on the surface, there is something furtive, unapproachable, mysterious about him. At all events, he is a man not easy to know, and the Calvin of history is, therefore, largely the official Calvin. One could not say this of Luther, whose inner personality is as obtrusive as his shadow. Read his works and

---

[2] " Opera," ix. 891 f.
[3] *Ibid.*, xvii. 335, 351 f.
[4] *Ibid.*, xxi. 169. In a letter in the *Scotsman*, June 1921, the writer says that the tomb " is said to have been discovered in a Genevan cemetery." I wonder if this statement is reliable.

you know the man as well as the Reformer. His great contemporary and successor-in-chief of the Reformed movement is far more elusive. The soul of him was known only to his intimate friends, and his intimate friends were not numerous. He had not the capacity for friendship of the boisterous, headlong, open-mouthed Reformer of Wittenberg. It was not easy to penetrate the bar of the shyness and reserve, which almost made him miss the great chance of his career in 1536 and which clung to him throughout it. It is difficult to imagine him relaxing like Luther when the day's work was done, or the dinner-hour had come, and giving full play to the social instinct in the company of his associates, his visitors, his students. He was too self-concentrated to attract men of a stamp of intellect and character different from his own—men of the type of Castellion, whose freer standpoint he could not understand, or M. de Falais who broke with him over his harsh treatment of Bolsec. One could only be his friend by becoming his subordinate, except in the case of those of his fellow-Reformers like Farel, Viret, Bullinger, Bucer, who were his seniors and shared his views. So was it, it may be said, in the case of Luther, as Melanchthon found to his cost. But Luther attracted by his human magnetism as well as dominated by his imperious personality. Calvin had far less of this magnetism, whilst possessing in equal measure the dominating will of the born leader. He inspired submission rather than affection outside the narrow circle of his intimate associates and friends. Nevertheless, within this circle, he exercised an extraordinary. fascination, not merely in virtue of his gifts as the born leader in a common cause, but of what we might call the latent humanity of the man. It was this as well as his strength of character that attracted Melanchthon to him at once, and the same attraction is observable in the case of intimate friends like Beza, Colladon, Des Gallars, Michael Cop, Laurent de Normandie, and others of his close associates, who adored the man as well as subordinated themselves to the leader.

M. Doumergue has an illuminating, if enthusiastic, chapter on what we may call the inside life of Calvin, or Calvin at home, as he calls it (*Calvin chez lui*). As the result of his almost filial research, he may be said to have discovered the man behind the official, as portrayed by most previous historians.

He was, it seems, a keen observer of nature, admired and
enjoyed its beauties, especially as reflecting the goodness,
wisdom, and power of God.   He was by no means impervious
to the charm of the far-reaching panorama of lake, vineyard,
and mountain that faced the windows of his house in the
Rue des Chanoines.   Doumergue adduces appreciative passages
from his letters, his sermons, and even from his theological
masterpiece in proof of the fact.[5]   The religious note is very
characteristic of these appreciations, and, as M. Doumergue
admits, he does not look on nature with the rhapsodic fervour
of a Rousseau.   But he is sensible of its beauty and has
no sympathy with the ascetic conception—" the inhuman
philosophy," as he calls it—that would shun the enjoyment of
this gift of God to man.   He habitually sought relief and
refreshment from the harassing task of his official life in rustic
retirement in the country house of his brother, or M. de Falais,
or other friend.   One is apt to think of him as a morose and
somewhat atrabilious individual, who could hardly smile, far
less indulge in a hearty laugh.   M. Doumergue, in reply, bids
us listen to him preaching a sermon on happiness, not merely
in the strictly religious sense, but as a habit of life—the happiness
of enjoying all good things as God's gifts.   He quotes a letter
to Farel which expresses regret that he cannot be with him
for at least a few hours " in order to laugh with you."   From
another quotation it appears that, after all, he could enjoy a
joke and even make one himself in such restricted company.
He was, indeed, the most brilliant of conversationalists, quick
in repartee, in witty sallies, and joining in the laughter over
the pleasantries of Beza and Viret.   Castellion even reproaches
him with his taste for such literary badinage, whilst peppering
him with his severities because of a difference of opinion.   He
was in truth a master of facetious irony, as his tract on " Relics "
reminds us.   Nothing delighted him more than to make the
Romanists laughable as well as detestable, and it is certainly
rather novel to find him the champion of the human right
to laugh, or counselling consideration for human weakness
and folly, and making allowance for the liking of the people
for what he calls *divertissement*.   One would hardly have

[5] Imbart de la Tour has overlooked these passages in denying this
appreciation, " Calvin," 178.

expected this of the leader of the Genevan Consistory!
"Experience," aptly says Schaff, "teaches that even at this
day the severest Calvinism is not seldom found connected with
a sweet and amiable Christian temper." [6]   When his temper
was under control, he could show this sweetness in a remarkable
degree, as Beza testifies. Nor does one think of the puritan
censor of morals as an adept in the love affairs of his friends,
as an assiduous matchmaker in the interest of M. Viret or
M. Cop, for instance. Marriage in those days was largely a
matter of arrangement by the friends of the parties concerned,
and Calvin seems to have kept a list of young ladies for emer-
gencies of this kind and knew all the particulars about their
character, qualifications, dowry, etc. He was even prepared,
on occasion, to propose himself on behalf of a colleague and was
evidently rather a fastidious connoisseur of feminine charms.
He was, too, prompt to make the personal interests of others
his own, to recommend a housekeeper, or a tutor, or find
situations for parishioners out of work, or supervise the education
of the children of correspondents he had never seen, or select
a good cask of wine for M. de Falais. He exercised a vast
amount of disinterested patronage of this minor sort with the
same zeal that he bestowed on the greater affairs of his vocation
as the leader of an international movement.

He showed, in fact, a remarkable aptitude for practical
affairs, partly inherited from his father, partly due to his legal
training. At his suggestion the Council started a silk factory
in order to provide work for the unemployed, and thus mitigate
the poverty which, for various reasons, had become an urgent
social problem. He imparted an impulse to the practical life
by his conception of it as " a vocation " ordained by God, in
contrast to the mediæval monastic conception of it. To him
as well as to Luther we owe what has been called " the laicization
of holiness "—the consecration of everyday duty as a service
of God. Unlike Luther, he approved and defended against
the canonists the right to exact a moderate interest (five per cent.)
on capital lent for the promotion of industry and commerce.
At the same time, he sought to limit the nascent capitalism by
the supreme law of love, and set his face against the taking of
interest from the poor, and the selfish manipulation of finance

[6] " Swiss Reformation," ii. 840 (1893).

at the expense of others. It is a mistake to represent him as the patron of the capitalist system in this objectionable sense.[7]

He could, too, it seems, enjoy a game of quoits with the magistrates and join in the hilarity of the game of keys with his guests after dinner. He was given to hospitality and very gracious in dispensing it. M. Doumergue quotes many expressions of gratitude and affection on the part of those who had experienced his generous kindness as a host. " Your hospitality in the name of Christ," wrote one of them, " is known throughout Europe." Those who were privileged to know him thus intimately certainly carried away very agreeable impressions of their sojourn in his simple home, and speak warmly of his " humanity," the sweetness of his conversation, even " the suavity of his character." The Calvin of the Consistory, or the lecture-room, or the pulpit was evidently not the whole Calvin. M. Doumergue does not hesitate to dwell on " the feminine sensibility " of the man who sent Servetus to the stake. It is somewhat difficult to grasp the fact in the light of this and other grim incidents of his career. But his elaborate and admiring biographer can quote texts in confirmation of the tenderness of his heart, testimonies of Calvin himself among them. " You know," he writes to Viret, " to what a degree my heart is tender, even soft." " Yes, I know it," answers Viret. Bucer is another witness. The unmerited reproach of a friend like Bucer cost him sleepless nights and agitated days. The death of another is equally unnerving, and among the most beautiful effusions of his pen are the letters of sympathy to bereaved friends. M. Borgeaud does not deny these traits in Calvin's character. But he objects that they are predicable only of the younger Calvin and that in his maturer years they disappear, or are completely over-shadowed by the harder and harsher tendencies of his nature. M. Doumergue quotes Beza and Des Gallars for the defence. But the testimonies of Beza and Des Gallars are obituaries of the panegyrical type. M. Doumergue has, therefore, recourse to the texts bearing on the later period of his life. These

[7] See, in detail, Hauser, " L'Économie Calvinienne," *Bull. Soc. Hist. du Prot. Français*, 1935, 227 f.; R. Freschi, " Giovanni Calvino," II., xi. (1934).

texts are, however, comparatively few in number and hardly serve to refute the thesis of M. Borgeaud.[8]

BEZA'S DELINEATION

Beza concluded the Latin biography of Calvin with a general appreciation of the man and his work, which is interesting and valuable as reflecting the impression not merely of a contemporary but of an intimate friend and co-worker. " He was of moderate stature, of rather pale-dark complexion, clear of eye even unto his death—testifying to the penetration of his genius. In the care of the body he was neither over-refined nor slovenly, but observed a demeanour becoming his singular modesty. His mode of life was so temperate that it was entirely free from both meanness and luxury. He was most sparing of food and for many years took only one meal daily by reason of the weakness of his stomach. He did with very little sleep. His memory was incredible. Those whom he had once seen he immediately recognised after many years, and when disturbed whilst dictating his writings, as he often was for hours on end, he would return to his task and immediately take up the train of thought, without needing to refresh his mind on what he had already dictated. However great and varied the multitude of affairs by which he was oppressed, he never forgot a single detail. So clear and exact was his judgment on whatever affairs he was consulted that he almost seemed to be endowed with the gift of prophecy, nor do I ever remember that anyone went astray who followed his advice. He scorned fine speaking and was sparing of words. But he was the least inept of writers. No theologian of his day has written so lucidly and impressively, though he wrote more voluminously than any in our memory or that of the Fathers. He derived this facility from the studious application of his youth and from the natural acuteness of his intellect, which was strengthened by long practice in dictation, so that he was never at a loss to utter his thoughts with force and point.

[8] For details of the inner personality of Calvin see Doumergue, iii. 527 f. See also his essay on " Calvin : Epigone or Creator ? " in " Calvin and the Reformation " (1909), by various writers. For an attempt to elucidate the personality and thought of Calvin from the psychological point of view, see H. Weber, " Die Théologie Calvin's " (1930).

Indeed, he wrote much in the same style as he spoke. In the doctrine which he set forth at the beginning he remained constant to the end, changing hardly anything—a thing that has happened to few theologians of our time. Although nature had endowed him with a certain gravity of manner and character, no one could be more agreeable in intercourse than he. He was remarkably prudent in bearing with the faults of his fellow-men arising from human infirmity, so that he neither put to shame nor terrified weak brethren by unreasonable reproaches, nor encouraged their vices by conniving at, or flattering them. Flattery was altogether alien to his nature, and of dissimulation or dishonesty, especially in the matter of religion, he was as keen and vehement an enemy as he was a lover of the simplicity and candour of truth. He was by nature of a choleric temperament, and this failing was intensified by the very laborious kind of life which he led. Nevertheless, the spirit of God had taught him to moderate his anger so that no one ever heard him speak a word unworthy of a good man. Still less did he allow himself to go beyond the bounds of moderation or prudence, unless, indeed, when the question concerned religion or when he was engaged in bending the opposition of those who inflexibly resisted him." [9]

This is Calvin as he appeared to the partial eye of a devoted follower and fellow-worker, to whom he was both master and the closest of friends. Between him and Beza there was evidently nothing of the *constrained* friendship which, latterly at least, made the personality of Luther such a burden to Melanchthon. To Beza Calvin is a leader and a friend to be followed and admired and abetted through thick and thin. He is the prince of men as well as theologians. Impartial history substantially shares his appreciation of his supreme intellectual power, the simplicity of his life, his passionate loyalty to what he deemed the truth, his severe self-discipline, his brilliant gifts as a writer, the strength of his character and his indomitable will, the purity of his life and the greatness of his influence as a moralist and a religious teacher. At the same time, Beza is inclined in this generalisation and throughout his short biography of him to dwell exclusively on the good and great side of his friend, to praise without sufficient discrimina-

[9] " Opera," xxi. 169 f.

tion, to represent the great conflict of his life as waged with those who were always in the wrong against one who was always in the right, to treat his opponents as *ipso facto* enemies of God and the truth and misrepresent and even malign their character, to resent criticism as calumny, and to deal too apologetically with his failings of temper and character. He is too much of the partisan to be an impartial and discriminating judge.

CALVIN THROUGH HOSTILE EYES

The partial appreciation of his friends is offset by the detraction of hostile critics like Baudouin and Bolsec, both of them friends transformed into enemies and both renegades from Protestantism. Both, too, had reason to resent Calvin's harsh treatment. As we have seen, Bolsec had experienced to his cost what it meant to dissent from the doctrine of predestination, and ultimately gave full rein to his resentment in gross calumny. " There is no possible doubt," says the Roman Catholic Imbard de la Tour in reference to this calumny, " about the integrity of his life." [10] Baudouin had for a time enjoyed his complete confidence and his hospitality. He was a man of culture and a distinguished jurist with a keen interest in the religious question, which led him to visit Strassburg and Geneva. Calvin treated him with the utmost kindness and as his amanuensis he had the free use of his library and access to his private papers. The relation between them was more that of father and son than that of master and servant. Calvin believed that he had made an ardent convert, and the attractive and enthusiastic young man remained in affectionate epistolary intercourse with him after his return to France to fill the post of lecturer in law at Bourges, where he remained seven years. He signed himself in these epistles Peter Rochius, Peter the Rock, in testimony of the firmness of his Calvinist convictions. He seems, however, to have been one of those voluble natures, whose religion changes with the dominant influence of the hour, and at Bourges he compromised himself in Calvin's eyes by conforming to the old faith. Calvin had

[10] " Calvin," 174.

heard of this objectionable conduct and on his return to Geneva in 1556 reproached him with his infidelity. He succeeded, however, in disarming his suspicions of his religious honesty and in renewing the former close intimacy. From Geneva he proceeded to Strassburg to resume intercourse with Bucer, and was involved in a heated controversy with his fellow-jurists Duaren and Hotman. The quarrel strained his relations with Calvin, who was the friend of both his opponents, though he continued to write him letters full of professions of respect and affection. Ultimately in 1561 the strain resulted in a complete breach in connection with the religious negotiation between Catholics and Protestants at Poissy, in which Baudouin, whilst posing as the friend of conciliation, appears as the abetter of the Cardinal of Lorraine's policy of setting the Lutheran and Calvinist theologians by the ears. By this time Calvin had convinced himself that he was an intriguing dissembler and erroneously ascribed to him an anonymous pamphlet advocating a reconciliation of Protestants and Catholics, and in an attack on it bluntly described him as a fox and a turncoat. Baudouin was, however, only the inspirer of this effusion, which was written by Cassander, and replied in a tone very different from his previous profession of admiration and devotion. He now called Calvin a liar and a tyrant, who sought to insult and lord it over all the world. Calvin replied in his most violent strain. He accused him, *inter alia*, of having abused his hospitality by stealing his correspondence, and the fact is indubitable that Baudouin had pilfered some of his private papers, including a confidential letter from Bucer, in which the Reformer of Strassburg complained of his harsh temper. In his second response Baudouin garbled Bucer's words. He represents him as ascribing to Calvin " the malady of defamation," and calling him a false accuser, an *enragè*, a rabid madman, etc. He amplified his previous accusations, and it must be said that, if he gave full rein to his malice, he knew Calvin too intimately not to expose some of his weak points. Like Bolsec, he ended by publicly renouncing the Calvinist creed, and his polemics against his old master and patron materially contributed to form what M. Doumergue calls the " *legende Calvinienne* " — the Calvin of the calumniators. In the propagation of this legend both had assidious co-operators and successors in Florimond de Raymond, Papire Masson, Desmay, and Levasseur.[11]

CALVIN IN RIGHT PERSPECTIVE

From them the charges of ambition, tyranny, cruelty, avarice, even immorality, have descended to modern times and have coloured partisan biographies like that of the Roman Catholic Audin, and influenced historians like the two Galiffes, father and son, who take the side of the old Genevan opposition party, later known as the Libertines. Nor can it be denied that there was some ground for charges like that of ambition and tyranny, though we must be careful to discount the animus, the repulsion, on personal or religious grounds, of those who originally made them or afterwards made use of them. Calvin was in a sense an ambitious man. He had the dominating will to which the exercise of power is an essential. As we have seen, he shrank at the outset of his career from the responsibility of leadership. But once in office, he was nothing if not self-assertive, and struggled for nearly twenty years to establish and maintain his supremacy over Geneva. He quickly acquired the habit of command, and both the consciousness of his powers and the conviction of his duty as God's representative impelled him to exact submission to his rule. It will not do to say, as his panegyrists do, that he was actuated in all things by the grace of God, to assume the absence of the human strain in his motives and his actions. He was so made, was so strong-willed, so intellectually superior that he must needs be second to none, an equal only among equals. Once his mind was made up, the thing must be done, not only because God wills it, but also because Calvin wills it. There is un-doubtedly a strong strain of self in him, however piously, even depreciatingly, the self may utter itself. Calvinus locutus, causa finita. This is Calvin, and it is very human. At the same time he is not the ambitious man that his calumniators depict. He does not strive after power in itself. He does not aim at lordship in the vulgar sense. He cares nothing for what to meaner minds are the sweets of power. His life is

[11] For Baudouin, see Prolegomena to " Opera," ix., and Doumergue, i. 150 f. and 519 f.; ii. 762 f.

simplicity itself. The supremacy he seeks to wield is moral.
It is due to the strength of his character as well as his will
and his convictions, and is concerned with the realisation of the
highest ends.

That he could be tyrannical and even cruel in his treatment
of opponents is only too true. In what he considered matters
essential, he would allow no liberty of opinion or discussion.
There was no room in Geneva for a Castellion, a Bolsec, a
Trolliet, a Gentile, not to speak of a Servetus, and in his pursuit
of such opponents he played the despot pure and simple.
The Reformation principle of the right of private judgment
he reserved for himself and his adherents. His enemies, says
Beza apologetically, were the enemies of God, blasphemers,
and mockers of the Divine Word, and to condemn him was
to condemn the Holy Spirit. So said the tyrannical Inquisitors,
who tortured and burned his reformed brethren by the
thousand. Nor is it a sufficient exculpation or an excuse to
say that he was in this respect but a man of his age and could
not be expected to act otherwise. He professed to have discovered the Gospel. He studied the life and teaching of Jesus
and the apostles in the original, and one might reasonably
expect and demand that he should understand the Gospel
teaching to the disciple of Christ to suffer, not to inflict
persecution even for the sake of the faith. Ignorance of the
Gospel might be a valid plea, but ignorance of the Gospel is
the last thing that Calvin would have owned. He must,
therefore, be judged by an even stricter standard than his
fellow-inquisitors of the Roman Church, who appealed to the
canon law and ecclesiastical tradition in defence of their right
to persecute, and whom he denounced as ignorant of the truth.
True, Beza can say that when the Inquisition would have sent
heretics to the stake, he was content to banish the Anabaptists,
the Bolsecs, and the Gentiles. But he allowed Gruet to be
executed for his free thinking, recommended the Council to
sentence the repentant Gentile to death for his anti-Trinitarian
opinions, and did his utmost to secure the execution of Servetus,
if he suggested a milder form of death than the stake and the
faggot. He deliberately held the principle that heretics
should be punished by the sword and exhorted the young
King Edward VI. to use it against them. From this point of

view there is more truth than calumny in the accusation that
he was tyrannical and cruel towards those who criticised or
rejected a cardinal doctrine of his theological system, though
his conduct was actuated by a mistaken sense of duty rather
than by the passions ascribed to him.   Moreover, the fact of
the protests of a Castellion and many others proves that the
age was not so obsessed by the duty of persecution for the
sake of the truth as the argument adduced in his favour on
this ground presupposes.

His irascibility is admitted by Beza, though it is exaggerated
by Baudouin with malicious intent. He was too apt to get
into a rage with those who opposed him and play the bellicose
theologian, and when on the warpath to let his temper run away
with him, as in the philippics against Baudouin. At such
moments his victims might almost be pardoned for saying
that it was better to be with Beza in hell than with Calvin in
heaven.   To speak the truth in love, reproach gently and with
a due sense of human frailty in himself as well as others was
not Calvin's habit, though when not personally provoked he
could be patient and forbearing. This irascibility, which his
friends regretted and his enemies exaggerated, was admitted
by Calvin himself, and Beza ascribes it to a hasty and sensitive
temperament which opposition easily chafed, the strain of his
laborious life, and the ill-health which in his later years became
chronic.   His frequent maladies rendered him, he says,
" chagrin et difficile." It was his only failing in Beza's eyes,
and he hastens to add that it was tempered by great and lovable
qualities and was paired by none of the vices that usually
accompany it. The account which he adds of the recurring
and racking attacks of fever, acute indigestion, headache,
stone, gout, hæmorrhage, phthisis, piles during the last six years
of his life certainly inclines one to judge this failing very
indulgently, on which Baudouin enlarges so bitterly without
mentioning these extenuating facts. The root of this chronic
ill-health lay in his intense application as a student, which
permanently disordered his digestion and made a large
part of his life that of an invalid. He dictated many of his
works and his letters from his bed. He would, in fact, have
been a valetudinarian but for his inflexible will and his compelling sense of duty. " Anyone," says Beza, " who chanced

to meet him, judging from his delicate and careworn frame, would have wondered how he managed to live." Yet this spare and decrepit figure was the most laborious of workers, and even the days of sickness were days of exacting toil. In 1559 when prostrated by fever he completed the final edition of his theological masterpiece in Latin and French. During his last illness, when suffering from breathlessness and almost unable to move, he translated his "Harmony on Moses" from Latin into French, revised his translation of Genesis, wrote his Commentary on Joshua, and corrected the greater part of his annotations on the New Testament.[12] If he was irascible, he was also heroic in his long struggle with the complex maladies that racked his body without enfeebling his will or his capacity for work.

Varied and Laborious Activity

Apart altogether from his feeble health, the work he did merely as preacher and professor, not to speak of his productivity as a writer and his varied and exacting activity as chief leader of the widespread Reform movement, would have broken the most robust of constitutions. For sheer hard work Beza knew not his equal, and it would be difficult to find his equal in any age. He preached several times a week and usually twice on Sunday. He excelled in the homiletic treatment of the Word and its application to his hearers. He delivered three theological lectures weekly and usually gave an address every Friday at the meeting of the ministers. He took the chief part in the meetings of the Consistory, and he carried on these pastoral and professional labours year by year until his death, unless hindered by illness.[13] He was often in his pulpit and his chair when he should have been in bed. He found time to write thousands of letters on a complex variety of affairs in connection with the ecclesiastical, theological, and political questions affecting the contemporary history of the greater part of Europe. The letters written by and to him fill ten volumes of the standard edition of his works. Many

[12] " Opera," xxi. 41-42.
[13] Ibid., xxi. 33. On the characteristic features of his preaching, see Mülhaupt, " Die Predigt Calvin's " (1931), and I. de Saussure in the Preface and A. M. Schmidt in the Introduction to " Sermons de Calvin."

of these letters are really short treatises, and it is probable that more of his correspondence has been lost than preserved.

In the midst of this ceaseless and harassing activity he composed the greatest theological masterpiece of the age, which conclusively proves him to be the great systematising, as he was the great organising, genius of the movement. He poured forth commentary after commentary on the books of the Bible.[14]   It is a striking tribute to his powers as an exponent of the Bible that, in almost every modern commentary on its books, quotations from his are to be found. He is still regarded as a master of Biblical exposition, even if modern scholarship and critical skill have outrun his. His command of the original languages, surpassed by none, equalled by few in his own age, and his quick, penetrative mind, amply support this posthumous reputation. While he was abreast and even, to some extent, ahead of the Biblical scholarship of his age, and took the utmost pains to get at the exact significance of the original in the passage he comments, he makes no parade of his ample learning. His aim was to edify rather than impress his readers with his scholarship. His Commentaries, which are impregnated with his personal piety as well as his dogmatic convictions, were intended not only to increase an exact knowledge of the Scriptures, but to further the individual and communal religious life. With his all too narrow view of inspiration we may not, of course, look for an adequate insight into the problems raised by modern higher criticism. For the historian his preference, for instance, for the Fourth Gospel over the other three as a reflection of the authentic teaching of Jesus is quite untenable.

He only ceased to dictate, says Beza, eight hours before his death, when his voice failed him.[15] Nevertheless, what he wrote shows little trace of haste or mental fatigue. It bears constant witness to the intense working of a lucid, fertile, and orderly mind. From the concentrated force of his writings, one might infer that the writer was entirely undisturbed by any press of business and was absorbed only in the theme in question.

---

[14] On his characteristics as commentator, see Mitchell Hunter, " Teaching of Calvin," 15 f. See also H. Clavier, " Calvin Commentateur Biblique," " Études sur le Calvinisme," 99 f. (1936), and article by Schaff on " Calvin as Commentator," *Presbyterian Review*, 1892, 462 f.

[15] " Opera," xxi. 34.

But for the controversial or practical nature of many of them, he might, too, pass for the solitary student, who lived only in the realm of ideas, the scholar and the thinker whose toil was confined to his library, not the leader engaged in a harassing conflict to establish and maintain his supremacy at Geneva, or to extend and defend the Reform movement in France and other lands. His capacity for work and his versatility as preacher, theologian, organiser, and controversialist are truly amazing. From the parish politics of Geneva he could pass to the subtle and profound problems of existence, and from them again to the practical questions of international policy as they affected Church and State from Spain to Russia. His omnipotent memory greatly helped him in this marvellous productivity. It enabled him to work rapidly and easily. He had little time to prepare his lectures and sermons. But his knowledge was so extensive, his memory so strong, that he could, if necessary, improvise with all the effectiveness and ease of the master.

Reputed Affluence

An Anabaptist, whom he was badgering before the Council in 1546, called him a miser. The Councillors present laughed,[16] he remarks in a letter to Farel. It was the last thing they would think of laying to his charge. Nevertheless this calumny was a favourite with hostile critics of the Bolsec and Baudouin type. They tell us that he was in receipt of a big salary, hoarded his money, and died a rich man. The fact is that he earned only a very modest income and gave away much of it in charity—so much that he was at times at a loss to pay for the day's provisions and was forced to borrow. The Queen of Navarre sent him 4000 gold crowns for the poor. Calvin, of course, gave it to his friends at a fixed interest, which he avariciously pocketed ! This sort of story needs no refutation. " I have learned to be content with little." This is the simple truth in answer to all such malicious tales. He lived and died a poor man. His salary was 500 florins, perhaps about 3500 francs in modern value, and not the 5000 to 7000 francs which some have estimated it. His allowance in kind (grain and wine) was perhaps equivalent to another 500 francs—4000 in

16 " Opera," xii. 257.

all—with a free house,[17] and an occasional honorarium for extraordinary services to the Council. Even if we accept the larger figures, he was certainly not overpaid. That he grew rich on his salary and on the presents received from admirers, and that he strove to increase his income by a grasping greed is disproved by the fact that at his death he left only about 10,000 francs in money and personal belongings. His detractors further know of large sums received in return for the dedications of his books. Beza, on the other hand, assures us that he never derived from this source more than 20 *écus* in all. Unlike Erasmus, he never sought a patron in order to be paid for his homage. He addressed his writings to kings and other influential persons only in order to further the cause of the Reformation. Unlike Erasmus, too, he received hardly anything in payment of his works, and only the publishers and booksellers grew rich on the product of his brain. He had, moreover, an extreme delicacy in touching more than his salary, and refused the sums with which the Council, in view of his poverty and in case of illness, wished to present him.[18] On the other hand, he spent freely in entertaining in his hospitable but simple home the numerous strangers who visited Geneva.

EPOCH-MAKING SIGNIFICANCE

The work he accomplished on behalf of the Reformation was truly epoch-making. We may safely say that, without him, it would have been much more limited in its scope and historic effects. He was there to fill the gap that the death of Luther left, to inspire, strengthen, develop it when it had spent its force in Germany and had made little impression in the western lands. Rome felt his power and feared it as much as it had done that of Luther. What he accomplished as the defender and propagandist of the movement was of incalculable importance. His learning, his rare intellectual ability; his resource and strength in attacking the papal ecclesiastical system, his skill in defence of his own; his forcefulness and

---

[17] Doumergue, iii. 469 The franc is to be understood at its standard value of twenty-five to the pound, before its devaluation.
[18] Doumergue, iii. 475.

lucidity as a writer, the constructive gift which systematised its
doctrines and organised its forces ; the passionate faith in it
as the cause of God and in himself as God's instrument ; the
indomitable optimism based on the sovereignty of God and
assured of triumph in spite of persecution and apparent defeat
in France and elsewhere ; most important of all, perhaps, the
moral strength, the intense devotion and energy which his
consciousness of the Divine sovereignty inspired in himself and
his followers—all this was of immeasurable potency in the
extension of the movement in its later aggressive phase, as
exemplified in France, England, Scotland, the Netherlands.
What Huguenot France, evangelical England, Scotland, Holland
represent for the cause of the Reformation may be largely
traced to Calvin, to the influence of the man who, in his official
capacity, was only the minister of one of the parishes of an
insignificant city state, but who, in his unofficial capacity,
was the leader of an international religious revolution, the
uncrowned king of millions of his fellow-men in lands far and
near. No pope or king of them all could compare as a ruler
with John Calvin, because John Calvin in the moral and
religious sphere was the strongest, the most intense man of
his age, and because brute force is, in the long run, no match
for the spiritual force incorporated in such a character.

The secret of his power lies in the fact that he united strength
of character with a powerful mind and will and with depth and
tenacity of religious conviction. The type of character and
piety he represents was narrow and hard. But it was strong,
dynamic, and this is the striking feature of the type as per-
petuated in his followers, in the Calvinism which struggled to
vindicate itself against the religious and political forces of the
counter-Reformation and which produced leaders like Coligny
and William of Orange. It was this that contributed so
powerfully to frustrate the policy of crushing the spirit of
liberty—religious, intellectual, political—to which the Reformation, considered as an emancipating movement, gave birth
and which influenced so fundamentally the trend of modern
history. Calvin himself was no real apostle of this liberty.
He sought to repress the champions of a larger liberty of thought
and conscience than he could understand or admit. He had
not a keen sense of the importance of political liberty in itself,

though happily his lot was cast in a sphere in which the republican tradition and spirit had asserted themselves and perforce influenced his ecclesiastical organisation. But he was the leader of a larger movement than even he could grasp, a move-ment far more potential, in its fundamental principles, than its greatest leaders perceived, a movement which could not be permanently stereotyped in mere systems of doctrine, authori-tatively formulated for all time. The Reformation was a much bigger thing than the Lutheran or the Calvinist form of it. Lutheranism, Calvinism, were only phases of it, though, from the standpoint of organised influence, the dominating phases. The more independent thinkers and the more radical sects, whom the orthodox Reformers opposed and sought to repress, represent its emancipating principles and tendency more truly than they, and it was to them that the future really belonged. Fortunately, too, the movement, as it expanded under Calvin's auspices or influence in the western lands, had to struggle with the full force of the counter-Reformation, and in the struggle with this force the followers of Calvin learned to evaluate political liberty much more highly, to assert the inviolable right of liberty of thought and conscience, to under-stand toleration in a larger sense than their master. Even Beza, under the influence of the massacre of St Bartholomew, already goes beyond his master and proclaims the right of a people to depose a tyrannical ruler.[19] Knox, the most con-firmed of his disciples, went far beyond him in asserting the right of resistance to political tyranny. Whilst Calvin was content to wield the pen on behalf of this liberty—and this with large reservations—and only at the end of his career adopted a more bellicose tone towards the oppressors of his French brethren, Knox did not hesitate to grasp the sword in defence of his oppressed Scottish brethren and resolutely carry the decision to the battlefield. What Knox did the leaders of the French Huguenots, of the Dutch Beggars, and ultimately the English Puritans and the Scottish Covenanters, were equally prompt and determined to do in the cause not merely of the right to worship God in accordance with conscience, but of their rights as free men. Even so, they owed much of their achievement in this respect to the fact that they were trained

[19] Choisy, " Esquisse de l'Histoire Religieuse de Genève," 35 (1928).

in Calvin's school. Calvinism rather than Lutheranism was the moral force fitted for such a struggle. It gave greater scope for the militant individualism, the strength of character, the self-assertion in the political as well as the religious sphere which Lutheranism lost the chance of vindicating in this wider sphere by its subordination to the princely power, its sacrifice of democracy to autocracy. Though no democrat himself, Calvin was the author of a more democratic system of Church government than obtained where Luther reigned supreme. His teaching, by its greater emphasis on the Divine sovereignty, of which the individual as well as the community is the instrument, produced in his followers an overpowering sense of individual rights and nerved them for the struggle to vindicate them in the State as well as the Church.

Calvinism as a theological system has, on the other hand, ceased, in some respects, to influence the twentieth-century mind as it did that of the sixteenth and seventeenth centuries. The more important Reformed Churches have found it necessary to modify their Confessions, to a certain extent at least, in accordance with the progress of modern research and enlightenment, and progressive religious experience. Many within these Churches no longer regard the Bible in the light in which Calvin saw it. They no longer believe in predestination, election, and reprobation as Calvin believed in them. They no longer regard the theological formulas of the Greek Councils as necessarily tests of theological truth. Calvinist orthodoxy is not necessarily the sum of the truth to be accepted without question as the last word in theology, any more than is Roman Catholic orthodoxy, even with an infallible pope to back it with his imprimatur. Protestantism deposed the infallible pope in a large part of Europe and it did well. It was, unfortunately, too much disposed to make infallible popes of the Reformers and to place Luther and Calvin, the infallible theologians, in the place of Christ Himself as an authority that could not be gainsaid. This tendency was, perhaps, it strength at a time of conflict, when it avails much to have intense beliefs and no doubts, to march and do battle at the word of command. It was a source of weakness and stagnation when the battle was over and theology became more a matter of accepted dogmas than a creed to live by and fight for.

Calvinism, like Lutheranism, degenerated into a sort of scholasticism against which it had been, in part, a protest. The inevitable reaction intervened in due time as the scientific, the critical historical spirit, derived rather from the Renascence than the Reformation, came into operation. It has penetrated deeply into the Reformed Churches in spite of long and misdirected resistance, and the attempts to stem the flood of new life and new light in theology, as in other branches of knowledge, have been largely a forlorn hope. If John Calvin were to be born anew in the early twentieth century he would have difficulty in recognising himself in large numbers of his modern spiritual descendants, who nevertheless honour him as their spiritual ancestor and owe infinite gratitude to him as a pioneer, if not, in all respects, a master. He would seek in vain for the theocracy and the Consistory in Geneva or elsewhere. He would find the members of the theological Faculty of its University and of many other universities criticising his doctrine of predestination and reprobation [20] without the risk of being treated like Bolsec and Trolliet. He would find many critics in the theological schools applying the higher criticism to the Scriptures, without incurring disqualification for the ministerial office, as in the case of Castellion. He would find that historic investigation had gone considerably beyond his depth in its treatment of the origins and early development of Christianity. He would find leading theologians disposed to give even Servetus a judicial hearing in the debate over the Christology of the Greek Fathers, and he could not possibly send the heretic to the stake.

We hear, indeed, in books and conferences of a Calvinist

[20] " The whole history of the dogmatic theology of the Reformed Church," says the late Professor Hastie, in his Croall Lectures for 1892 (published in 1904 after his death under the editorship of Professor Fulton, with a preface by Professor Flint), " might be written under the one heading of the Principle of Absolute Predestination ; it has been, generally speaking, at once the basis of all its orthodoxy, the occasion of all its heresies, and the indirect cause of all its schisms. Yet there have not been wanting voices even in the bosom of the Reformed Church that have disclaimed or repudiated the principle, and they never spoke out their dissent or revolt more boldly than now. . . . Indeed a learned nobleman who in our time stood out conspicuously as representing the living spirit of the Scottish Church deemed it a ground of valid apology for its continued maintenance that through his long life he never heard the doctrine of predestination once referred to in a Scottish sermon. Such a statement is significant of the change that has come over Scottish theology," " Theology of the Reformed Church," 224 f.

Revival.[21] But even among the votaries of orthodox Calvinism
there is perforce some reservation in regard to certain aspects
of his thought and practice, which the modern world, to the
advantage of Christianity, has outlived. Whilst the neo-Calvinism
of Karl Barth and his school, with its insistence on the sovereignty
of God and the Word of God as the revelation of His will,
has evoked a widespread interest, it is not a return to Calvinism
pure and simple, if the tone of its founder is dogmatic enough.[22]
A literal Calvinist Revival is neither possible nor desirable,
though the Reformed Churches may be trusted to appreciate
and preserve what is of permanent interest, abiding value in
his thought and work. They will, too, whatever the shade of
their Confession, continue to cherish his memory as that of a
great moral and religious personality and the greatest, after
Luther, of the Reformers. The large recent literature devoted
to him and his work shows that he retains the power of quicken-
ing the interest not only of theologians, but of historians and
philosophers, even if this literature shows disagreement as well
as partial agreement with his theology. At the same time, it
is perhaps not superfluous to remind the perfervid Calvin
Revivalists that our common Christian faith, as taught by its
Founder, is not necessarily identical with any " ism," and that
it is incumbent on His disciples to have recourse for themselves,
in a free, if reverent, spirit, to His teaching as its supreme and
ultimate fountain and norm.

[21] On the Calvinist Revival, see Clavier, " Études sur le Calvinisme,"
141 f. See also article by Professor Henderson, " Calvinism in Europe,"
in *British Weekly*, 17th September 1936.

[22] See his " Dogmatik," i., 1932, English translation by Professor Thomson
(1936). It is very wordy, and lacks the lucid and precise style of Calvin.
Apart from his prominence as a theologian, Barth has distinguished himself
by his sturdy defence of spiritual liberty, in the spirit of Calvin, against a
dictatorial government. He is indeed " a bonnie fechter." For an exposition of his theology in English by an ardent disciple, see M'Connachie,
" The Significance of Karl Barth " (1931). Another of the numerous
monographs on his teaching is Max Strauch's " Die Theologie Karl
Barth's " (1926). Dissentients and critics are not lacking, see, for instance,
in English, Hoyle, " The Teaching of Karl Barth." Adolf Keller gives a
discriminating exposition of the movement in " Religion and the European
Mind," 45 f. (1934). In his most recent work, " Credo " (1936), Barth
seems to have modified some of his earlier ultra-deliverances.

INDEX

C

Calvin, distinctive influence on Reformation, 1 f.; education, 39 f.; studies law, 40 f.; humanist studies, 41 f.; Commentary on " De Clementia " of Seneca, 42 f.; conversion, 43 f.; reputed author of Cop's rectorial discourse, 43 f.; religious development, 45 f.; early evangelism, 48 f.; escapes from France, 49; publication of " Institutes," 50; plea for true religion, 50 f.; visits Duchess of Ferrara, 56; associates himself with Farel at Geneva, 57; tentative organisation of Genevan Church, 57 f.; Catechism and Confession of Faith, 58 f.; enforced acceptance, 60 f.; question of excommunication, 61 f.; dispute with Caroli on Trinity, 62 f.; conflict with Government and banishment, 64 f.; at Strassburg, 68 f.; Epistle to Sadolet, 70 f.; recall to Geneva, 73 f.; reorganisation of Genevan Church, 76 f.; relation of Church and State, 81 f.; formulary of public worship, 82 f.; the Calvinist régime, theocratic tendency of, 85 f.; Consistory as its instrument, 89 f.; abetment by the Government, 91 f.; Calvin's sense of authority, 93; renewed opposition to, 93 f.; renewed conflict, 96 f.; prosecution of Gruet, 99 f.; Calvinist régime in danger, 101 f.; the turning point, 106 f.; significance of conflict, 109 f.; Calvin and Castellion, 112 f.; Calvin and Bolsec, 116 f.; Servetus' correspondence with, 130 f.; complicity in denunciation of, 139 f.; part in trial of, 142 f.; criticism, 152 f.; Calvin's defence, 154 f.; Castellion's attack and plea for toleration, 156 f.; Beza's defence, 158 f.; Calvin supreme, 161 f.; government according to the Word, 162 f.; Geneva under Calvinist régime, 165 f.; Revision of Ordinances of 1541, 169 f.; perfect school of Christ, 170 f.; Calvin and educational reform, 172 f.; founding of college and academy, 173 f.; champion of Reformation, 178 f.; " On Necessity of Reformation," 179 f.; Calvin and Pope Paul III, 183 f.; exposure of relic mania, 184 f.; Calvin and Council of Trent, 185 f.; denounces Augsburg Interim, 187; mediator between Reformed Churches, 188 f.; conciliatory towards Lutherans, 189 f.; other conciliatory endeavours, 191 f.; director of evangelical mission, 195 f.; militant evangelism, 195 f.; international propaganda, 197 f.; mission to the New World, 204 f.; Calvin and international politics, 206 f.; diplomatic activity on behalf of German Reformation, 206 f.; of Reformation in France, 208 f.; Calvin as theologian, 214 f.; his dogmatic faculty, 215; influence of Luther and others on, 215 f.; Biblical theologian, 217; remarkable erudition, 218 f. (for main doctrines, see under " Institutes "); passing of Calvin, 271 f.; the man, 273 f.; Beza's delineation, 278 f.; Calvin through hostile eyes, 280 f.; Calvin in right perspective, 282 f.; varied and laborious activity, 285 f.; reputed affluence, 287 f.; epoch-making significance, 288 f.; the Reformed Churches and Calvin, 291 f.; Calvinist Revival, 292 f.
Camillus, 234
Capito, 68, 123, 146, 194
Cappel, War of, 36 f.
Carlstadt, 31
Caroli, P., 57, 62 f.
Cassander, 281
Castellion, S., 91, 112 f., 151, 155 f., 274 f., 283 f., 292